Hibernate Quickly

Hibernate Quickly

Patrick Peak
Nick Heudecker

MANNING

Greenwich
(74° w. long.)

Manning Publications Co.   Copyeditor: Liz Welch
209 Bruce Park Avenue   Typesetter: Dottie Marsico
Greenwich, CT 06830   Cover designer: Leslie Haimes

ISBN 1932394419

Printed in the United States of America
1 2 3 4 5 6 7 8 9 10 – VHG – 10 09 08 07 06 05

For my brother, Matthew

—P.G.P.

For Trevin

—N.J.H.

Brief contents

1 ○ Why Hibernate?   1

2 ○ Installing and building projects with Ant   26

3 ○ Hibernate basics   50

4 ○ Associations and components   88

5 ○ Collections and custom types   123

6 ○ Querying persistent objects   161

7 ○ Organizing with Spring and data access objects   189

8 ○ Web frameworks: WebWork, Struts, and Tapestry   217

9 ○ Hibernating with XDoclet   274

10 ○ Unit testing with JUnit and DBUnit   313

11 ○ What's new in Hibernate 3   346

Appendix ○ The complete Hibernate mapping catalog   364

Contents

preface   *xv*

acknowledgments   *xvii*

about this book   *xviii*

about the cover illustration   *xxiv*

1   Why Hibernate?   1

   1.1   Understanding object persistence   3

     Identity   4 ○ Inheritance   5 ○ Associations   5
Object/relational mapping   6

   1.2   Using direct JDBC   9

     Example application   10 ○ Retrieving object graphs
using JDBC   11 ○ Persisting object graphs to a relational model   15 ○ Deleting object graphs   18
Querying object graphs   19

   1.3   Persistence with Hibernate   20

     Simplicity and flexibility   20 ○ Completeness   22
Performance   23

   1.4   Summary   25

2   Installing and building projects with Ant   26

   2.1   Getting a Hibernate distribution   28

     Installing Ant   30 ○ Getting Ant   30 ○ Extracting
and installing Ant   30

2.2   Setting up a database   31
      Getting MySQL   32 ○ Testing MySQL   32
      MySQL drivers   34

2.3   Setting up a project   34
      Defining directories   35 ○ Ant 101   36
      Running Ant   39

2.4   Habits of highly effective build files   41
      Connecting Hibernate   42 ○ Reusable build
      files   46 ○ Expanding your horizons   48

2.5   Summary   49

3   Hibernate basics   50

3.1   Configuring Hibernate   51
      Basic configuration   53

3.2   Creating mapping definitions   56
      IDs and generators   58 ○ Properties   59
      Many-to-one element   60 ○ Proxies   62
      Collections   63 ○ Cascades   64
      Fetching associated objects   66

3.3   Building the SessionFactory   66
      Configuring the SessionFactory   66

3.4   Persisting objects   68

3.5   Retrieving objects   70

3.6   The Session cache   72

3.7   Advanced configuration   74
      Connection pools   74 ○ Transactions   76
      Cache providers   79

3.8   Inheritance   83
      Table per class hierarchy   83
      Table per subclass   85

3.9   Summary   86

4   Associations and components   88

4.1   Associations   89

Many-to-one relationships, in depth   90
The central configuration file   95
Defining sample data   96

4.2   Building tables with Ant and SchemaExport   99

Logging with log4j and Commons Logging   102
Running SchemaExport   104 ○ Loading the
Events   106 ○ Refactoring   108 ○ Finding
Events   113 ○ Cascades   115

4.3   Components   116

What's in a component?   117 ○ Mapping a
component   119 ○ Why use a component?   121

4.4   Summary   122

5   Collections and custom types   123

5.1   Persisting collections and arrays   125

Using interfaces   126 ○ Mapping persistent
collections   128 ○ Collection types   131
Lazy collections   138 ○ Sorted collections   139
Bidirectional associations   142 ○ Cascading
collections   145

5.2   Implementing custom types   147

UserTypes   148 ○ Implementing
CompositeUserTypes   154

5.3   Summary   159

6   Querying persistent objects   161

6.1   Using HQL   162

session.find(...)   163 ○ The Query interface   164
Outer joins and HQL   168 ○ Show SQL   169
Query substitutions   169 ○ Query parser   170

6.2   Querying objects with HQL   171

The FROM clause   171 ○ Joins   172
Selects   174 ○ Using functions   176
HQL properties   178 ○ Using expressions   179

6.3   Criteria queries   183

6.4   Stored procedures   185

6.5   Hibern8IDE   186

6.6   Summary   187

7   Organizing with Spring
      and data access objects   189

7.1   The ubiquitous DAO pattern   190

Keeping the HQL together   191

7.2   Analyzing the DAO   196

Boilerplate code   196 ○ Potential
duplication   196 ○ Detached objects only   197

7.3   The Layer Supertype pattern   198

Creating an AbstractDao   199

7.4   The Spring Framework   202

What's in a template?   204
Beans and their factories   208

7.5   Summary   215

8   Web frameworks: WebWork, Struts,
      and Tapestry   217

8.1   Defining the application   219

8.2   A quick overview of MVC   219

Service Layer pattern   222

8.3   Decoupling Hibernate from the web layer   227

Working with detached objects   227 ○ Session
scope   229 ○ Accessing the Session from the
Controller   230 ○ Accessing the Session from
the Service layer   235

8.4 WebWork 238
      WebWork fundamentals 238
      Creating controllers 239

8.5 Struts 253
      Struts fundamentals 254
      Building Struts Actions 256

8.6 Tapestry 261
      Getting started 261 ○ Tapestry
      fundamentals 261 ○ HTML views 262
      Page controller 264 ○ Page specification 267
      web.xml 269

8.7 Hibernate in the view layer 270

8.8 Summary 272

9   Hibernating with XDoclet 274

9.1 Essential XDoclet 276
      JavaDoc basics 276 ○ XDoclet: Building your own
      tags 277 ○ Installing XDoclet 279
      Configuring Ant 280

9.2 Making single objects persistent 282
      The @hibernate.class tag 283 ○ The @hibernate.id
      tag 284 ○ The @hibernate.property tag 287
      The @hibernate.column tag 289

9.3 Basic relationships 292
      The @hibernate.many-to-one tag 292
      The @hibernate.component tag 295

9.4 Building collections 300
      One-to-many: a kicking set of Speakers 301
      The @hibernate.set tag 303
      The @hibernate.collection-key 304
      The @hibernate.collection-one-to-many tag 305

9.5 Going where no XDoclet has gone before 306
      Merge points 306 ○ Property substitution 308

9.6 Generating the hibernate.cfg.xml file 310

9.7 Summary 311

10   Unit testing with JUnit and DBUnit   313

10.1   *Introduction to unit testing   314*
Automate those tests   315   ○   Assertions   316
Expect failures   317

10.2   *JUnit   318*
Test-infecting your build file   318
Polishing off the build file   321

10.3   *Testing the persistence layer   324*
What do we want to test?   324   ○   Testing basic
persistence   325   ○   Testing queries   329
General database testing tips   331

10.4   *Testing with DBUnit   336*
Loading test data   336
ProjectDatabaseTestCase   340

10.5   *Summary   345*

11   What's new in Hibernate 3   346

11.1   *Filters   347*

11.2   *Mapping improvements   348*
Multiple table mapping   348   ○   Discriminator
formulas   349   ○   Union subclasses   351
Property references   352

11.3   *Dynamic classes   352*

11.4   *Annotations   354*

11.5   *Stored procedures and SQL   357*

11.6   *Persistence events   359*

11.7   *Lazy properties   361*

11.8   *Summary   363*

Appendix   The complete Hibernate mapping catalog   364

Index   411

Preface

Like many others, I started writing my own persistence framework before I discovered Hibernate. In 2002, I was working on a large business-to-business portal that underwent frequent changes. It seemed that the persistence code changed weekly, making it impossible to both maintain the SQL and have a stable system. My first attempt at a persistence framework covered a few of the basics: associations and SQL generation. When these proved insufficient for my needs, I realized the task was large and began looking at the available persistence options for Java applications. I soon decided to go with Hibernate.

Hibernate was still relatively new at the time; version 1.0 had just been released. However, it seemed the logical choice—it wasn't overly complicated and offered the features that I needed and didn't have time to implement. Hibernate also didn't require that I change my existing code to accommodate it.

I quickly became impressed by Hibernate, having used it on a few projects. In the developer community, its popularity skyrocketed with version 2.0. I wrote a well received introductory article about Hibernate for TheServerSide, and eventually received an offer to contribute to the upcoming book *Hibernate in Action* from Manning. Shortly after that, Manning asked if I would be interested in writing another, complementary book on Hibernate with co-author Patrick Peak.

Patrick too had written articles on TheServerSide and we discovered a mutual interest in working together. The idea of writing a complete book loomed as a daunting undertaking but we could not resist. We decided to write the book as quickly as possible, while still publishing a first rate product.

Hibernate Quickly is the end result. Unlike *Hibernate in Action* which is an exhaustive reference, this book attempts to introduce the reader quickly to the core knowledge needed to start being productive with Hibernate. It uses the remaining pages to cover the larger environment that Hibernate operates in—the Hibernate "ecosystem." Hibernate 3 was released as we were finishing the writing and the book covers the newest, version 3.0 features.

Of course, we couldn't have done it alone—writing a book is a team effort and our team included reviewers, friends, colleagues, and the staff at Manning. I hope you will learn as much from reading this book as we did writing it.

NICK HEUDECKER

Acknowledgments

Although only our names appear on the cover, this book would not have been possible without a dedicated team of individuals who assisted in helping us get the job done.

We'd like to start by thanking the Hibernate developers for creating a great product and working to build a community around it. Without community, Hibernate wouldn't have the vibrancy that it currently enjoys.

We also appreciate the contributions of our technical reviewers, including Will Lopez, Richard Brewster, Peter Eisentraut, Jack Herrington, Mark Monster, Doug Warren, Michael Koziarski, Norman Richards, Sang Shin, Christopher Bailey, Andrew Grothe, Anjan Bacchu, Will Forster, Christopher Haupt, Ryan Daigle, and Ryan Cox. You helped us focus the book in the right places and for the right audience.

The production of this book owes a great deal to everyone at Manning, including our publisher, Marjan Bace. We owe a special debt to our developmental editor, Jackie Carter, whose endless patience and guidance made this book possible. Thanks to our review editor Karen Tegtmayer, our technical editor Doug Warren, our copy editors Liz Welch and Tiffany Taylor, proofreader Barbara Mirecki, typesetter Dottie Marsico, cover designer Leslie Haimes, publicist Helen Trimes, project editor Mary Piergies, and Manning web master Iain Shigeoka.

To everyone involved in the project: Without your assistance, *Hibernate Quickly* wouldn't be the book we wanted it to be.

About this book

Hibernate is a solid, productive Object Relational Mapping (ORM) tool that lets developers think and work with objects rather than tables and columns. It has grown over the years, been used by many developers, and has gone through three major versions. This book's goal is to make you productive with Hibernate.

Hibernate Quickly is a gradual introduction to the features of Hibernate, covering the latest version, Hibernate 3. Each chapter introduces a series of concepts that form a foundation for the next chapter, but should illustrate those concepts completely. We set out to write the book we would have liked to have when we first learned Hibernate. We both think that studying good code examples is one of the best ways to learn, so we included as many as we could. We also wanted to make our own reference, a book we could have on our desk and turn to when we forgot just how that one mapping needed to be written.

Developers don't work with Hibernate in a vacuum. In addition to standard Java, developers often use Hibernate with a host of other third-party (often open source) tools and libraries, including J2EE (web applications); build tools like Ant; unit-testing frameworks like JUnit; and frameworks like XDoclet, Struts, WebWork, Tapestry, and Spring. This book shows how Hibernate fits into your development projects by demonstrating how these third party tools can be integrated with Hibernate. Because this book is about Hibernate, and we didn't want it to be 1,000 pages long or weigh as much as a battleship, we assume that developers are partially familiar with the third-party libraries with which they want to integrate Hibernate. We provide some introduction, so you should be able to follow along if you've used, say, Tapestry; but you should consult Manning's In Action series for more details about those tools.

Roadmap

Hibernate Quickly is logically divided into two parts. The first half of the book introduces the core concepts and features of Hibernate. The second half puts Hibernate into context by showing you how to integrate it with a number of open source tools and frameworks.

Chapter 1 is both a justification and an introduction. It covers the reasons why Hibernate is useful, and it compares and contrasts Hibernate with JDBC. It also covers the basics of what object relational mapping is and provides an introduction to how Hibernate's particular brand of persistence works.

Chapter 2 is the project kickoff. It covers setting up a Hibernate project and using Ant, an open source Java build tool. It shows you where to find both Ant and Hibernate and how to organize your project. We also discuss setting up and integrating a database, MySQL. By the end of this chapter, you should have a solid foundation for your project to build on in the subsequent chapters.

Chapter 3 is about the core concepts of Hibernate. It covers mapping files, configuration, and the essential classes developers use to persist and find objects from the database. Finally, this chapter touches on a few more advanced topics like inheritance, caching, and transactions.

Chapter 4 discusses relationships. Specifically, we cover in detail two of the most common relationships between persistent objects: many-to-one and components. This chapter also explains how to generate your database from Hibernate mappings using the SchemaExport tool.

Chapter 5 covers collections and custom types. Hibernate allows you to use basic java.util collections classes to express both one-to-many and many-to-many relationships between entities, and we show how to map and use them here. In addition, we demonstrate both how and why you can use Hibernate's custom types, which let you define new datatypes that can map to database columns.

Chapter 6 discusses finding objects. Hibernate uses a SQL-like query language that allows you to express queries using classes and properties rather than tables and columns. This chapter covers Hibernate Query Language's (HQL) syntax and usage in depth, including parameters, joins, from/select clauses, and projection. So that you can test your HQL, the chapter also touches on Hibern8IDE, a tool that lets you rapidly test and try your queries.

Chapter 7 is about patterns and architecture. We show you how to better organize your project with a few patterns like the Data Access Object (DAO) and Layer Super types. We also explain how to introduce a popular application framework, Spring, into your project. Spring integrates extremely well with Hibernate; it streamlines the DAO pattern along with some of the productive boosting features.

Chapter 8 discusses "webifying" your Hibernate application. We cover the basics of the Model View Controller pattern; and we build our sample application, the Event Calendar, using three open source web frameworks. The same application is written three times using a similar core architecture but integrated with Struts, WebWork, and Tapestry. Our intent is to show the general principles you need to consider when writing Hibernate applications for the Web.

Chapter 9 covers code generation with XDoclet. Until JDK 1.5/Java 5.0 becomes more widely accepted, Hibernate developers can either hand-write their mapping files or, better yet, use XDoclet to generate them. This chapter shows you how to do the latter. We go in depth to show you how to set up, configure, and generate mapping files for single objects, many-to-one, components, and collections. In addition, we explain how to generate your configuration files, hibernate.cfg.xml, using XDoclet.

Chapter 10 is about testing. It shows you how to use two tools, JUnit and DBUnit, to verify that your Hibernate application works as expected. We cover the general principles of unit testing and how to apply them to testing a database.

Chapter 11 discusses Hibernate 3. It's a brief guide for those who are familiar with Hibernate 2 and want to know what's new. This chapter covers the important new features, including filters, mapping file improvements, dynamic classes, and the new persistent event model.

The appendix is the reference we wanted for ourselves. It's a complete reference guide to all the common relationships that Hibernate allows. For each relationship, the appendix shows an object model, table models, Java classes (with XDoclet markup), and the resulting mapping file.

Who should read this book?

In short, Java developers who work with databases. More specifically, we aimed this book at two main groups of developers:

- Developers who are new to Hibernate and who want a step-by-step guide to getting started painlessly
- Hibernate intermediate/expert users who want to learn how to integrate Hibernate into their existing projects and make it work with all the other tools they already know

We assume you're familiar with basic object-oriented programming techniques as well as the Java language. We discuss a lot of third-party tools, like Ant and XDoclet, but no in-depth familiarity with them is needed. Because Hibernate builds on JDBC and uses databases, it's helpful if you're familiar with SQL and how to use it to work with databases using Java.

Code

The code for this project is available at this book's website, www.manning.com/books/peak.

Much of the source code shown early in the book consists of fragments designed to illustrate the text. When a complete segment of code is given, it's shown as a numbered listing; code annotations accompany some listings. When we present source code, we sometimes use a bold font to draw attention to specific elements.

In the text, a `monospaced font` is used to denote code (JSP, Java, and HTML) as well as Java methods, JSP tag names, and other source code identifiers:

A reference to a method in the text generally doesn't include the signature, because there may be more than one form of the method call.

A reference to a JSP tag includes the braces and default prefix but not the list of properties the tag accepts (`<c:out>`).

A reference to an XML element in the text includes the braces but not the properties or closing tag (`<class>`).

Author Online

Purchase of *Hibernate Quickly* includes free access to a private web forum run by Manning Publications where you can make comments about the book, ask technical questions, and receive help from the authors and from other users. To access the forum and subscribe to it, point your web browser to www.manning.com/peak. This page provides information on how to get on the forum once you are registered, what kind of help is available, and the rules of conduct on the forum.

Manning's commitment to our readers is to provide a venue where a meaningful dialog between individual readers and between readers and the authors can take place. It is not a commitment to any specific amount of participation on the part of the authors, whose contribution to the AO remains voluntary (and unpaid). We suggest you try asking them some challenging questions lest their interest stray!

The Author Online forum and the archives of previous discussions will be accessible from the publisher's website as long as the book is in print.

About the authors

PATRICK PEAK is the chief technology officer of BrowserMedia, a Java/J2EE web development/design firm in Bethesda, MD. His focus is on using open source frameworks/tools as a competitive advantage for rapid custom software development. He has been using Hibernate in numerous production applications for almost two years. He runs a Java/Technology weblog at www.patrickpeak.com.

NICK HEUDECKER is the president and founder of System Mobile, a software consulting firm headquartered in Chicago, IL. He has more than nine years of commercial development experience, and he has developed software products and solutions for multiple Fortune 500 clients as well as media, lobbying, and government organizations.

About the cover illustration

The figure on the cover of *Hibernate Quickly* is called "An Officer of the Janissaries." The illustration is taken from a collection of costumes of the Ottoman Empire published on January 1, 1802, by William Miller of Old Bond Street, London. Janissaries were soldiers of the Ottoman Turkish Army, loyal to the sultan, rather than to tribal leaders. These "New Soldiers," which is what the name means in Turkish, were the elite troops of the Ottoman Empire, renowned for their bravery and skills. The title page is missing from the collection and we have been unable to track it down to date. The book's table of contents identifies the figures in both English and French, and each illustration bears the names of two artists who worked on it, both of whom would no doubt be surprised to find their art gracing the front cover of a computer programming book...two hundred years later.

The collection was purchased by a Manning editor at an antiquarian flea market in the "Garage" on West 26th Street in Manhattan. The seller was an American based in Ankara, Turkey, and the transaction took place just as he was packing up his stand for the day. The Manning editor did not have on his person the substantial amount of cash that was required for the purchase and a credit card and check were both politely turned down.

With the seller flying back to Ankara that evening the situation was getting hopeless. What was the solution? It turned out to be nothing more than an old-fashioned verbal agreement sealed with a handshake. The seller simply proposed that the money be transferred to him by wire and the editor walked out with the bank information on a piece of paper and the portfolio of images under his arm. Needless to say, we transferred the funds the next day, and we remain grateful and impressed by this unknown person's trust in one of us. It recalls something that might have happened a long time ago.

The pictures from the Ottoman collection, like the other illustrations that appear on our covers, bring to life the richness and variety of dress customs of two centuries ago. They recall the sense of isolation and distance of that period—and of every other historic period except our own hyperkinetic present.

Dress codes have changed since then and the diversity by region, so rich at the time, has faded away. It is now often hard to tell the inhabitant of one continent from another. Perhaps, trying to view it optimistically, we have traded a cultural and visual diversity for a more varied personal life. Or a more varied and interesting intellectual and technical life.

We at Manning celebrate the inventiveness, the initiative, and, yes, the fun of the computer business with book covers based on the rich diversity of regional life of two centuries ago, brought back to life by the pictures from this collection.

1

Why Hibernate?

In this chapter

- *Understanding persistence and object/relational mapping*
- *Introducing Hibernate*

We've all been there. Six weeks into a cumbersome project, updated requirements are received from the client that result in massive changes to your application code. Weeks of work have to be scrapped or changed to comply with the new requirements. Updating the web pages or GUI is relatively simple, but hundreds or thousands of lines of database code, including your beautiful, handcrafted SQL, have to be updated and tested.

There needs to be a better way to build database-backed applications.

This book presents Hibernate, an object/relational mapping framework for Java applications. Hibernate provides the bridge between the database and the application by storing application objects in the database for the developer, rather than requiring the developer to write and maintain mountains of code to store and retrieve objects.

You may wonder why Manning decided to publish a second book on Hibernate. After all, *Hibernate in Action* is the authoritative source, written by the project founders and widely regarded as the best reference on the topic. Manning feels there are two distinct needs. One calls for a focused and comprehensive book on the subject of Hibernate. It serves as the place

1

to turn to when any Hibernate questions occur. The other need is for a book that gives readers the proverbial 20% of information they require 80% of the time, including all the peripheral technologies and techniques surrounding Hibernate. This is the book you are likely to turn to if you want to get up and running quickly.

Since Hibernate is a persistence service, it's rarely the only framework or tool used in an application. You'll typically use Hibernate alongside a web application or inversion-of-control framework, or even a GUI toolkit such as Swing or SWT. After covering the basics of Hibernate in the first few chapters, we'll move on to discuss development tools like Ant and XDoclet. The majority of applications using Hibernate will be web applications, so we'll look at how Hibernate integrates with three popular web frameworks: Struts, Webwork, and Tapestry. We'll also look at some support frameworks and utilities, like Spring and JUnit.

This chapter is meant primarily for developers who haven't been exposed to object/relational mapping in the past and are wondering what all the fuss is about. We start by introducing the concept of object persistence and some of the difficult problems encountered when storing objects in a relational database. Then we examine the shortcomings of storing objects in a database using Java Database Connectivity (JDBC). After reviewing the popular methods used to persist objects, we discuss how Hibernate solves most, if not all, of these issues.

Chapter goals

The goals for this chapter are as follows:

- Explain the concept of object persistence.
- Describe the object/relational mismatch and how JDBC fails to resolve it.
- Introduce object persistence with Hibernate.

Assumptions

Because object/relational mapping can be a complicated subject, we assume that you

- Are comfortable building Java applications using JDBC
- Have built database-centric applications
- Understand basic relational theory and Structured Query Language (SQL)

1.1 Understanding object persistence

The common definition of persistence, related to software, is data that outlives the process that created it. When data is persistent, you can obtain the data at a later point in time and it will be the same as when you left it, assuming an outside process didn't change it.

There are a few kinds of persistence. When you're editing a source file, that file is persisted to disk for later retrieval and use. Files stored on disk are probably the most common form of persistence. When we refer to persistence in this book, we're referring to storing application data in a relational database. Applications, such as an online shopping cart, typically persist data in a relational database.

Relational databases are a popular choice for storing data for a number of reasons. They're relatively easy to create and access, using the SQL. Vendors also offer relational databases with a variety of features, allowing you to select the ideal database for your application's needs. Because relational databases are so common, finding developers with relevant experience is less difficult than for niche technologies.

The model used by relational databases, called the relational model, represents data in two-dimensional tables. This logical view of the data is how database users see the contained data. Tables can relate to each other through the use of primary and foreign keys. Primary keys uniquely identify a given row in a table, whereas foreign keys refer to a primary key stored in another table.

Relational databases are designed to manage the data they contain, and they're very good at it. However, when you're working with object-oriented applications, you may encounter a problem when you try to persist objects to a relational model. As just stated, relational databases manage data. Object-oriented applications are designed to model a business problem. With two radically different purposes in mind, getting the models to work together can be challenging. Resolving the differences has been the subject of much debate over the years and has been referred to as the object/relational impedance mismatch or just impedance mismatch.

The impedance mismatch is caused by the differences between object and relational schemas. Most developers who have used direct JDBC to store objects are aware the mismatch exists, even if they don't know the name for it. We'll look at a few areas of the impedance mismatch next.

1.1.1 Identity

One of the more significant areas of the impedance mismatch is in regard to identity. Java objects exist independently of the values they contain, which is to say that

```
objectA == objectB;
```

is different from

```
objectA.equals(objectB);
```

So, objects can either be identical or equal. If two objects are identical, they're the same object. If the objects are equal, they contain the same values. These different notions of identity don't exist in relational models. Rows in a relational database are only identified by the values they contain. How can you identify objects with their relational counterparts?

A common way to overcome this problem in relational models is to introduce a unique identifier column, typically called a sequence or identifier. The relational identifier is also represented in the object model and becomes a surrogate for identity checking.

Although the object identity problem can be resolved, a more significant mismatch occurs when your object model uses inheritance.

1.1.2 Inheritance

A core feature of object-oriented languages is the ability to have one object inherit from one or many parent objects. Figure 1.1 illustrates an object hierarchy used in our example application.

Relational databases don't support the notion of inheritance, so persisting a rich object hierarchy to a relational schema can be complex. Since inheritance is difficult to translate to a relational model, why can't you just design your object model without hierarchies?

Object-oriented languages were developed to model real-world problems. Inheritance is vital because it allows you to create a precise model of the problem while allowing shared properties and behavior to cascade down the hierarchy. You shouldn't be forced into sacrificing this feature because the relational model doesn't support it.

1.1.3 Associations

The last portion of the impedance mismatch we'll look at is the differences in associations between object and relational models. Associations are probably one of the easiest portions of the mismatch to overcome since both models support this notion. The relational model understands only one type of association: a foreign key reference to a

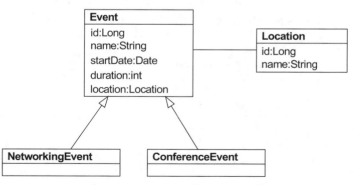

Figure 1.1 Simple object hierarchy

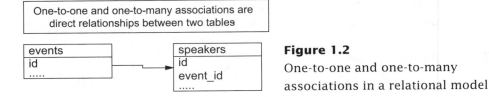

Figure 1.2
One-to-one and one-to-many associations in a relational model

primary key stored in another table. Compare that to the associations available in an object model: one-to-one, one-to-many and many-to-many.

Converting an object-based one-to-one association to a relational schema is simple: Reference the primary key of the associated objects. If you have a one-to-many association, you can repeat this process for each row on the "many" side. The only problem is that the database doesn't understand the one-to-many association—it only knows that a foreign key refers to a primary key. Let's look at a diagram of one-to-one and one-to-many associations in a relational schema, shown in figure 1.2.

Mapping a many-to-many association is typically done with a join table. The join table contains two foreign key columns referencing two tables, allowing multiple entries for each side of the association. Figure 1.3 illustrates a many-to-many join table.

1.1.4 Object/relational mapping

We've touched on a few problems illustrating the impedance mismatch, but we haven't covered all areas of the mismatch. Our goal was simply

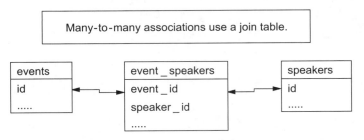

Figure 1.3 Many-to-many associations in a relational model

to explain what most developers realize intrinsically: Merging objects with a relational schema isn't easy. Object/relational mapping was developed to solve these problems.

Object/relational mapping (ORM) is the process of persisting objects in a relational database. ORM bridges the gap between object and relational schemas, allowing your application to persist objects directly without requiring you to convert objects to and from a relational format. There are many types of ORM solutions, offering varying levels of mapping support. Some ORM frameworks require that persistent objects inherit from a base class or perform post-processing of bytecode.

Hibernate, on the other hand, requires a small amount of metadata for each persistent object. Hibernate is a noninvasive ORM service. It doesn't require bytecode processing or a base persistent class. Hibernate operates independently of application architecture, allowing it to be used in various applications. It provides full object/relational mapping, meaning that it supports all the available object-oriented features that relational databases lack.

Developers accustomed to using the standard JDBC API may wonder why a tool like Hibernate is needed. After all, JDBC provides a simple and complete interface to relational databases. Using JDBC directly is ideal for basic applications, since you can quickly persist objects with well-understood code. However, JDBC can get out of hand with larger applications or when requirements change. If an object changes, the code that persists the object must be changed and tested, as well as all the SQL used to manage the object's state.

Using Hibernate for application persistence helps avoid the drawbacks of raw JDBC. In section 1.2, we demonstrate the shortcomings of these techniques; then, in section 1.3, we explain how Hibernate allows you to bypass them.

Of course, object/relational mapping isn't a silver bullet for persistence problems. There are instances where ORM, and therefore Hibernate, isn't the best solution.

When to use ORM

Although powerful, object/relational mapping is fundamentally limited by the underlying database schema, particularly in legacy databases. For instance, if tables refer to each other through columns other than primary keys, your chosen ORM solution may have trouble adapting to the legacy schema. Let's look at a good example of a bad design, shown in figure 1.4.

Admittedly, this schema is a contrived example; but before you dismiss it, realize that schemas even more poorly designed than this exist in enterprise applications. Just what's wrong with this schema? None of the tables have a surrogate primary key. By a surrogate key, we mean that the table's primary key has no business significance. All the columns in the tables are relevant to the business problem.

You can certainly map these tables to objects with an ORM solution, but that may not be the best way to handle the domain model. You may spend more time working around how your ORM framework manages the data than is desirable. Alternative solutions, such as iBATIS, may be a better candidate for persisting legacy databases.[1]

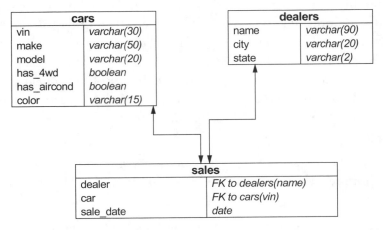

Figure 1.4 Poorly designed database schema

---

[1] iBATIS (www.ibatis.com) is an alternative to Hibernate.

ORM is a good solution for legacy databases when the schema

- Is highly normalized
- Has primary keys
- Has foreign key relationships referring to primary keys, not columns

Thankfully, the Hibernate developers have been responsive to developers working with legacy database schemas. Hibernate 3, discussed in chapter 11, adds many new features to support legacy database schemas.

Before diving into what Hibernate offers, let's take a brief look at why using JDBC is so painful for large applications. If you're still clinging to direct JDBC for application persistence, the next section is for you.

1.2 Using direct JDBC

The core drawback of JDBC is that it doesn't allow you to store objects directly to the database—you must convert the objects to a relational format. For instance, if you want to persist a new instance of the Event class to the database, you must first convert the Event object to a SQL statement that can be executed on the underlying database. Similarly, when rows are returned from the database, you must convert each result row into an instance of Event. Let's look at some of the difficulties presented when converting objects and graphs of objects between the relational and object models.

When working with objects, you're generally using a number of connected objects. This is called an object graph. An object graph represents an internally consistent view of application data. Internally consistent means that a change made to one object is reflected throughout the graph. The objects within a graph are typically connected using one-to-one or one-to-many associations.

Using direct JDBC for persistence presents distinct problems for each of the persistence operations: creation, updating, retrieval, and deletion. Some of the problems we describe expand on the object/relational mismatch, discussed earlier. We examine those problems in detail in a moment, using an example application that will reappear throughout this book.

1.2.1 Example application

To address the drawbacks of traditional application persistence with JDBC, we must first introduce an example that we'll use as the basis of comparison. The application that we use throughout the book is an event-management application used to manage a conference with speakers, attendees, and various locations, among other things. To demonstrate the problems with JDBC, we'll discuss persisting one of the central objects in the domain model, Event.

We use the term domain model frequently. A domain model is the collection of related objects describing the problem domain for an application. Each object in the domain model represents some significant component in the application, such as an Event or Speaker.

Diagrams of the Event object and the relational table used to store the Event are shown in figure 1.5.

The parallel between the Event object and the relational table is clear. Each property in the Event class is reflected as a column in the events table. The id column in the events table is the primary key for the table. We've intentionally kept the Event object simple for the opening discussion. With the object and relational table defined, we can move forward with examining the drawbacks of application persistence with direct JDBC.

Event
id:Long
name:String
startDate:java.util.Date
duration:int

events	
id	bigint (pk)
name	varchar (255)
start _date	date
duration	int

Figure 1.5 The Event object and the events table

1.2.2 Retrieving object graphs using JDBC

Looking at the diagram of the Event object in figure 1.5, it appears that converting between relational and object models presents little difficulty. Problems arise when we want to retrieve a complete object graph from a relational schema. Figure 1.6 presents a domain model for our event-management application.

The Event class has three associations: a one-to-one association to the Location object and two one-to-many associations to the Speaker and Attendee objects. Figure 1.7 shows the relational tables for the domain model. (The speakers table is omitted since it's identical to the attendees table.)

Let's look at the one-to-one association of the events and locations tables. The tables can be joined to retrieve the data from the locations table for a given row in the events table with the following SQL:

```
select e.id, e.name, e.start_date, e.duration, l.id, l.name
from events e join locations l on e.location_id = l.id
where e.id = 1000;
```

Executing this SQL returns a single row with columns containing data from both the events and locations tables.

The associations between the Event object and the Attendee and Speaker objects can be more difficult to manage because they involve

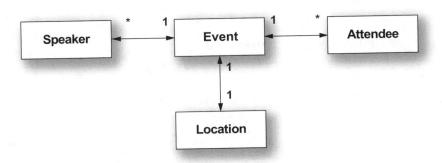

Figure 1.6 A domain model for an Event

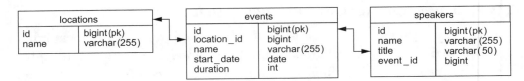

Figure 1.7 The foreign keys for events and speakers

one-to-many associations. Object associations are directional, from one object to another object. To navigate from both ends of the association, you must define the association in both objects. Listing 1.1 illustrates the one-to-many association between the Event and Speaker objects, using the following Java classes.

Listing 1.1 Creating a bidirectional association

```
package com.manning.hq.ch01;
import java.util.List;

public class Event {

    private String name;
    private List speakers;
    private Location location;

    public String getName() {
      return name;
    }

    public void setName(String name) {
      this.name = name;
    }

    public List getSpeakers() {
        return this.speakers;
    }

    public void setSpeakers(List speakers) {
        this.speakers = speakers;
    }

    public Location getLocation() {
      return location;
```

```
    }

    public void setLocation(Location location) {
      this.location = location;
    }
}

package com.manning.hq.ch01;
public class Speaker {

    private Event event;

    public Event getEvent() {
        return this.event;
    }

    public void setEvent(Event event) {
        this.event = event;
    }
}

package com.manning.hq.ch01;

public class Location {

    private Long id = null;
    private String name = null;
    private Event event = null;

    public Long getId() {
      return id;
    }

    public void setId(Long id) {
      this.id = id;
    }

    public String getName() {
      return name;
    }

    public void setName(String name) {
      this.name = name;
    }

    public Event getEvent() {
      return event;
```

```
    }
    public void setEvent(Event event) {
      this.event = event;
    }
  }
```

By defining the association in both objects, you can navigate in either direction: from the Speaker to the Event or from the Event to the Speaker. When translating this association to the relational database, you'll realize that whereas the database has the notion of the association through the use of foreign keys, it lacks the notion of association multiplicity. The database doesn't know that there are multiple rows in the speakers table linked to the events table. You must write the logic to retrieve relevant rows from the database to populate the one-to-many associations.

To retrieve associated rows from the speakers table for a row in the events table, you must execute separate queries for each table. Why can't you use another table join to the speakers table to retrieve the data for the object graph, as you did for the locations table?

Suppose you want to retrieve one row in both the events and locations table, and they're linked with a foreign key. The row in the events table is linked to four rows in the speakers table, also with a foreign key. The SQL to retrieve all data associated to the event data is shown here:

```
select e.name, l.name, s.first_name, s.last_name from events e
join locations l on e.location_id = l.id
join speakers s on s.event_id = e.id
where e.id = 1000;
```

Executing this SQL results in a Cartesian product of the data, as shown in figure 1.8. (If you're unfamiliar with the term, a Cartesian product is the combination of all pairs of elements in two sets.)

e.name	l.name	s.name
Opening Presentation	Hilton Convention Center	Amy Watkins
Opening Presentation	Hilton Convention Center	Mark Johannson
Opening Presentation	Hilton Convention Center	Diane Davies
Opening Presentation	Hilton Convention Center	Marcus Smith

Figure 1.8 Cartesian product result

Although all the data was retrieved with a single query, Cartesian products are generally inefficient. For this reason, to retrieve the data for one-to-many associations, you should execute a separate query for each object.

Remember that the domain model in figure 1.2 also has a one-to-many association of Attendee instances. To retrieve the data for the Attendee objects, you must write operations similar to the Speaker association. Since an object graph often contains many objects, the amount of code needed to retrieve a full object graph for an Event can be quite large.

Usually you only need to retrieve a portion of the object graph for a specific view that is presented to the user, such as displaying the Attendee instances assigned to an Event. Retrieving the extra objects results in needless calls to the database and overhead in converting the ResultSet into the corresponding domain objects.

A direct JDBC persistence layer would need to provide the ability to return specific portions of the object graph, including the ability to populate collections of associations when required. These aren't trivial tasks and require a significant investment for the developers and organization.

To this point, we have discussed retrieving objects. New problems arise when you try to persist an object graph to a relational database.

1.2.3 Persisting object graphs to a relational model

If a new instance of Event needs to be persisted, you must first convert the instance into a format for inclusion in a SQL statement. Assuming that Speaker and Attendee instances have been associated with the

Event, you must also convert and persist these associations, maintaining their link to the parent Event. Some of the objects in the graph may already exist in the database, but other new objects may have been added to the graph. How can you determine which objects in the graph should be inserted and which should be updated?

You can usually determine the operation to execute by examining the object's id property. If the ID type is an object, such as a Long or Integer, you can assume that the object is transient and hasn't yet been persisted if the ID's value is null. If the ID type is a primitive, such as int or long, a value of 0 indicates a transient object. (Recall that ints and longs are initialized to 0.) In both cases, a SQL INSERT should be issued after converting the object to a relational format. Otherwise, an UPDATE would be issued for the object, keyed on the value of the ID.

At what point is the value of the id property assigned? If the database supports identity columns or sequences, you can let the database assign the ID value. Alternatively, you can have the application assign the ID value, but this must be handled carefully. Application-managed identity generators must ensure that the generator is thread-safe, is efficient, and won't deadlock under heavy load. For the examples in this book, we use database-generated identifier values.

Let's examine this process with an example of persisting an object graph. Start by creating a new graph, shown in listing 1.2.

Listing 1.2 Creating a new object graph

```java
package com.manning.hq.ch01;

import java.util.ArrayList;
import java.util.List;

public class Example2 {

  private Event event = null;
  private List speakers = null;

  public static void main(String[] args) {
    Example2 app = new Example2();
```

```
    app.doMain(args);
  }

  private void doMain(String[] args) {
    // Create the Event instance
    event = createEvent();
    // Create two Speaker instances
    speakers = createSpeakers();
    // and add them to the Event
    event.setSpeakers(speakers);
  }

  private Event createEvent() {
    Event event = new Event();
    event.setName("Opening Presentation");
    // ... set date and duration
    return event;
  }

  private List createSpeakers() {
    List speakers = new ArrayList();
    Speaker speaker0 = new Speaker();
    Speaker speaker1 = new Speaker();
    // ... set properties for speakers
    speakers.add(speaker0);
    speakers.add(speaker1);
    return speakers;
  }
}
```

When persisting the object graph, you first need to save the Event instance and retrieve the created ID value from the database. This new ID value is used as the foreign key for each of the associated objects — the Speaker instances — when they're persisted.

Although cumbersome, this method works as long as the object graph is persisted from the parent to the children. This is referred to as a cascading save. If you add a new Location to the object graph, as in listing 1.3, the direct JDBC persistence layer must specify that the Location instance needs to be persisted before the Event to avoid a foreign key violation when the row is inserted into the events table.

Listing 1.3 Setting a newly created Location for the Event

```
private Location location = null;

private void doMain(String[] args) {
  // Create location
  location = createLocation();
  // Create Event instance
  event = createEvent(location);
  // Create two Speaker instances
  speakers = createSpeakers();
  // and add them to the Event
  event.setSpeakers(speakers);
}

private Location createLocation() {
  Location location = new Location();
  location.setName("Grand Hyatt - Convention Room A");
  return location;
}

private Event createEvent(Location location) {
  Event event = new Event();
  event.setName("Opening Presentation");
  // Assign location to event
  event.setLocation(location);
  // Establish bi-directional association
  location.setEvent(event);
  // ... set date and duration
  return event;
}
```

A persistence layer implemented with direct JDBC must be able to persist all or part of a complex object graph while avoiding foreign key violations. Similar behavior is required when deleting objects and object graphs from a relational database.

1.2.4 Deleting object graphs

Suppose that an Event has been cancelled and the associated data should be removed from the database. The direct JDBC persistence layer must handle deleting not only the Event, but also the objects associated to the Event, such as the Speakers and Attendees. The delete operation should not cascade to the Location, however, since multiple Events can be held at a given Location. Assuming that a Location needs to be deleted, each of the corresponding Events held at the Location should also be deleted, being careful to cascade to the child objects of the Event.

Deleting, or making a persistent object transient, is the easiest persistence operation when you're using direct JDBC for application persistence. Still, you must be careful to delete only the relevant objects from the graph.

1.2.5 Querying object graphs

Although JDBC's Statement and PreparedStatement classes provide the ability to query a database, you must still write the SQL statement and process the results. Most direct JDBC persistence layers have some form of SQL generation for the objects in the domain model, but it's often incomplete and lacks the flexibility needed for an enterprise application. The SQL generation component must also be updated as the application matures and requirements change.

Executing a query with the Statement or PreparedStatement class returns a ResultSet object containing the query results. The ResultSet is essentially a list of key-value pairs. Each entry in the list represents one result row: The key is the column name, and the value is the data returned.

Now that you have the results, how should you return the data to the application? There are two options: You can convert the results either into a list of Event objects or into a list of Map instances. The latter solution may seem more appealing because it's easier to code (you can add the properties as Map.Entry objects), but this method also introduces some problems.

A plain old Java object (POJO), such as the Event object, support primitive type properties, such as int, char, and boolean, as well as objects, such as `String` and `Date`. The Java Collections classes only support objects. To return a list of `Map` instances, you would need to convert each primitive type into its object representation.

By using `Map` instances, you also forfeit any behavior that the `Event` class provides. Recall that a domain model contains both the data and the behavior for the objects. Clearly, the benefit of the domain model is lost if the `Event` instances aren't used.

To return a list of `Event` instances from a `ResultSet`, you must convert each result row into a corresponding `Event` instance. Data returned for associated objects, like `Location`, must also be converted and set for the `Event`. While this may not seem like a huge chore, writing code to convert every object to and from a relational schema quickly becomes tedious and error-prone.

There are clearly a number of open issues when persisting objects with direct JDBC. You can certainly try to answer all of them, but this results in a large number of classes, repetitive and complicated code, as well as a huge time commitment in maintenance and testing.

Next, we'll look at how to use Hibernate to overcome some of the problems that JDBC presents.

1.3   Persistence with Hibernate

After examining the shortcomings in our persistence techniques using direct JDBC, let's discuss the benefits of using Hibernate for application persistence. Hibernate addresses all the shortcomings of the previous persistence methods and offers a number of additional features. The core benefits of Hibernate are simplicity, flexibility, completeness, and performance.

1.3.1   Simplicity and flexibility

Rather than the handful of classes and configuration properties required by some persistence solutions, such as EJBs, Hibernate requires a single runtime configuration file and one mapping document for each application object to be persisted. The runtime configuration file can be a standard key-value properties file or an XML file. Alternatively, you can configure the runtime portion of Hibernate programmatically.

The XML-formatted mapping documents can be very short, leaving the framework to determine the remainder of the mapping. Optionally, you can provide the framework with more information by specifying additional properties, such as an alternative column name for a property. Listing 1.4 show the mapping document for the Event class.

Listing 1.4 Hibernate mapping document for the Event class

```xml
<?xml version="1.0"?>
<hibernate-mapping package="com.manning.hq.ch01">
    <class name="Event" table="events">
        <id name="id" column="uid" type="long">
            <generator class="native"/>
        </id>
        <property name="name" type="string"/>
        <property name="startDate" column="start_date"
                  type="date"/>
        <property name="duration" type="integer"/>
        <many-to-one name="location" column="location_id"/>
        <set name="speakers">
            <key column="event_id"/>
            <one-to-many class="Speaker"/>
        </set>
        <set name="attendees">
            <key column="event_id"/>
            <one-to-many class="Attendee"/>
        </set>
    </class>
</hibernate-mapping>
```

Don't worry if aspects of the mapping document are confusing. We'll cover this document in detail in chapters 2 and 3.

To use some persistence frameworks, such as EJBs, your application becomes dependent on that framework. Hibernate doesn't create this additional dependency. Persistent objects in your application don't have to inherit from a Hibernate class or obey specific semantics: You simply create your Java objects and the associated mapping documents. Persisting the application objects is then left to Hibernate.

Also, unlike EJBs, Hibernate doesn't require a special container in order to function. Hibernate can be used in any application environment, from standalone applications to enterprise application servers.

In the next section, you'll see that the functionality and ease provided by Hibernate don't come at the cost of limited support for object-oriented features.

1.3.2 Completeness

Unlike most homegrown persistence layers, Hibernate supports the full range of object-oriented features, including inheritance, custom object types, and collections. Without support for these features, you may be forced to alter the application domain model to meet the limitations of the persistence layer. Hibernate frees you to create a domain model without concern for persistence layer limitations.

Hibernate provides a SQL abstraction layer called the Hibernate Query Language (HQL). HQL strongly resembles SQL, with object property names taking the place of table columns. HQL has special support for collections, object indexes, and named query parameters, as shown in the following examples.

This query returns a `List` of `String` objects containing the names of the `Event` instances in the database:

```
select e.name from Event e;
```

Note the e shorthand notation for query objects. Of course, you aren't limited to basic queries:

```
from Event e where size(e.speakers) > 2;
```

This time, we're returning all Event instances with more than two Speakers. The size(...) function requires a database that supports subselects. You'll notice that we didn't need to include a SELECT clause. (We'll revisit this topic in chapter 6.) Let's look at one more example:

```
select s from Event e join e.speakers s where e.id = :eventId;
```

Here, we're selecting all the Speaker instances for a given Event ID. The example in the previous listing demonstrates named queries. Hibernate's Query interface provides methods to populate named parameters in addition to standard JDBC parameters. HQL statements are compiled into database-specific SQL statements by the Hibernate framework and cached for reuse. We cover HQL in detail in chapter 6.

In the next section, we discuss a concern that most people have when examining a new framework: performance.

1.3.3 Performance

A popular misconception is that ORM frameworks severely impact application performance. This isn't the case with Hibernate. The key performance measure for an ORM framework is whether it performs its tasks using the minimum number of database queries. This holds for inserting and updating objects as well as retrieving them from the database. Many hand-coded JDBC persistence frameworks update the state of an object in the database even if the object's state hasn't changed. Hibernate issues an update for an object only if its state has actually changed.

Lazy collections provide another performance enhancement. Rather than load collections of objects when the parent object is loaded, collections are populated only when they're accessed by the application. Developers new to Hibernate often misunderstand this powerful feature.

If you were using direct JDBC for persistence, you would need to explicitly populate the collection of Speaker instances for an Event. This would occur either when the object was initially loaded or from a separate call after the Event object was loaded. With Hibernate, you just load the Event instance from the database. The collection of Speaker instances is populated only when accessed. This ensures that you aren't retrieving unnecessary objects, which can severely impact performance.

Another performance-enhancing feature is the ability to selectively disable which associated objects are retrieved when the primary object is retrieved. This is accomplished by setting the outer-join property for the association. For instance, let's say you have a User class with a one-to-one association to a Department class. When you're retrieving a User instance, you don't always need the associated Department instance, so you can declare that the object should be retrieved only when needed by setting outer-join to false.

It's also possible to declare proxies for objects, resulting in the objects being populated only when accessed by the developer. When you declare a proxy, Hibernate creates an unpopulated representation of the persistent class. The proxy is replaced with the actual instance of the persistent class only when you access the object by calling one of its methods.

Proxies are related to the outer-join setting we just mentioned. Using the same brief example, if the Department class is declared to have a proxy, you don't need to set the outer-join from the User to the Department to false—the Hibernate service will only populate the Department instance when needed.

Object caching also plays a large role in improving application performance. Hibernate supports various open-source and commercial caching products. Caching can be enabled for a persistent class or for a collection of persistent objects, such as the collection of Speaker instances for an Event. (We'll look at how to configure caches in chapter 3.) Query results can also be cached, but doing so only benefits queries that run with the same parameters. Query caching doesn't significantly benefit application performance, but the option is available for appropriate cases.

1.4 Summary

We've covered a lot of ground in this chapter. We introduced the concepts of persistence and object/relational mapping as well as the problems that exist when you're persisting objects to a relational database. We also reviewed the shortcomings of using JDBC for persistence in Java applications and introduced Hibernate as an alternative persistence technique.

We started this chapter by introducing the object/relational impedance mismatch. The mismatch occurs because of the fundamental differences between the object and relational models. The three areas of the mismatch we examined were identity, inheritance, and associations. The impedance mismatch is solved to varying degrees by ORM frameworks.

Applications with basic persistence requirements typically use JDBC because the API is simple and most developers are familiar with it. However, JDBC requires application developers to write, maintain, and test a great deal of repetitive code. JDBC doesn't handle domain objects directly, requiring you to map domain objects to relational tables. This problem is further complicated as the domain model increases in complexity.

Hibernate is designed to address the shortcomings in direct JDBC and other ORM frameworks. Using Hibernate doesn't require that your domain objects implement specific interfaces or use an application server. It supports collections, inheritance, and custom data types, as well as a rich query language.

Throughout this book, we'll introduce the core features of Hibernate as well as how to build applications with Hibernate. But first, you have to install it. The next chapter discusses installing Hibernate, Ant, and MySQL so that you can begin using Hibernate immediately.

2

Installing and building projects with Ant

This chapter covers

- Getting and installing Hibernate
- Installing and learning the basics of Ant
- Setting up and testing MySQL
- Creating a basic project using Ant

Now that we've laid out the case why Hibernate is a useful tool for developers, this chapter discusses how you can get the tools, set up a project, and start persisting your Java objects. All nontrivial tools, including open-source ones like Hibernate, have quite a few moving parts that need to be set up in order to work correctly. Often the most difficult part of any project is getting started—and if you've never set up a project that uses Hibernate, figuring out where to start can be a bit overwhelming.

In this chapter, we'll cover setting up three essential open-source tools: Hibernate; MySQL, the most popular open-source database; and Ant, the premier Java build tool. Ant isn't strictly necessary for our example project, but it can make life easier; not using it would be like coding with one hand tied behind your back.

Chapter goals

The main purpose of this chapter is to get you ready to start building Hibernate projects. To achieve this, you'll accomplish a few general tasks by the close of the chapter:

- Find a copy of Hibernate and install it on your computer.
- Download and install Ant.
- Set up MySQL, which you'll use as your database for the example projects.
- Create a basic project using Ant, which will serve as a model for more complex projects.

Accomplishing these goals will put you in a good position to explore Hibernate's concepts further in subsequent chapters. And as a side bonus, you should also be able to set up a complete Hibernate project from scratch.

Assumptions

To keep the scope of this chapter manageable, we'll start by making a few assumptions:

- You have a copy of Sun JDK installed already—preferably JDK 1.4.x, because Hibernate requires it for a few of its nice features. If you don't have Sun JDK, visit http://java.sun.com/j2se/ and follow the instructions to download and install the JDK.
- You have configured the JAVA_HOME correctly to point where the JDK has been installed.
- You haven't installed Ant, Hibernate, or a database (MySQL) before. This chapter is all about getting set up, so if you already have or know how to install these systems, feel free to skim sections or skip ahead to chapter 3. You may want to note where you're installing things, because examples will build on this information later.

NOTE Most of the examples in this chapter involve running Ant and MySQL from the command line. They should work roughly the same on Windows, Unix, Linux, and Macintoshes. To avoid confusion, all command-line fragments use a generic $ command prompt (from Mac), rather than repeat the example for each platform. So, when you see this

```
$ ant clean build
```

it's essentially the same as seeing

```
C:\applications>ant clean build
```

When there are differences between the platforms, consult the tool's documentation for platform-specific considerations.

NOTE   For paths, we typically use forward slashes (/) rather than the Windows backslash (\) convention. If you're using a Windows system, reverse the slashes as needed.

2.1   Getting a Hibernate distribution

The first step in creating your Hibernate project is to get the latest copy from the website. Go to Hibernate's homepage at www.hibernate.org. There is wealth of information here, including solid reference documentation, a mailing list, and an active community Wiki.[1] For now, you just want the code. Click the Download link from the menu, and choose the latest 3.x version of the Hibernate distribution. Hibernate distributions come in two flavors: .zip and the .tar.gz versions.

Choose the appropriate bundle for your platform (Windows users probably want the .zip, and Linux/Unix users might prefer the .tar.gz). Then select a mirror site near you, choosing from a list similar to that displayed in figure 2.1.

While Hibernate is downloading, create an application directory where you can unzip it. On Windows, create a c:\applications directory. On

---

[1] What's a Wiki? Think of it as a massively multiplayer website where any visitor can read, learn, and add their knowledge to the community. See http://c2.com/cgi/wiki?WikiWikiWeb, the original Wiki, for more information.

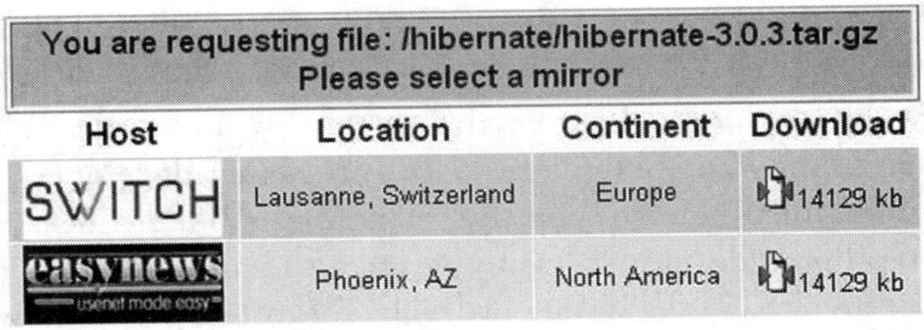

Figure 2.1 Select a mirror site for the Hibernate distribution.

Linux\Unix, create /applications. Extract the Hibernate distribution into that directory. On Windows, you'll have c:\applications\hibernate-3.0, as shown in figure 2.2.

Some of the highlights to note include hibernate3.jar, which contains all the framework code; the /lib directory, which holds all the Hibernate dependencies; and the /doc directory, which has the JavaDocs and a copy of the reference documentation. For now, you have everything you need from Hibernate, so let's move on to the next task.

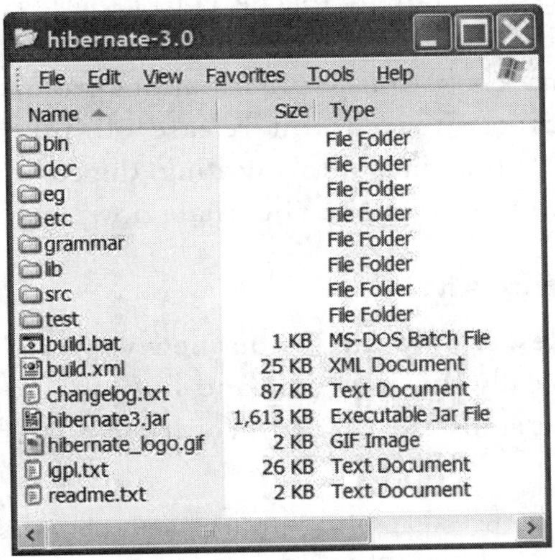

Figure 2.2
Extracted Hibernate distribution on Windows

2.2 Installing Ant

Any software project needs to be able to reliably and repeatably compile, package, and distribute its files. The steps that developers take to put everything together are typically referred as a build process. Every manual step that a developer has to perform to build the project is one that will be invoked in the wrong order, be forgotten, or be known only to a guy who is inconveniently out getting a root canal. To prevent these manual missteps, you can turn to build tools, which let you automate the process. For Java projects, that tool is commonly Ant.

Since its creation, Ant has proven its worth on many diverse Java projects and has become the de facto standard for Java build tools. So, it's a natural choice to help you build a new Hibernate project. First, you need to get a copy of it.

2.2.1 Getting Ant

Ant's homepage is located at http://ant.apache.org/. It's hosted by the Apache Software Foundation, which plays host to some of the most popular open-source projects, including Apache HTTP Server. There is a lot of useful information at this site, especially the excellent Ant User's Manual.[2] To get Ant, click Binary Distributions from the left menu. Scroll down, and choose the current release of Ant in .zip, .tar.gz, or .tar.bz2 format. (At this time of this writing, the current version is 1.6.2.) Save the file right next to the Hibernate download.

2.2.2 Extracting and installing Ant

After the download completes, extract Ant to your newly created applications directory. Ant is typically run as a command-line tool. To install it, a few more configuration steps are needed. You need to define an

---

[2] In our opinion, the Ant User's Manual (http://ant.apache.org/manual/index.html) is one of the best examples of great documentation, which in many open-source projects tends to be fairly poor. What makes it so useful is that in addition to displaying the available parameters and tasks, it gives working examples for each task, which you can easily copy and modify.

environment variable called ANT_HOME to point to Ant's directory (set ANT_HOME=/applications/apache-ant-1.6.2). Also, add the Ant bin directory to your command-line path (on Windows XP, for example, set PATH=%ANT_HOME%\bin;%PATH%).

If everything is set up correctly, you should be able to open a command line and enter the ant command:

```
$ ant

Buildfile: build.xml does not exist!
Build failed
```

As you can see, Ant gives you an error message, because it expects a build file called build.xml.

Once Ant is installed, you can start setting up your project, beginning with an Ant build file (typically named build.xml). You'll do this in section 2.4. Before you start creating your project, you need a database.

2.3 Setting up a database

Hibernate is all about seamlessly connecting your Java objects to a database. By defining mapping files, it can automatically convert objects into SQL statements to shuttle data back and forth between live memory and the persistent file systems that databases typically use.

If you have spent any time working with SQL, you know that not all databases are created equal. Although SQL is technically standardized, every database vendor has its own slightly different version of "standard." By using Hibernate, you can avoid writing vendor-specific JDBC code. You can generally write applications that can be deployed against any database, such as Oracle, MySQL, or SQL Server. As long as you aren't writing your own database engine, odds are pretty good that Hibernate will work with it.

For our example application, you'll use MySQL—a popular open-source database that many developers are already familiar with. You need to take one caveat into consideration: MySQL versions 4.0 and earlier don't support subselects, which Hibernate uses for some queries. You certainly can use older versions; you just need to write queries a bit differently. To avoid this complication, this chapter's example uses MySQL 4.1, which supports subselects.

2.3.1 Getting MySQL

Installing MySQL can be a complicated procedure, so we'll only cover the basics of installing it on Windows. Complete documentation is available at http://dev.mysql.com/doc/ for other databases. Happily, installations are getting easier since MySQL 4.1.5; there is a Windows installer that will handle most of the messy setup details and should generally suit your needs.

Get a copy of MySQL 4.1 (or later) from http://dev.mysql.com/downloads/. Select the 4.1 database server, choose the appropriate binary version for your platform, and download it. Then, extract it to a /applications/mysql directory. Run the installer, and follow along. As part of the installation, choose to install MySQL as a Windows service; doing so eliminates the need to manually start the server from the command line.

In addition, if you have firewall software installed, such as Norton Internet Security, you'll need to configure the firewall to permit access for outgoing connections from your local computer with IP address 127.0.0.1 (localhost) to your MySQL server at port 3306.

2.3.2 Testing MySQL

Let's verify that MySQL is working:

1 Open another command line, and start the command-line console. The console lets you interact with the MySQL server and run SQL statements against it.

2 Change to the mysql/bin directory:

```
$ cd applications/mysql/bin
```

Alternatively, you could add the /bin directory to the path, which would allow you to run MySQL anywhere.

3   From the mysql/bin directory, log in as the root user, with complete access privileges:

```
$ mysql -u root -p
```

The –u option specifies the username, and –p tells MySQL to request a password.

4   When MySQL asks for the password, you can press Enter, since the default password is blank:

```
Enter password:
```

The server will respond with

```
Welcome to the MySQL monitor.  Commands end with ; or \g.
Your MySQL connection id is 35 to server version: 4.1.10-nt
Type 'help;' or '\h' for help. Type '\c' to clear the buffer.
```

5   To give Hibernate a database to work with, use SQL to create the events_calendar database, like so:

```
mysql> CREATE database events_calendar;
```

The server should respond with

```
Query OK, 1 row affected (0.00 sec)
```

6   Verify that the database has been created by querying for a list of databases:

```
mysql> show databases;
+------------------+
| Database         |
+------------------+
| events_calendar |
| mysql            |
| test             |
+------------------+
3 rows in set (0.02 sec)
```

Sure enough, events_calendar is there, along with MySQL's built-in databases (mysql and test).

7 Quit the MySQL console by typing the following:

```
mysql> quit;
```

The server responds with a pithy

```
Bye
```

At this point you have successfully set up MySQL, installed it as a Windows service, and verified that it's running. Complete information is included in the installation instructions at www.mysql.com. If you had any problems along the way getting this to work, the installation instructions are a good place to start to debug them.

2.3.3 MySQL drivers

In addition to needing a database server, in this case, you need to get the JDBC driver. The driver is the piece of software that allows Java code to access and send SQL commands to the database server. Drivers are database-specific, but implement the necessary `javax.sql.Driver` interface, which allows JDBC to remain ignorant of which database it's talking to. At its core, Hibernate is just a fancy wrapper around JDBC, so you need the MySQL driver as well for your project.

Go to http://dev.mysql.com/downloads/, and look for MySQL Connector/J, which is the name of the driver (the current version is 3.1). Select the latest production release, and download the .zip file to the /applications directory. Extract the .zip file into that directory; it should end up in a directory named something like /applications/mysql-connector-java-3.1.6 (depending on the version, of course). If you look in that directory, you should see a JAR file named mysql-connector-java-3.1.6-bin.jar, which contains the driver.

2.4 Setting up a project

To help illustrate how to use Hibernate, you'll build a sample application—Event Calendar 2005, an event/calendar-planning program—which can be used to create events, schedule speakers, and manage attendees.

An event calendar program is a good candidate for a Hibernate application for a number of reasons. Calendars and scheduling are common pieces of many business applications, so this should be familiar territory for many readers. In addition, Hibernate shines when it's applied to a rich domain model. A realistic event application has to handle a number of complex relationships, including conferences, lecture sessions, hotels, room reservations, and guests.

Each chapter of this book expands the application a bit more, adding new relationships with Hibernate. But before you develop any code, you need to set up the project. Now that you have all the necessary building blocks (Hibernate, Ant, and a MySQL database), you can begin.

2.4.1 Defining directories

The first thing any successful project needs is a directory. Create it as follows:

1 Create a directory, /work. This is a base directory where all your future projects can go.

2 For now, you have one project to worry about: the new Event Calendar application. So, create a /work/calendar directory. This is will be referred to as the project directory from now on.

3 Create an src/java directory in the project directory. All the Java sources files you create will go under this directory. It also leaves room for other source files that aren't .java files, like JSP, SQL, or Hibernate mapping files (hbm.xml), which you'll learn about in the next chapter.

4 Open your favorite text editor or Integrated Development Environment (IDE)[3], and create a file called `build.xml` in the project

---

[3] Discussing the "right" IDE can be about as contentious as talking religion or politics at a dinner party. That said, most of the modern IDEs have built-in support for Ant and even plug-ins for Hibernate, and can make managing a project a bit easier. The authors' favorites include IDEA (www.intellij.com) and Eclipse (www.eclipse.org/).

directory. For the moment, leave the file empty. This will be the Ant build file for your Event Calendar program.

Let's do a quick check to be sure you're on track. If all is well, you should have a directory structure that looks like this.

```
/applications/apache-ant-1.6.2
/applications/hibernate-3.0
/applications/mysql
/applications/mysql-connector-java-3.1.6
/work
```

With your project directory set up, let's go ahead and develop the Ant build file.

2.4.2 Ant 101

Your first Ant build file won't be too complicated, just enough to show the basics of what it can do. You're going to have it create a directory, compile a Java class, and run that class. You'll also learn about several important Ant concepts, including targets, tasks, paths, and properties.

Typing everything will certainly build character, but you can also download the book's source code from www.manning.com/peak. Look in the ch02 directory for a file name build.xml, and open it in your preferred text editor (see listing 2.1). Throughout the chapter, you'll modify this file, and saving versions of it at various stages of development.

Listing 2.1 First Ant build file, build.xml

```xml
<?xml version="1.0"?>                          Basic root element    Defines reusable
<project name="build.xml" default="build">  ◄──                       properties
    <property name="src.java.dir" location="src/java"/>    ◄──
    <property name="build.classes.dir" location="build/classes"/>

    <path id="project.classpath">   ◄── Defines classpath
        <pathelement location="${build.classes.dir}"/>
    </path>
    <target name="init" >       ◄────────────────────────    Task that creates
        <mkdir dir="${build.classes.dir}"/>                 directory to compile to
```

```
    </target>
    <target name="compile" depends="init" >          ←——  Task that
        <javac srcdir="${src.java.dir}"                     compiles src files
  destdir="${build.classes.dir}">
            <include name="**/EventCalendar.java" />
        </javac>
    </target>
    <target name="build" depends="compile" >         ←——  Task that runs
        <java classname="com.manning.hq.ch02.EventCalendar"     compiled classes
  failonerror="true">
            <classpath refid="project.classpath"/>      ——  What you
        </java>                                               see if code
        <echo>If you see this, it works!!!</echo>     ←——    works
    </target>
</project>
```

Since this may be the first build file you have seen, let's discuss some of the concepts Ant uses, in light of this example.

Projects

All well-formed XML files need a root element, and Ant is no different. The basic element is <project>. The two attributes you see are name and default. The name attribute is a descriptive name for your project and can be anything. The default attribute sets the target that will be invoked if you don't specify one from the command line when you run Ant. Here we want a target called build to be invoked:

```
<project name="build.xml" default="build">
```

Properties

Properties are Ant's version of variables. Most projects define a number of properties (best kept organized together at the top of the project) for directories or file names that are frequently used throughout the file. Once you define a property, you can substitute its value back again by using the ${property.name} syntax you see here:

```
<property name="src.java.dir" value="src/java"/>
```

Defining a property this way lets you use the property ${src.java.dir} anywhere you might otherwise need to type out the full directory path. The property is converted back into a relative directory, /work/calendar/src/java. Relative directories like src/java are always resolved relative to the location of the build.xml file. You define two properties: one for your Java source files directory and another for the directory to which you want your compiled Java .class files to be sent.

Paths

Paths allow you to define a series of directories and/or JAR files that tasks will use. Paths are generally used to define class paths for compiling .java files or running .class files. Creating a `<path>` element with an id attribute lets you reuse the same classpath several times. Here we give the `<path>` element an id called `project.classpath` and point it at our compiled .class file directory:

```
<path id="project.classpath">
        <pathelement location="${build.classes.dir}"/>
</path>
```

This path is simple — just one lonely directory by itself. When you start to add more third-party JAR files (like Hibernate), and the classpath becomes more complicated, its value will be apparent. Classpaths can be tricky beasts to get right, and the fact that Ant helps manage their complexities is worth the price of entry.

Targets

Targets are Ant's public methods. They contain tasks, which you'll read about next. By dividing your build file into several targets, you can make it more organized and readable. Targets can depend on other targets, if you specify a `depends` attribute. When you invoke a target before it executes, Ant invokes any targets that your target depends on.

In our file, note that the `build` target depends on the `compile` target, which in turn depends on the `init` target. This is helpful because we can type

```
$ ant build
```

Ant will execute the init, compile, and build targets, in that order. This is also where the default attribute comes into play. Refer back to the "Projects" section, where we talk about the default attribute. Since we defined build as the default attribute, we can type

```
$ ant
```

Ant will call the same init, compile, and build targets again.

Tasks

If targets are Ant's public methods, then tasks are its private methods and statements. A build file uses several tasks, including the following:

- mkdir creates the ${build.classes.dir}. Since this directory contains only derived files, you can easily delete the entire directory to have a clean build.
- javac compiles Java files into .class files and places them into ${build.classes.dir}.
- java runs the compiled class files.
- echo is Ant's version of System.out.println(). It writes a message out to the command line.

Tasks tend to be simple in their basic usage, but there are quite a few attributes you can configure if you want to get fancy. We recommend you check out the Ant User's Manual for complete details.

2.4.3 Running Ant

The build file is now complete, but one obvious piece is missing: the actual EventCalendar class. Let's create that now. In the src/java directory, create a new com/manning/hq/ch02 directory and then an EventCalendar.java file. No programming book would be complete without the quintessential Hello World application; so as not to disappoint you, here it is:

```
package com.manning.hq.ch02;

public class EventCalendar {
```

```
        public static void main(String[] args) {
            System.out.println("Welcome to Event Calendar 2005.");
        }
    }
```

When it runs, your class welcomes prospective users to the Event Calendar.

Now that you have all the necessary classes in place, you should run the build file. At the command line, change directories so that you're in the same directory as the build.xml file. Type the following at the command line:

```
$ ant
Buildfile: build.xml

init:

compile:
    [javac] Compiling 1 source file to
  C:\work\calendar\build\classes

build:
    [java] Welcome to Event Calendar 2005.
    [echo] If you see this, it works!!!

BUILD SUCCESSFUL
Total time: 2 seconds
```

If you have set everything up correctly, then you should see something similar. If this is the first time you have seen output from Ant, take note of the following:

- Since you didn't supply the name of a build file, Ant implicitly used build.xml, but it's nice enough to remind you which file it's using on the first line of output.
- Although you never specified which target to invoke, Ant used the project's default attribute and invoked the build target.

- As it executes each target, Ant states the name of that target. This is why you see `init:`, `compile:`, and `build:`.

- Most of the tasks you defined log some of their own information.

When you look at the output of an Ant file, you aren't really concerned about the interesting prose you put into your `<echo>`s and `System.out.println`s, since you just want to know that tasks were executed and where Ant is putting the files. So, the most useful debugging information is typically what you see from the `javac` task, where Ant is resolving properties:

```
[javac] Compiling 1 source file C:\work\calendar\build\classes
```

This output tells you where Ant is dumping the compiled Java .class files. Remember the build file, which specifies the `destdir` attribute using an Ant property:

```
<javac destdir="${build.classes.dir}" />
```

One tricky thing to get right, as a build file grows in size, is making sure all properties resolve correctly to the directory or file you thought they would. In this case, by inspecting the output, you know that `${build.classes.dir}` has been turned into /work/calendar/build/classes at runtime.

You have created a basic build file and put it through its paces. In the next section, you'll expand on this example and update it to use a few Hibernate files.

2.5 Habits of highly effective build files

Creating an organized, consistent project structure takes a bit of thought up front, but that work pays dividends later as the project grows in size. As a tool, Ant gives you a great deal of flexibility in how you can organize a project; but without structure, too much flexibility can lead to overly complicated build files.

Open-source projects are usually fast-moving targets, and new distributions are released fairly often. An ideal project setup would let you get the latest copy of Hibernate and easily compile and test your code against the newest version.

As helpful as Ant is, one of the chief historical criticisms against it is that there tends to be a lot of duplication between projects. Two projects each have their own build files that basically perform the same steps, just on different directories. For example, if you like Hibernate, you'll probably want to use it on your next project. Why rewrite (or, nearly as bad, copy and paste) the build file from your last project? A new feature of Ant 1.6.2 allows you to create a single build file, which can be imported and reused between all your projects. One of this book's goals is to create a reusable build file that you can use on all your future Hibernate projects.

2.5.1 Connecting Hibernate

So far, all you have done with Hibernate is download and install it. Let's put it to use in a project. You're going to modify the build.xml file so that all the Hibernate JAR files are in the classpath, along with a few more embellishments.

Updating the build file

If you're following the source code, to show the progress of each modification, you've sequentially numbered the build files in the source code. If you want to run those (rather than modify your existing file), type `ant -f build2.xml` to specify a file other than the default build.xml. For now, open build.xml and make the modifications shown in listing 2.2.

Listing 2.2 Updated build file (build2.xml)

```
<?xml version="1.0"?>
<project name="build2.xml" default="build">
    <property name="src.java.dir" value="src/java"/>
    <property name="build.classes.dir" value="build/classes"/>
    <property name="hibernate.version" value="3.0"/>
```

Sets Hibernate version **❶**

```
<property name="hibernate.lib.dir"
 location="/applications/hibernate-${hibernate.version}"
 />
<path id="project.classpath">
    <pathelement location="${build.classes.dir}"/>
</path>
<path id="hibernate.lib.path"
    <fileset dir="${hibernate.lib.dir}/lib">
        <include name="**/*.jar"/>
    </fileset>
    <fileset dir="${hibernate.lib.dir}">
        <include name="hibernate3.jar"/>
    </fileset>
</path>
<target name="init" >
    <mkdir dir="${build.classes.dir}"/>
</target>
<target name="compile" depends="init" >
    <javac srcdir="${src.java.dir}"
destdir="${build.classes.dir}">
        <classpath refid="hibernate.lib.path"/>
    </javac>
</target>
<target name="build" depends="compile" >
    <java classname="com.manning.hq.ch02.EventCalendar2">
        <classpath refid="project.classpath"/>
        <classpath refid="hibernate.lib.path"/>
    </java>
    <echo>If you see this, it works!!!</echo>
</target>
<target name="clean">
    <delete dir="${build.classes.dir}"/>
</target>
</project>
```

② Sets base directory where Hibernate is installed

③ Defines classpath with Hibernate and all its JARs

④ Adds Hibernate for compiling

⑤ Uses new class

⑥ Adds Hibernate to run Java file

⑦ Adds self cleaning target

① By parameterizing the version of Hibernate you're using, you can easily install a new version of Hibernate. Just download the new version, rename the directory to the exact version number (such as 3.0), and update the hibernate.version property. Build your project, and make sure everything works. No need to copy lots of JAR files.

❷ The `hibernate.lib.dir` shows a little more advanced usage of properties; part of the directory is static, with the version number as a property.

❸ Here you create a new `path` element that includes the hibernate3.jar file and all the dependencies.

❹ This code adds the Hibernate classpath when compiling.

❺ Change the class you're going to run to `com.manning.hq.ch02.EventCalendar2`.

❻ Here you add the Hibernate classpath when running the Java file.

❼ This lets you clean up the build artifacts for a fresh build.

The improved Ant build file now constructs a classpath for Hibernate and uses it for both compilation and running the Java class.

A sample class with Log4j

`EventCalendar2` is a slightly modified version of the first class, `EventCalendar`, which uses a few classes from Hibernate and some of its dependencies. The new class uses two dependencies: one from Hibernate and another from a Hibernate dependency, log4j.jar. Let's take a quick look the newly modified class:

```
package com.manning.hq.ch02;

import org.hibernate.cfg.Configuration;
import org.apache.log4j.*;

public class EventCalendar2 {
    public static void main(String[] args) {
        BasicConfigurator.configure();    ◀── Configures Log4j logger
        Configuration configuration = new Configuration();   ◀─┐
        Logger log = Logger.getLogger(EventCalendar2.class);   │
                                                          Uses a
        log.warn("Welcome to Event Calendar v2 2005.");  Hibernate
    }                                                    dependency
}
```

There isn't much happening here. You configure Log4j, an open-source logging framework, to log messages to the command line. Then you create a basic configuration for Hibernate (which you'll learn more about in the next chapter). This doesn't accomplish much, but it's enough to ensure that if you haven't correctly set up your classpath, your file won't compile or run. The `org.hibernate.cfg.Configuration` class comes from the Hibernate3.jar file, and the `org.apache.log4j.*` classes comes from the log4j.jar file, which is in the hibernate/lib directory. Finally, you use your obtained Log4j logger to log a success message to console. This ensures that you have both sets of JAR files in the classpath.

Now you can run your new build file. You should see this:

```
$ ant -f build2.xml clean build
Buildfile: build2.xml

init:

compile:
    [java] 0 [main] INFO org.hibernate.cfg.Environment  - Hibernate
3.0.3
    [java] 15 [main] INFO org.hibernate.cfg.Environment  -
hibernate.properties not found
    [java] 15 [main] INFO org.hibernate.cfg.Environment  - using
CGLIB reflection optimizer
    [java] 15 [main] INFO org.hibernate.cfg.Environment  - using
JDK 1.4 java.sql.Timestamp handling
    [java] 31 [main] WARN com.manning.hq.ch02.EventCalendar2  -
Welcome to Event Calendar v2 2005.
    [echo] If you see this, it works!!!

BUILD SUCCESSFUL
Total time: 2 seconds
```

At the command line, you ran two targets from the build file. The `clean` target deletes the build/classes directory, to start with a fresh empty build/classes directory. Both your `EventCalendar` and `EventCalender2` files are compiled successfully. Ant then runs the `EventCalendar2` Java class. The "Welcome to Event Calendar" message you see confirms that you have successfully configured Hibernate.

2.5.2 Reusable build files

Now that you have connected Hibernate into your build file, you have something you can use to demonstrate Ant's reusable import feature. The build file includes two reusable pieces: `fileset` and `path` elements that define where Hibernate is installed. They look through the installed Hibernate directory and define where the needed JAR files are. You should extract these fragments into a reusable build file, which can be used on other projects. Later, if you upgrade to a new version of Hibernate, you can easily extract the new versions, point your build.xml at the new Hibernate directory, and everything should go.

The next step is to create a new file, hibernate-build.xml, which will be the base for your reusable build file. You'll extract the `hibernate.lib.path` element from the build2.xml file and move it to hibernate-build.xml (listing 2.3).

Listing 2.3 hibernate-build.xml: Defines a generic classpath for any Hibernate installation

```
<?xml version="1.0"?>
<project name="hibernate-build" default="default">
    <path id="hibernate.lib.path">
        <fileset dir="${hibernate.lib.dir}\lib">
            <include name="**/*.jar"/>
        </fileset>
        <fileset dir="${hibernate.lib.dir}">
            <include name="hibernate3.jar"/>
        </fileset>
    </path>
    <target name="default"/>
</project>
```

This file is a complete build file in its own right. Starting from an externally specified directory, ${hibernate.lib.dir}, it builds the classpath. This allows hibernate-build.xml to be imported into a project, which can specify where Hibernate is installed, and can use the path as if it was part of the project build file. Next, modify your build.xml file to import the hibernate-build.xml file (see listing 2.4).

Listing 2.4 build3.xml: Refactored build file imports a classpath from hibernate-build.xml

```xml
<?xml version="1.0"?>
<project name="build3.xml" default="build">

    <property name="src.java.dir" value="src/java"/>
    <property name="build.classes.dir" value="build/classes"/>
    <property name="hibernate.version" value="3.0"/>
    <property name="hibernate.lib.dir" location=" /applications/
hibernate-${hibernate.version}"/>

    <import file="hibernate-build.xml" />     <—— Replaces path with import

    <path id="project.classpath">
        <pathelement location="${build.classes.dir}"/>
    </path>

    <target name="clean">
        <delete dir="${build.classes.dir}"/>
    </target>
    <!-Other targets omitted -->
</project>
```

The new line is the import task, which replaces the path statement in build2.xml. It pulls the hibernate-build.xml file directly into build.xml. As far as Ant is concerned, hibernate.lib.path is still defined, and the build file should work. Test this by running the new file:

```
$ ant -f build3.xml clean build
Buildfile: build3.xml

init:
```

```
compile:

build:
    [java] Welcome to Event Calendar v2 2005.
    [echo] If you see this, it works!!!

BUILD SUCCESSFUL
Total time: 1 second
```

Running the newly modified file successfully should give you something like this output. It runs the javac and java tasks, which rely on hibernate.lib.path being configured correctly.

But what if the file doesn't work? If you see something like the following, it means the import isn't configured correctly.

```
compile:
    [javac] Compiling 2 source files to
  C:\work\calendar\build\classes

BUILD FAILED
C:\work\calendar\build.xml:21: Reference hibernate.lib.path not
found.
```

Double-check to see whether you have imported the hibernate-build.xml file and that the build file has hibernate.lib.path configured.

2.5.3 Expanding your horizons

This section has only discussed some of the basics of how Ant works, demonstrating a basic build file. This should be enough information to get you started, and there are quite a few useful things you can do with it. Be sure to check the Ant User's Manual (specifically, the Ant Core tasks), where you can learn more about specifics of tasks like import and javac.

2.6 Summary

In this chapter, we looked at the necessary steps to setup a Hibernate project, including obtaining Hibernate itself, MySQL database, and Ant build tool. Hibernate is distributed in a big zip file; it includes documentation (if you read that sort of thing), source code, and JAR files, including the essential hibernate3.jar and all the JAR files Hibernate depends on. For more information, you can find the Hibernate homepage at www.hibernate.org; it includes the User's Manual and the community area, both of which are useful sources of Hibernate wisdom.

Ant is a build tool written in Java. It allows developers to build repeatable projects on any platform. Its home is at http://ant.apache.org. Ant uses XML files to define the steps in a build process. The default name is build.xml. As of Ant 1.6, build files can be made modular and reusable between projects.

Hibernate can generally work with most databases, including MySQL, as long as they have a JDBC driver. MySQL is the most popular open-source database and can be found at www.mysql.com.

3

Hibernate basics

This chapter covers

- *Configuring Hibernate*
- *Mapping persistent classes*
- *Advanced Hibernate configuration*

As a persistence service, Hibernate must work with multiple databases and within various application environments. Supporting these variations requires Hibernate to be highly configurable to adapt to different environments. After all, running a standalone application can be quite different from running a web application. Differences in obtaining database connections, for instance, can be significant. Hibernate is typically configured in two steps.

First, you configure the Hibernate service. This includes database connection parameters, caching, and the collection of persistent classes managed by Hibernate. Second, you must provide Hibernate with information about the classes to be persisted. Persistent class configuration allows you to bridge gaps between the class and databases.

Although it's commonly used within J2EE application servers, such as WebSphere and JBoss, Hibernate can also be used in standalone applications. Requirements vary for different environments, and Hibernate can be configured to adapt to them. Hibernate works with various support services, such as connection pools, caching services, and transaction managers. It also lets you maintain additional support services by implementing simple interfaces.

Individual persistent classes are also highly configurable. Each class may have a different method to generate identifier values, and it's possible to persist complex object hierarchies. You can also customize specific object properties mapping to a SQL type, depending on the data types available in the database. There is much more to configuring persistent classes, as we'll discuss in this chapter.

Chapter goals

In this chapter, we'll cover configuring Hibernate at the framework and persistent class level. More specifically, we'll discuss the following:

- Creating a basic hibernate.cfg.xml file
- Building mapping definition files to provide Hibernate with information about persistent classes
- The primary Hibernate classes used to persist and retrieve classes
- Advanced Hibernate configuration, including object caching and transaction management
- Persisting class hierarchies (inheritance) with Hibernate

Assumptions

This chapter requires that you've completed these steps outlined in chapter 2:

- Ant, Hibernate, and MySQL are installed correctly.
- The basic project from chapter 2 is installed.

In addition, you're required to have basic knowledge of XML for the configuration file and mapping documents.

3.1 Configuring Hibernate

Hibernate must peacefully coexist in various deployment environments, from application servers to standalone applications. We refer to these as managed and nonmanaged environments, respectively. An application server is an example of a managed environment, providing services to hosted applications like connection pools and transaction management. Two of the commonly used application servers include WebSphere and JBoss.

The alternative is a nonmanaged environment, in which the application provides any required services. Nonmanaged environments typically lack the convenience services found in managed environments. A standalone Swing or SWT application is an example of a nonmanaged environment.

Hibernate supports a number of different configuration methods and options to support these scenarios. Configuring all of Hibernate's properties can be overwhelming, so we'll start slowly. Before we jump into configuration, look at figure 3.1, which shows the major Hibernate classes and configuration files.

The light gray boxes in the figure are the classes your application code will use most often. The dark gray boxes are the configuration files used by the Configuration class to create the SessionFactory, which in turn creates the Session instances. Session instances are your primary interface to the Hibernate persistence service.

Let's begin with the basic configuration that can be used in any Hibernate deployment. We'll discuss advanced configuration later in this chapter.

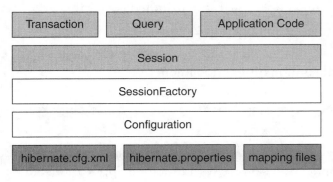

Figure 3.1 Primary Hibernate components

3.1.1 Basic configuration

Hibernate provides two alternative configuration files: a standard Java properties file called hibernate.properties and an XML formatted file called hibernate.cfg.xml. We'll use the XML configuration file throughout this book, but it's important to realize that both configuration files perform the same function: configuring the Hibernate service. If both the hibernate.properties and hibernate.cfg.xml files are found in the application classpath, then hibernate.cfg.xml overrides the settings found in the hibernate.properties file. (Actually, we use both files in the example source code to avoid putting the database connection information throughout the project directory tree.)

Before configuring Hibernate, you should first determine how the service obtains database connections. Database connections may be provided by the Hibernate framework or from a JNDI DataSource. A third method, user-provided JDBC connections, is also available, but it's rarely used.

Using Hibernate-managed JDBC connections

The sample configuration file in listing 3.1 uses Hibernate-managed JDBC connections. You would typically encounter this configuration in a nonmanaged environment, such as a standalone application.

Listing 3.1 Example hibernate.cfg.xml file

```
<?xml version="1.0"?>
<!DOCTYPE hibernate-configuration PUBLIC
 "-//Hibernate/Hibernate Configuration DTD 3.0//EN"
 "http://hibernate.sourceforge.net/hibernate-configuration-
   3.0.dtd">

<hibernate-configuration>
  <session-factory>
    <property name="connection.username">uid</property>
    <property name="connection.password">pwd</property>
    <property name="connection.url">
        jdbc:mysql://localhost/db
    </property>
    <property name="connection.driver_class">
        com.mysql.jdbc.Driver
```

```
        </property>
        <property name="dialect">
            org.hibernate.dialect.MySQLDialect
        </property>
        <mapping resource="com/manning/hq/ch03/Event.hbm.xml"/>
        <mapping resource="com/manning/hq/ch03/Location.hbm.xml"/>
        <mapping resource="com/manning/hq/ch03/Speaker.hbm.xml"/>
        <mapping resource="com/manning/hq/ch03/Attendee.hbm.xml"/>
    </session-factory>
</hibernate-configuration>
```

To use Hibernate-provided JDBC connections, the configuration file requires the following five properties:

- connection.driver_class — The JDBC connection class for the specific database
- connection.url — The full JDBC URL to the database
- connection.username — The username used to connect to the database
- connection.password — The password used to authenticate the username
- dialect — The name of the SQL dialect for the database

The connection properties are common to any Java developer who has worked with JDBC in the past. Since you're not specifying a connection pool, which we cover later in this chapter, Hibernate uses its own rudimentary connection-pooling mechanism. The internal pool is fine for basic testing, but you shouldn't use it in production.

The dialect property tells Hibernate which SQL dialect to use for certain operations. Although not strictly required, it should be used to ensure Hibernate Query Language (HQL) statements are correctly converted into the proper SQL dialect for the underlying database.

The dialect property tells the framework whether the given database supports identity columns, altering relational tables, and unique indexes, among other database-specific details. Hibernate ships with more than 20 SQL dialects, supporting each of the major database vendors, including Oracle, DB2, MySQL, and PostgreSQL.

Hibernate also needs to know the location and names of the mapping files describing the persistent classes. The mapping element provides the name of each mapping file as well as its location relative to the application classpath. There are different methods of configuring the location of the mapping file, which we'll examine later.

Using a JNDI DataSource

To use Hibernate with database connections provided by a JNDI DataSource, you need to make a few changes to the configuration file, as shown in listing 3.2.

Listing 3.2 Modified hibernate.cfg.xml file

```xml
<?xml version="1.0"?>
<!DOCTYPE hibernate-configuration PUBLIC
  "-//Hibernate/Hibernate Configuration DTD 3.0//EN"
  "http://hibernate.sourceforge.net/hibernate-configuration-
    3.0.dtd">

<hibernate-configuration>                            Sets JNDI name
  <session-factory                                   of SessionFactory
    name="java:comp/env/hibernate/SessionFactory">
    <property name="connection.datasource">
        jdbc/myDataSource              Specifies name of
    </property>                        JNDI DataSource
    <property name="dialect">
        org.hibernate.dialect.MySQLDialect
    </property>
    <mapping resource="com/manning/hq/ch03/Event.hbm.xml"/>
    <mapping resource="com/manning/hq/ch03/Location.hbm.xml"/>
    <mapping resource="com/manning/hq/ch03/Speaker.hbm.xml"/>
    <mapping resource="com/manning/hq/ch03/Attendee.hbm.xml"/>
  </session-factory>
</hibernate-configuration>
```

You would typically use this type of configuration when using Hibernate with an application server. The connection.datasource property must have the same value as the JNDI DataSource name used in the application server configuration. The dialect property serves the same purpose as the previous configuration file example.

At this point, you have almost enough information to configure Hibernate. The next step is to create mapping definitions for the objects you intend to persist.

3.2 Creating mapping definitions

Mapping definitions, also called mapping documents, are used to provide Hibernate with information to persist objects to a relational database. The mapping files also provide support features, such as creating the database schema from a collection of mapping files.

Mapping definitions for persistent objects may be stored together in a single mapping file. Alternatively, the definition for each object can be stored in an individual mapping file. The latter approach is preferred, since storing the definitions for a large number of persistent classes in one mapping file can be cumbersome. We use the file-per-class method to organize our mapping documents throughout this book.

There is another advantage to having multiple mapping files: If you have all mapping definitions in a single file, it may be hard to debug and isolate any error to a specific class definition.

The naming convention for mapping files is to use the name of the persistent class with the hbm.xml extension. The mapping file for the Event class is thus Event.hbm.xml. The Event.hbm.xml file is shown in listing 3.3.

Listing 3.3 The Event.hbm.xml mapping file

```xml
<?xml version="1.0"?>
<!DOCTYPE hibernate-mapping PUBLIC
  "-//Hibernate/Hibernate Mapping DTD 3.0//EN"
  "http://hibernate.sourceforge.net/hibernate-mapping-3.0.dtd">
<hibernate-mapping package="com.manning.hq.ch03">
    <class name="Event" table="events">
```

```
            <id name="id" column="uid" type="long" unsaved-
    value="null">
            <generator class="native"/>
        </id>
        <property name="name" type="string" length="100"/>
        <property name="startDate" column="start_date"
                type="date"/>
        <property name="duration" type="integer"/>
        <many-to-one name="location" column="location_id"
                class="Location"/>
        <set name="speakers">
            <key column="event_id"/>
            <one-to-many class="Speaker"/>
        </set>
        <set name="attendees">
            <key column="event_id"/>
            <one-to-many class="Attendee"/>
        </set>
    </class>
</hibernate-mapping>
```

Let's examine this mapping file in detail. The mapping definition starts with the `hibernate-mapping` element. The `package` attribute sets the default package for unqualified class names in the mapping. With this attribute set, you need only give the class name for other persistent classes listed in the mapping, such as the `Speaker` and `Attendee` classes. To refer to a persistent class outside the given package, you must provide the fully qualified class name within the mapping document.

If Hibernate has trouble locating a class because of a missing package on, for instance, a many-to-one element, Hibernate throws a `MappingException`. This doesn't mean that Hibernate can't find the actual class file, but that it isn't able to navigate from one mapping definition to another.

Immediately after the `hibernate-mapping` tag, you encounter the `class` tag. The `class` tag begins the mapping definition for a specific persistent class. The `table` attribute names the relational table used to store the state of the object. The `class` element has a number of attributes available, altering how Hibernate persists instances of the class. (Appendix contains all the elements and attributes for each element available in a mapping document.)

3.2.1 IDs and generators

The `id` element describes the primary key for the persistent class as well as how the key value is generated. Each persistent class must have an `id` element declaring the primary key for the relational table. Let's look at the `id` element:

```
<id name="id" column="uid" type="long" unsaved-value="null">
    <generator class="native"/>
</id>
```

The `name` attribute defines the property in your persistent class that will be used to store the primary key value. The `id` element implies that the `Event` class has a property also named `id`:

```
public Long getId() {
    return this.id;
}

public void setId(Long id) {
    this.id = id;
}
```

If the column for the primary key has a different name than your object property, the `column` attribute is used. For our example's purposes, this column name is `uid`. The values of the `type` and `unsaved-value` attributes depend on the generator used.

The generator creates the primary key value for the persistent class. Hibernate provides multiple generator implementations that use various methods to create primary key values. Some implementations increment a value stored in a shared database table, whereas others create hexadecimal strings. Another generator, called `assigned`, lets you generate and assign the object ID. The `assigned` generator allows applications to reuse legacy code, such as the UUID generator from an EJB application. A recent introduction is the `select` generator, which retrieves the primary key value by selecting a value from a database trigger. The generator type you choose determines its behavior based on the underlying database.

You've used the `native` generator class in mapping definitions. `native` generators provide portability for mapping documents since the framework can determine the generator method supported by the database. Generators using the `native` class will use identity or sequence columns depending on available database support. If neither method is supported, the `native` generator falls back to a high/low generator method to create unique primary key values. Databases supporting identity columns include Sybase, MySQL, Microsoft SQL Server, and IBM DB2. Oracle, PostgreSQL, and SAP DB support sequence columns.

The `native` generator returns a `short`, `integer`, or `long` value. You've set the `type` attribute to `long`, and the `id` property in the Event object has a type of `java.lang.Long`. The value of the `type` attribute and the property type in the object must be the same.

The `unsaved-value` attribute describes the value of the `id` property for transient instances of this class. The `unsaved-value` attribute affects how objects are stored. We'll discuss the impact of this attribute later in the chapter.

3.2.2 Properties

Property elements for the Event object are similar to the `id` element:

```
<property name="name" type="string" length="100"/>
<property name="startDate" column="start_date" type="date"/>
<property name="duration" type="integer"/>
```

Each `property` element corresponds to a property in the Event object. The `name` attribute contains the property name, whereas the `type` attribute specifies the property object type. The column used to store the property value defaults to the property name. The `column` attribute overrides this default behavior, as shown in the `startDate` property.

If the `type` attribute is omitted, Hibernate determines the type using runtime reflection. In certain cases, you must provide the property type, since reflection may not be able to determine the desired type (such as differentiating between the Hibernate `DATE` and `TIMESTAMP` types). Valid property types include the Hibernate basic types, such as `integer`, `string`, and `timestamp`, as well as the corresponding Java objects and primitives. However, you aren't limited to basic data types.

The `property` element may also contain the name of a serializable Java class or a user-defined type. You create a new user-defined type by implementing either the `org.hibernate.UserType` or `org.hibernate.CompositeUserType` interface. The fully qualified class name of the user type or the serializable Java class is used as the property type value. We explore custom user types in chapter 5.

3.2.3 Many-to-one element

The `many-to-one` element defines the association to the `Location` class. In chapter 1, we referred to this association as one-to-one — why did we call this association a many-to-one instead? Hibernate classifies one-to-one associations as two objects sharing the same primary key. One-to-one associations aren't often used with Hibernate, so we won't cover them in detail. Many-to-one associations use foreign keys to maintain the association between two persistent classes. Let's examine many-to-one associations using the association shown in figure 3.2.

From this figure, you can deduce that many `Event` instances are associated with a single `Location` instance. Although the figure doesn't display it, this association is unidirectional, meaning you can navigate

Figure 3.2
Association between
`Location` and `Event`

from the Event instance to the Location but not from the Location to the Event instance. At this point, it's worthwhile to present the mapping file for the Location class, shown in listing 3.4.

Listing 3.4 Location.hbm.xml

```xml
<?xml version="1.0"?>
<hibernate-mapping package="com.manning.hq.ch03">
    <class name="Location" table="locations">
        <id name="id" column="uid" type="long">
            <generator class="native"/>
        </id>
        <property name="name" type="string"/>
        <property name="address" type="string"/>
    </class>
</hibernate-mapping>
```

The mapping for the Location class is similar to the Event mapping, although it doesn't have as many properties and lacks associations to other persistent objects. The association from Event to Location is a simple object reference.

For the Event mapping, the many-to-one element defines object references between persistent objects. Mapping a many-to-one association is straightforward:

```xml
<many-to-one name="location" column="location_id" class="Location"/>
```

The name attribute gives the name of the property in the object, and the optional column attribute specifies the column used to store the foreign key to the locations table. If you don't give a column attribute, the name attribute is used as the column name. The class attribute names the associated persistent class. Remember that you don't need to give the fully qualified name of the Location class if it's in the package defined in the hibernate-mapping element.

A common question from developers new to Hibernate is how to make a many-to-one relationship lazy, meaning that the associated object won't be retrieved when the parent object is retrieved. The solution is to use proxied objects.

3.2.4 Proxies

An object proxy is just a way to avoid retrieving an object until you need it. Hibernate 2 does not proxy objects by default. However, experience has shown that using object proxies is preferred, so this is the default in Hibernate 3.

Object proxies can be defined in one of two ways. First, you can add a proxy attribute to the class element. You can either specify a different class or use the persistent class as the proxy. For example:

```
<class name="Location"
proxy="com.manning.hq.ch03.Location"...>...
</class>
```

The second method is to use the lazy attribute. Setting lazy="true" is a shorthand way of defining the persistent class as the proxy. Let's assume the Location class is defined as lazy:

```
<class name="Location" lazy="true"...>...</class>
```

The lazy attribute is true by default in Hibernate 3. An easy way to disable all proxies, including lazy collections, is to set the default-lazy attribute to true in the hibernate-mapping element for a given mapping file. Let's look at an example of using a proxied Location instance:

```
Session session = factory.openSession();
Event ev = (Event) session.load(Event.class, myEventId);
Location loc = ev.getLocation();
String name = loc.getName();
session.close();
```

The returned Location instance is a proxy. Hibernate populates the Location instance when getName() is called.

You'll be dealing with a proxy of Location generated by CGLIB until you call an instance method.[1] What happens when you retrieve the

---

[1] CGLIB is a code generation library used by Hibernate. You can find out more about it at http://cglib.sourceforge.net/.

Event instance from the database? All the properties for the Event are retrieved, along with the ID of the associated Location instance. The generated SQL looks something like this:

```
select event0_.id as id0_, event0_.name as name0_,
    event0_.location_id as location_id0_ from events event0_
    where event0_.id=?
```

When you call loc.getName(), the following generated SQL is executed:

```
select location0_.id as id0_ as id0_, location0_.name as name0_
    from locations location0_ where location0_.id=?
```

If you've guessed that you can call loc.getId() without invoking a call to the database, you're correct. The proxied object already contains the ID value, so it can be safely accessed without retrieving the full object from the database.

Next, we'll look at collections of persistent objects. Like proxies, collections can also be lazily populated.

3.2.5 Collections

The mapping file defines the collections for Speakers and Attendees. Since the two collections are essentially the same, we're just going to look at the Speaker collection here. The collections are defined as sets, meaning Hibernate manages the collections with the same semantics as a java.util.Set:

```
<set name="speakers">
    <key column="event_id"/>
    <one-to-many class="Speaker"/>
</set>
```

This definition declares that the Event class has a property named speakers, and that it's a Set containing instances of the Speaker class. The Event class has the corresponding property:

```
public class Event {
    private Set speakers;
    ...

    public void setSpeakers(Set speakers) {
        This.speakers = speakers;
    }

    public Set getSpeakers() {
        return this.speakers;
    }
    ...
}
```

The key element defines the foreign key from the collection table to the parent table. In this case, the speakers table has an event_id column referring to the id column in the events table. The one–to–many element defines the association to the Speaker class.

We've only touched on persisting collections with Hibernate. In addition to Sets, Hibernate also supports persistent Maps and Lists, as well as arrays of objects and primitive values. Persistent collections are covered in detail in chapter 5.

ORGANIZING YOUR MAPPING FILES   Let's take a quick break from discussing Hibernate's persistence features and discuss a matter of practice: the location of mapping files. After you create mapping files for each persistent class, where should they be stored so the application can access them? Ideally, mapping files should be stored in the same JAR file as the classes they describe. Suppose the class file for the Event object is stored in the com/manning/hq directory and therefore in the com.manning.hq package. The Event.hbm.xml file should also be stored in the com/manning/hq directory inside the JAR archive.

3.2.6 Cascades

If you've worked with relational databases, you've no doubt encountered cascades. Cascades propagate certain operations on a table (such as a delete) to associated tables. (Remember that tables are associated through the use of foreign keys.) Suppose that when you delete an Event, you also want to delete each of the Speaker instances associated with the Event. Instead of having the application code perform the deletion, Hibernate can manage it for you.

Hibernate supports ten different types of cascades that can be applied to many-to-one associations as well as collections. The default cascade is none. Each cascade strategy specifies the operation or operations that should be propagated to child entities. The cascade types that you are most likely to use are the following:

- all—All operations are passed to child entities: save, update, and delete.
- save-update—Save and update (INSERT and UPDATE, respectively) are passed to child entities.
- delete—Deletion operations are passed to child entities.
- delete-orphan—All operations are passed to child entities, and objects no longer associated with the parent object are deleted.

The cascade element is added to the desired many-to-one or collection element. For example, the following configuration instructs Hibernate to delete the child Speaker elements when the parent Event is deleted:

```
<set name="speakers" cascade="delete">
  <key column="event_id"/>
  <one-to-many class="Speaker"/>
</set>
```

That's all there is to configuring cascades. It's important to note that Hibernate doesn't pass the cascade off to the database. Instead, the Hibernate service manages the cascades internally. This is necessary because Hibernate has to know exactly which objects are saved, updated, and deleted.

With the configuration and mapping files in hand, you're ready to persist objects to the database with Hibernate.

3.2.7 Fetching associated objects

When an object has one or more associated objects, it's important to consider how associated objects will be loaded. Hibernate 3 offers you two options. You can either retrieve associated objects using an outer join or by using a separate SELECT statement. The fetch attribute allows you to specify which method to use:

```
<many-to-one name="location" class="Location" fetch="join"/>
```

When an Event instance is loaded, the associated Location instance will be loaded using an outer join. If you wanted to use a separate select, the many-to-one element would look like this:

```
<many-to-one name="location" class="Location" fetch="select"/>
```

This also applies to child collections, but you can only fetch one collection using a join per persistent object. Additional collections must be fetched using the SELECT strategy.

If you're using Hibernate 2, the fetch attribute is not available. Instead, you must use the outer-join attribute for many-to-one associations. (There is no support for retrieving collections using a SELECT in Hibernate 2.) The outer-join attribute takes either a true or false value.

3.3 Building the SessionFactory

Hibernate's SessionFactory interface provides instances of the Session class, which represent connections to the database. Instances of SessionFactory are thread-safe and typically shared throughout an application. Session instances, on the other hand, aren't thread-safe and should only be used for a single transaction or unit of work in an application.

3.3.1 Configuring the SessionFactory

The Configuration class kicks off the runtime portion of Hibernate. It's used to load the mapping files and create a SessionFactory for those mapping files. Once these two functions are complete, the

Configuration class can be discarded. Creating a Configuration and SessionFactory instance is simple, but you have some options. There are three ways to create and initialize a Configuration object.

This first snippet loads the properties and mapping files defined in the hibernate.cfg.xml file and creates the SessionFactory:

```
Configuration cfg = new Configuration();
SessionFactory factory = cfg.configure().buildSessionFactory();
```

The configure() method tells Hibernate to load the hibernate.cfg.xml file. Without that, only hibernate.properties would be loaded from the classpath. The Configuration class can also load mapping documents programmatically:

```
Configuration cfg = new Configuration();
cfg.addFile("com/manning/hq/ch03/Event.hbm.xml");
```

Another alternative is to have Hibernate load the mapping document based on the persistent class. This has the advantage of eliminating hard-coded filenames in the source code. For instance, the following code causes Hibernate to look for a file named com/manning/hq/Event.hbm.xml in the classpath and load the associated class:

```
Configuration cfg = new Configuration();
cfg.addClass(com.manning.hq.ch03.Event.class);
```

Since applications can have tens or hundreds of mapping definitions, listing each definition can quickly become cumbersome. To get around this, the hibernate.cfg.xml file supports adding all mapping files in a JAR file. Suppose your build process creates a JAR file named application.jar, which contains all the classes and mapping definitions required. You then update the hibernate.cfg.xml file:

```
<mapping jar="application.jar"/>
```

Of course, you can also do this programmatically with the Configuration class:

```
Configuration.addJar(new java.io.File("application.jar"));
```

Keep in mind that the JAR file must be in the application classpath. If you're deploying a web application archive (WAR) file, your application JAR file should be in the /WEB-INF/lib directory in the WAR file.

The four methods used to specify mapping definitions to the Hibernate runtime can be combined, depending the requirements for your project. However, once you create the SessionFactory from the Configuration instance, any additional mapping files added to the Configuration instance won't be reflected in the SessionFactory. This means you can't add new persistent classes dynamically.

You can use the SessionFactory instance to create Session instances:

```
Session session = factory.openSession();
```

Instances of the Session class represent the primary interface to the Hibernate framework. They let you persist objects, query persistent objects, and make persistent objects transient. Let's look at persisting objects with Hibernate.

3.4 Persisting objects

Persisting a transient object with Hibernate is as simple as saving it with the Session instance:

```
Event event = new Event();
// populate the event
Session session = factory.openSession();
session.save(event);
session.flush();
```

Calling save(...) for the Event instance assigns a generated ID value to the instance and persists the instance. (Keep in mind that Hibernate doesn't set the ID value if the generator type is assigned.) The flush()

call forces persistent objects held in memory to be synchronized to the database. `Sessions` don't immediately write to the database when an object is saved. Instead, the `Session` queues a number of database writes to maximize performance.

If you would like to update an object that is already persistent, the `update(...)` method is available. Other than the type of SQL operation executed, the difference between `save(...)` and `update(...)` is that `update(...)` doesn't assign an ID value to the object. Because of this minor difference, the `Session` interface provides the `saveOrUpdate(...)` methods, which determine the correct operation to execute on the object. How does Hibernate know which method to call on an object?

When we described the mapping document, we mentioned the `unsaved-value` attribute. That attribute comes into play when you use the `saveOrUpdate(...)` method. Suppose you have a newly created `Event` instance. The `id` property is `null` until it's persisted by Hibernate. If the value is `null`, Hibernate assumes that the object is transient and assigns a new `id` value before saving the instance. A non-null `id` value indicates that the object is already persistent; the object is updated in the database, rather than inserted.

You could also use a `long` primitive to store the primary key value. However, using a primitive type also means that you must update the `unsaved-value` attribute value to 0, since primitive values can't be null.

> **TIP** In general, we suggest that you use object wrapper classes for primitive types in your persistent classes. To illustrate this, suppose you have a legacy database with a `boolean` column, which can be null. Your persistent class, mapped to the legacy table, also has a `boolean` property. When you encounter a row in the legacy table with a null `boolean` value, Hibernate throws a `Property-AccessException` since a `boolean` primitive can't be null—only `true` or `false`. However, you can avoid this problem if your persistent class property is of type `java.lang.Boolean`, which can be null, `true`, or `false`.

Here's the necessary code to persist an `Event` instance:

```
Configuration cfg = new Configuration();
SessionFactory factory = cfg.buildSessionFactory();

Event event = new Event();
// populate the Event instance

Session session = factory.openSession();
session.saveOrUpdate(event);
session.flush();
session.close();
```

The first two lines create the `SessionFactory` after loading the configuration file from the classpath. After the `Event` instance is created and populated, the `Session` instance, provided by the `SessionFactory`, persists the `Event`. The `Session` is then flushed and closed, which closes the JDBC connection and performs some internal cleanup. That's all there is to persisting objects.

Once you've persisted a number of objects, you'll probably want to retrieve them from the database. Retrieving persistent objects is the topic of the next section.

3.5 Retrieving objects

Suppose you want to retrieve an `Event` instance from the database. If you have the `Event` ID, you can use a `Session` to return it:

```
Event event = (Event) session.load(Event.class, eventId);
session.close();
```

This code tells Hibernate to return the instance of the `Event` class with an ID equal to `eventId`. Notice that you're careful to close the `Session`, returning the database connection to the pool. There is no need to flush the `Session`, since you're not persisting objects—only retrieving them. What if you don't know the ID of the object you want to retrieve? This is where HQL enters the picture.

The Session interface allows you to create Query objects to retrieve persistent objects. (In Hibernate 2, the Session interface supported a number of overloaded find methods. They were deprecated in Hibernate 3.) HQL statements are object-oriented, meaning that you query on object properties instead of database table and column names. Let's look at some examples using the Query interface.

This example returns a collection of all Event instances. Notice that you don't need to provide a select ... clause when returning entire objects:

```
Query query = session.createQuery("from Event");
List events = query.list();
```

In chapter 6, you'll see how the SELECT clause works with HQL.

This query is a little more interesting since we're querying on a property of the Event class:

```
Query query = session.createQuery("from Event where name = "+
                                  "'Opening Presentation'");
List events = query.list();
```

We've hardcoded the name value in the query, which isn't optimal. Let's rewrite it:

```
Query query = session.createQuery("from Event where name = ?",
                                  "Opening Presentation");
query.setParameter(0, "Opening Presentation", Hibernate.STRING);
List events = query.list();
```

The question mark in the query string represents the variable, which is similar to the JDBC PreparedStatement interface. The second method parameter is the value bound to the variable, and the third parameter tells Hibernate the type of the value. (The Hibernate class provides constants for the built-in types, such as STRING, INTEGER, and LONG, so they can be referenced programmatically.)

One topic we haven't touched on yet is the cache maintained by the Session. The Session cache tends to cause problems for developers new to Hibernate, so we'll talk about it next.

3.6 The Session cache

One easy way to improve performance within the Hibernate service, as well as your applications, is to cache objects. By caching objects in memory, Hibernate avoids the overhead of retrieving them from the database each time. Other than saving overhead when retrieving objects, the Session cache also impacts saving and updating objects. Let's look at a short code listing:

```
Session session = factory.openSession();
Event e = (Event) session.load(Event.class, myEventId);
e.setName("New Event Name");
session.saveOrUpdate(e);
// later, with the same Session instance
Event e = (Event) session.load(Event.class, myEventId);
e.setDuration(180);
session.saveOrUpdate(e);
session.flush();
```

This code first retrieves an Event instance, which the Session caches internally. It then does the following: updates the Event name, saves or updates the Event instance, retrieves the same Event instance (which is stored in the Session cache), updates the duration of the Event, and saves or updates the Event instance. Finally, you flush the Session.

All the updates made to the Event instance are combined into a single update when you flush the Session. This is made possible in part by the Session cache.

The Session interface supports a simple instance cache for each object that is loaded or saved during the lifetime of a given Session. Each object placed into the cache is keyed on the class type, such as com.manning.hq.ch03.Event, and the primary key value. However, this cache presents some interesting problems for unwary developers.

A common problem new developers run into is associating two instances of the same object with the same Session instance, resulting in a NonUniqueObjectException. The following code generates this exception:

```
Session session = factory.openSession();
Event firstEvent = (Event) session.load(Event.class, myEventId);
// ... perform some operation on firstEvent
Event secondEvent = new Event();
secondEvent.setId(myEventId);
session.save(secondEvent);
```

This code opens the Session instance, loads an Event instance with a given ID, creates a second Event instance with the same ID, and then attempts to save the second Event instance, resulting in the Non-UniqueObjectException.

Any time an object passes through the Session instance, it's added to the Session's cache. By passes through, we're referring to saving or retrieving the object to and from the database. To see whether an object is contained in the cache, call the Session.contains() method. Objects can be evicted from the cache by calling the Session.evict() method. Let's revisit the previous code, this time evicting the first Event instance:

```
Session session = factory.openSession();
Event firstEvent = (Event) session.load(Event.class, myEventId);
// ... perform some operation on firstEvent
if (session.contains(firstEvent)) {
        session.evict(firstEvent);
}
Event secondEvent = new Event();
secondEvent.setId(myEventId);
session.save(secondEvent);
```

The code first opens the Session instance and loads an Event instance with a given ID. Next, it determines whether the object is contained in the Session cache and evicts the object if necessary. The code then creates a second Event instance with the same ID and successfully saves the second Event instance.

If you simply want to clear all the objects from the Session cache, you can call the aptly named Session.clear() method.

So far, we've covered the basics of Hibernate configuration and use. Now we'll address some of the advanced configuration options that come into play when you deploy Hibernate in an application server.

3.7 Advanced configuration

Applications usually require more than a simple database connection. Scalability, stability, and performance are core aspects of any enterprise application. Popular solutions to achieve these goals include database connection pooling, transaction strategies, and object caching. Hibernate supports each of these solutions.

3.7.1 Connection pools

Connection pools are a common way to improve application performance. Rather than opening a separate connection to the database for each request, the connection pool maintains a collection of open database connections that are reused. Application servers often provide their own connection pools using a JNDI DataSource, which Hibernate can take advantage of when configured to use a DataSource.

If you're running a standalone application or your application server doesn't support connection pools, Hibernate supports three connection pooling services: C3P0, Apache's DBCP library, and Proxool. C3P0 is distributed with Hibernate; the other two are available as separate distributions.

When you choose a connection pooling service, you must configure it for your environment. Hibernate supports configuring connection pools from the hibernate.cfg.xml file. The `connection.provider_class` property sets the pooling implementation:

```
<property name="connection.provider_class">
  org.hibernate.connection.C3P0ConnectionProvider
</property>
```

Once the provider class is set, the specific properties for the pooling service can also be configured from the hibernate.cfg.xml file:

```
<property name="c3p0.minPoolSize">
  5
</property>
...
<property name="c3p0.timeout">
  1000
</property>
```

As you can see, the prefix for the C3P0 configuration parameters is `c3p0`. Similarly, the prefixes for DBCP and Proxool are `dbcp` and `proxool`, respectively. Specific configuration parameters for each pooling service are available in the documentation with each service. Table 3.1 lists information for the supported connection pools.

Hibernate ships with a basic connection pool suitable for development and testing purposes. However, it should not be used in production. You should always use one of the available connection pooling services, like C3P0, when deploying your application to production.

If your preferred connection pool API isn't currently supported by Hibernate, you can add support for it by implementing the `org.hibernate.connection.ConnectionProvider` interface. Implementing the interface is straightforward.

Table 3.1 Connection pooling services

Pooling Service	Provider Class	Configuration Prefix
C3P0	`org.hibernate.connec-tion.C3P0ConnectionProvider`	`c3p0`
Apache DBCP	`org.hibernate.connection.Proxool-ConnectionProvider`	`dbcp`
Proxool	`org.hibernate.connection.DBCPCon-nectionProvider`	`proxool`

There isn't much to using a connection pool, since Hibernate does most of the work behind the scenes. The next configuration topic we'll look at deals with transaction management with the Hibernate Transaction API.

3.7.2 Transactions

Transactions group many operations into a single unit of work. If any operation in the batch fails, all of the previous operations are rolled back, and the unit of work stops. Hibernate can run in many different environments supporting various notions of transactions. Standalone applications and some application servers only support simple JDBC transactions, whereas others support the Java Transaction API (JTA).

Hibernate needs a way to abstract the various transaction strategies from the environment. Hibernate has its own `Transaction` `Session` interface, demonstrated here:

```
Session session = factory.openSession();
Transaction tx = session.beginTransaction();
Event event = new Event();
// ... populate the Event instance
session.saveOrUpdate(event);
tx.commit();
```

In this example, `factory` is an initialized `SessionFactory` instance. This code creates an instance of the `org.hibernate.Transaction` class and then commits the `Transaction` instance.

Notice that you don't need to call `session.flush()`. Committing a transaction automatically flushes the `Session` object. The `Event` instance is persisted to the database when the transaction is committed. The transaction strategy you use (JDBC or JTA) doesn't matter to the application code — it's set in the Hibernate configuration file.

The `transaction.factory_class` property defines the transaction strategy that Hibernate uses. The default setting is to use JDBC transactions since they're the most common. To use JTA transactions, you need to set the following properties in hibernate.cfg.xml:

```
<property name="transaction.factory_class">
    org.hibernate.transaction.JTATransactionFactory
</property>
<property name="jta.UserTransaction">
    java:comp/UserTransaction
</property>
```

The `transaction.factory_class` property tells Hibernate that you'll be using JTA transactions. Currently, the only other option to JTA is JBDC transactions, which is the default. JTA transactions are retrieved from a JNDI URI, which is specified using the `jta.User-Transaction` property. If you don't know the URI for your specific application server, the default value is `java:comp/UserTransaction`.

There is some confusion about another property related to JTA transactions: `transaction.manager_lookup_class`. You only need to specify the manager lookup class when you're using a transactional cache. (We discuss caches in the next section — don't worry.) However, if you don't define the `jta.UserTransaction` property and `transaction.manager_lookup_class` is defined, the user transaction name in the lookup factory class is used. If neither of the properties are used, Hibernate falls back to `java:comp/UserTransaction`.

What's the benefit of using JTA transactions? JTA transactions are useful if you have multiple transactional resources, such as a database and a message queue. JTA allows you to treat the disparate transactions as a single transaction. Combining multiple transactions also applies within Hibernate. If you attempt to create multiple transactions from the same `Session` instance, all of the operations are batched into the first transaction. Let's look at an example that includes two transactions:

```
Transaction tx0 = session.beginTransaction();
Event event = new Event();
// ... populate the event instance
session.saveOrUpdate(event);

Transaction tx1 = session.beginTransaction();
Location location = new Location();
// ... populate the Location instance
session.saveOrUpdate(location);
tx0.commit();
tx1.commit();
```

This example begins by creating a new transaction. The second use of `session.beginTransaction()` just returns the first transaction instance. `session.saveOrUpdate(location)` commits the first transaction, and `tx0.commit()` recommits the first transaction.

Although you explicitly create two `Transaction` objects, only one is used. Of course, this creates a problem. Let's assume you have a `Session` object being used by two application threads. The first application thread begins the JTA transaction and starts adding objects. Meanwhile, the second thread, using the same transaction, deletes an object and commits the transaction. Where does this leave the first thread?

The first thread won't be committed, which is what you'd expect. The problem is that this issue can be hard to debug, bringing up an important point: Sessions should be used by only one application thread at a time. This is a common concern in web applications, which are multithreaded by their very nature. We discuss using Hibernate with web applications in chapter 8.

In the next section, we discuss Hibernate's support for various caching providers.

3.7.3 Cache providers

As we mentioned earlier, caching is a common method used to improve application performance. Caching can be as simple as having a class store frequently used data, or a cache can be distributed among multiple computers. The logic used by caches can also vary widely, but most use a simple least recently used (LRU) algorithm to determine which objects should be removed from the cache after a configurable amount of time.

Before you get confused, let's clarify the difference between the Session-level cache, also called the first-level cache, and what this section covers. The Session-level cache stores object instances for the lifetime of a given Session instance. The caching services described in this section cache data outside of the lifetime of a given Session. Another way to think about the difference is that the Session cache is like a transactional cache that only caches the data needed for a given operation or set of operations, whereas a second-level cache is an application-wide cache.

> NOTE   Caching services are typically referred to as second-level caches elsewhere in this book and in other Hibernate documentation. When you see it mentioned in the text, we're referring to external caching services.

By default, Hibernate supports four different caching services, listed in table 3.2. EHCache (Easy Hibernate Cache) is the default service. If you prefer to use an alternative cache, you need to set the cache.provider_class property in the hibernate.cfg.xml file:

```
<property name="cache.provider_class">
  org.hibernate.cache.OSCacheProvider
</property>
```

This snippet sets the cache provider to the OSCache caching service.

Table 3.2 Caching services supported by Hibernate

Caching Service	Provider Class	Type
EHCache	org.hibernate.cache.EhCacheProvider	Memory, disk
OSCache	org.hibernate.cache.OSCacheProvider	Memory, disk
SwarmCache	org.hibernate.cache.SwarmCacheProvider	Clustered
TreeCache	org.hibernate.cache.TreeCacheProvider	Clustered

The caching services support the caching of classes as well as collections belonging to persistent classes. For instance, suppose you have a large number of Attendee instances associated with a particular Event instance. Instead of repeatedly fetching the collection of Attendees, you can cache it. Caching for classes and collections is configured in the mapping files, with the cache element:

```
<class name="Event" table="events">
    <cache usage="read-write"/>

    ...
</class>
```

Collections can also be cached:

```
<set name="attendees">
    <cache usage="read-write"/>

    ...
</set>
```

Once you've chosen a caching service, what do you, the developer, need to do differently to take advantage of cached objects? Thankfully, you don't have to do anything. Hibernate works with the cache behind the scenes, so concerns about retrieving an outdated object from the cache can be avoided. You only need to select the correct value for the usage attribute.

The usage attribute specifies the caching concurrency strategy used by the underlying caching service. The previous configuration sets the usage to read-write, which is desirable if your application needs to update data. Alternatively, you may use the nonstrict-read-write strategy if it's unlikely two separate transaction threads could update the same object. If a persistent object is never updated, only read from the database, you may specify set usage to read-only.

Some caching services, such as the JBoss TreeCache, use transactions to batch multiple operations and perform the batch as a single unit of work. If you choose to use a transactional cache, you may set the usage attribute to transactional to take advantage of this feature. If you happen to be using a transactional cache, you'll also need to set the transaction.manager_lookup_class mentioned in the previous section.

The supported caching strategies differ based on the service used. Table 3.3 shows the supported strategies.

Table 3.3 Supported caching service strategies

Caching Service	Read-only	Read-write	Nonstrict-read-write	Transactional
EHCache	Y	Y	Y	N
OSCache	Y	Y	Y	N
SwarmCache	Y	Y	Y	N
TreeCache	Y	N	N	Y

Clearly, the caching service you choose will depend on your application requirements and environment. Next, let's look at configuring EHCache.

Configuring EHCache

By now you're probably tired of reading about configuring Hibernate, but EHCache is pretty simple. It's a single XML file, placed in a directory listed in your classpath. You'll probably want to put the ehcache.xml file in the same directory as the hibernate.cfg.xml file.

Listing 3.5 shows a simple configuration file for EHCache.

Listing 3.5 ehcache.xml file

```
<ehcache>
  <diskStore path="java.io.tmp"/>
  <defaultCache
    maxElementsInMemory="10"
    eternal="false"
    timeToIdleSeconds="120"
    timeToLiveSeconds="120"
    overflowToDisk="true"/>
  <cache name="com.manning.hq.ch03.Event"
    maxElementsInMemory="20"
    eternal="false"
    timeToIdleSeconds="120"
    timeToLiveSeconds="180"
    overflowToDisk="true"/>
</ehcache>
```

In this example, the diskStore property sets the location of the disk cache store. Then, the listing declares two caches. The defaultCache element contains the settings for all cached objects that don't have a specific cache element: the number of cached objects held in memory, whether objects in the cache expire (if eternal is true, then objects don't expire), the number of seconds an object should remain the cache after it was last accessed, the number of seconds an object should remain in the cache after it was created, and whether objects exceeding maxElementsInMemory should be spooled to the diskStore. Next, for custom settings based on the class, the code defines a cache element with the fully qualified class name listed in the name attribute. (This listing only demonstrates a subset of the available configuration for EHCache. Please refer to the documentation found at http://ehcache.sf.net for more information.)

With pooling, transactions, and caching behind us, we can look at a difference topic: how Hibernate handles inheritance.

3.8 Inheritance

Inheritance is a fundamental concept of object-oriented languages. Through inheritance, objects can inherit the state and behavior of their ancestor, or superclass. The most common use of object inheritance in applications is to create a generic base type with one or more specialized subclasses. Persisting a class hierarchy can be difficult, since each hierarchy can have its own unique requirements.

To address the problems found in hierarchy persistence, Hibernate supports three different inheritance persistence strategies:

- Table per class hierarchy
- Table per subclass
- Table per concrete class

Each mapping strategy is incrementally more complicated. In the following sections, we'll discuss the first two inheritance strategies. We've never needed to use the third, and most complicated, strategy.

3.8.1 Table per class hierarchy

This strategy is the most basic and easiest to use. All the classes in the hierarchy are stored in a single table. Suppose you have the base `Event` class, with `ConferenceEvent` and `NetworkingEvent` as subclasses. The mapping definition for this hierarchy is shown in listing 3.6.

Listing 3.6 Table per class hierarchy mapping

```
<class name="Event" table="events" discriminator-value="EVENT">
    <id name="id" type="long">
        <generator class="native"/>
    </id>
    <discriminator column="event_type" type="string" length="15"/>
    ...
    <subclass name="ConferenceEvent" discriminator-
    value="CONF_EVENT">
        <property name="numberOfSeats" column="num_seats"/>
        ...
```

```
    </subclass>
    <subclass name="NetworkingEvent" discriminator-
  value="NET_EVENT">
        <property name="foodProvided" column="food_provided"/>
        ...
    </subclass>
</class>
```

We've introduced a few new features in the mapping definition. The most important is the inclusion of the discriminator element. The discriminator column is what Hibernate uses to tell the different subclasses apart when retrieving classes from the database. If you don't specify a discriminator value, Hibernate uses the object's class name. The discriminator element in the example mapping tells Hibernate to look in the event_type column for a string describing the class type.

The discriminator is only a column in the relational table—you don't need to define it as a property in your Java object. In chapter 6, you'll see how the discriminator value can be used to retrieve specific subclasses in a query.

The subclass element contains the properties and associations belonging to the subclass. Any association element is allowed between subclass tags. You can't have an id element or a nested subclass element.

The table per class hierarchy strategy requires a single table, events, to store the three types of Event instances. Let's look at what our events table would look like with the table per hierarchy strategy, as shown in figure 3.3.

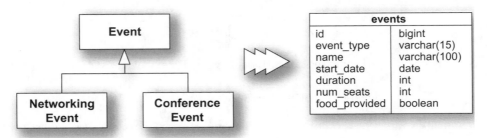

Figure 3.3 Table per hierarchy mapping

As you can see, one table contains the fields for all the objects in the hierarchy. The only obvious limitation is that your subclasses can't have columns declared as NOT NULL. Subclasses can't have non-null attributes because inserting the superclass, which doesn't even have the non-null attribute, will cause a null column violation when it's inserted into the database. The next inheritance strategy, table per subclass, doesn't have this limitation.

3.8.2 Table per subclass

Instead of putting all the classes into a single table, you can choose to put each subclass into its own table. This approach eliminates the discriminator column and introduces a one-to-one mapping from the subclass tables to the superclass table. The mapping definition for this strategy is shown in listing 3.7.

Listing 3.7 Table-per-subclass mapping

```
<class name="Event" table="events">
    <id name="event_id" type="long">
        <generator class="native"/>
    </id>
    <joined-subclass name="ConferenceEvent" table="conf_events">
        <key column="event_id"/>
        ...
    </joined-subclass>
    <joined-subclass name="NetworkingEvent" table="net_events">
        <key column="event_id"/>
        ...
    </joined-subclass>
</class>
```

The joined-subclass element can contain the same elements as the subclass element. The key element contains the primary key association to the superclass, Event. Figure 3.4 shows the resulting relational schema.

Creating an association to an Event or one of its subclasses is a simple many-to-one element:

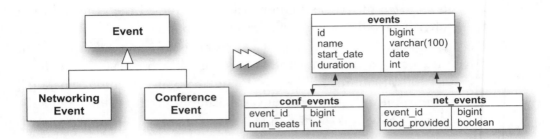

Figure 3.4 Table per subclass hierarchy

```
<many-to-one class="Event" column="event"/>
```

Since this association can refer to any class in the Event hierarchy, the association is referred to as a polymorphic association. You can also create a concrete association by giving the name of the specific subclass:

```
<many-to-one class="NetworkingEvent" column="event"/>
```

Persisting class hierarchies may seem like a complicated proposition, but Hibernate makes it fairly straightforward.

3.9 Summary

We've covered quite a bit of ground in this chapter. Starting with the most basic Hibernate configuration, we explored mapping file definitions and advanced configuration options.

As a persistence service, Hibernate operates in managed and nonmanaged environments. The configuration file, hibernate.cfg.xml, specifies how Hibernate obtains database connections—either from a JNDI DataSource or from a JDBC connection pool. Additionally, the mapping definition files describing the persistent classes may be specified in the configuration file.

Mapping files provide Hibernate with the necessary information to persist objects to a relational database. Each persistent property of a class is defined in the mapping file, including collections and associations to other persistent objects. The mapping file also defines the mandatory primary key for persistent objects.

The primary key is defined using the id element. The id element provides the name of the object property, the column used to persist the primary key, and the strategy used to generate the primary key value. Hibernate supports 10 generator strategies, including the assigned strategy that lets you assign a primary key value outside of Hibernate.

Once the configuration and mapping files are written, the Configuration object loads the files and is used to create a SessionFactory. The SessionFactory only needs to be initialized once and can be reused throughout the application. The SessionFactory creates instances of the Session interface. Session instances are basically database connections with some additional functionality.

The Session interface is the primary developer interface to Hibernate. Using it, you can persist transient objects and make persistent objects transient. It also provides querying capabilities and transaction support. Unlike the SessionFactory, Session instances should not be reused throughout the application. Instead, a new Session instance should be obtained for each transaction.

Additional pluggable components supported by Hibernate include database connection pool services, transaction management, and object caching services. These components can improve performance by reusing or caching objects and improving transaction management.

Hibernate is flexible enough to be used in any Java application environment. In this chapter, we examined how to configure it to support application persistence in managed and nonmanaged environments, as well as how to create the SessionFactory and persist objects. In the next chapter, we'll look at how Hibernate handles associations and components.

4

Associations and components

This chapter covers

- *Using many-to-one relationships to join tables*
- *Building the database with Ant and SchemaExport*
- *Using components to make finely grained object models*

Up until now, you have seen simple queries that basically pull data from a single table. The additional work of mapping a single persistent object might not seem worth the trouble. The real value of using an ORM framework like Hibernate is that you can connect objects together and then fetch an entire object graph with a simple query. Take a seemingly insignificantly small query like the following:

```
List list = session.find("from Event");
```

This query could return 1, 10, or 1000 persistent objects from the database, including not only Events but other objects linked to each Event. This approach is extremely efficient if you need all of them, and Hibernate even allows you to expand or shrink the scope of which objects are pulled from the database. One of the ways to do this is to define associations between persistent objects.

Nearly any relationship between two objects you can write can be mapped to a relational database by Hibernate. Powerful stuff indeed. This chapter covers how you can build those rich object models and turn over the heavy lifting to Hibernate to convert them back and forth between Java and the database.

Chapter goals

This chapter is all about relationships and rich object models. We expand our sample application a bit, and along the way we explore how Hibernate can bring objects together. You'll accomplish the following:

- Create a unidirectional many-to-one association between the Event and Locations.
- Automatically build a database table from our mapping documents using SchemaExport and Ant.
- Use a component to create an Address object, a finely grained object that doesn't get its own table, as entities do.

Assumptions

This chapter builds on what you have learned in previous chapters, so we assume you should be able to do the following:

- Configure a Hibernate SessionFactory using the hibernate.cfg.xml file.
- Make a single object persistent using a Hibernate mapping document.
- Obtain a session from the SessionFactory and use it to persist and load objects.

4.1 Associations

The simplest association that Hibernate supports is linking two entities together. Entity is a term for an object that has its own persistent identity.[1] For example, the Events you have worked with so far are entities. Even if two events had the same name and date, they might be completely different events, differing only by their identity. In your applications, Locations are also entities; each one has a unique identity. After all, there is probably an Oak Street in every suburb in America, but each one is a different street.[2]

In our application, every Event is held at a single Location only. The way you would represent this in Java is to have an Event object with a Location field. When you retrieve an Event, you usually want the Location too. So you are going to link Event and Location together using a many-to-one relationship.

4.1.1 Many-to-one relationships, in depth

In section 3.2, you saw a sample mapping file for an Event. Here we go a little deeper and explore a many-to-one relationship in a bit more depth.

Defining the Event and Location classes

In this section you'll create an Event class, with a many-to-one relationship to Location. From a detailed UML perspective, figure 4.1 shows what this relationship will look like.

In other words, many events can be in single location. First, create two classes (shown in listing 4.1 and listing 4.2), in the /work/calendar/src/java/com/manning/hq/ch04 directory.

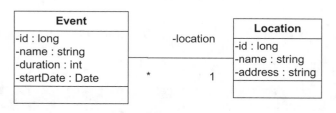

Figure 4.1
UML diagram of Event and Location

---

[1] The generic term "entity" is not to be confused with entity beans, which EJB uses to make objects unique.

[2] Old joke: Suburbs are where they cut down trees and then rename the streets after them.

Listing 4.1 Basic Event.java class

```java
package com.manning.hq.ch04;

import java.io.Serializable;
import java.util.Date;
import com.manning.hq.ch04.Location;

public class Event implements Serializable {
    private Long id;
    private int duration;
    private String name;
    private Date startDate;
    private Location location;

    public Event() { }
    public Event(String name) {
        this.name = name;
    }

    public Long getId() { return id; }
    public void setId(Long id) {
        this.id = id;
    }

    public String getName() { return name; }
    public void setName(String name) {
        this.name = name;
    }

    public Date getStartDate() { return startDate; }
    public void setStartDate(Date startDate) {
        this.startDate = startDate;
    }

    public int getDuration() { return duration; }
    public void setDuration(int duration) {
        this.duration = duration;
    }

    public Location getLocation() { return location; }
    public void setLocation(Location location) {
        this.location = location;
    }
}
```

Listing 4.2 Basic Location class

```
package com.manning.hq.ch04;

import java.io.Serializable;

public class Location implements Serializable {
    private Long id;
    private String name;
    private String address;

    public Location() { }
    public Location(String name) {
        this.name = name;
    }

    public Long getId() { return id; }
    public void setId(Long id) {
        this.id = id;
    }

    public String getName() { return name; }
    public void setName(String name) {
        this.name = name;
    }

    public String getAddress() { return address; }
    public void setAddress(String address) {
        this.address = address;
    }
}
```

As you can see, both of these are basic classes, which follow the Java-Bean specification for getter/setter fields. In listing 4.1, note that Event has a location field, which links it to a Location object. Also note that in listing 4.2, to keep the example simple for now, we have made the address field of Location a simple String. Later in this chapter, you will create the Address object you saw on Location in the previous chapter.

Mapping the database

Given the Java classes Event and Location that you have created so far, you need to map them to the database structure. Figure 4.2 shows

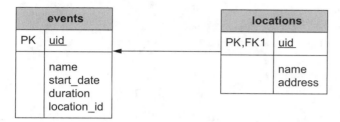

Figure 4.2 ER diagram for the events and locations tables

what the entity-relationship (ER) diagram for the two relational database tables will look like.

It might be worth pointing out that a database ER diagram for the data model shows the arrow pointing from locations to events based on the FK-PK relationship, whereas the corresponding UML object model focuses on association navigation from the Event object to the Location. This highlights a very simple example of the Object-Relational paradigm mismatch. So we need some more information to explain how the two objects are mapped to the database.

As discussed in section 3.2, each of the classes needs a corresponding mapping file, in this case, Event.hbm.xml and Location.hbm.xml, which will define the persistent fields and the relationship between the two files. Put the files in the same directory as the Event.java and Location.java files. Listing 4.3 shows these two mapping files.

**Listing 4.3   Location.hbm.xml, which makes Location a
               persistent entity**

```xml
<?xml version="1.0"?>
<!DOCTYPE hibernate-mapping PUBLIC
  "-//Hibernate/Hibernate Mapping DTD 3.0//EN"
  "http://hibernate.sourceforge.net/hibernate-mapping-3.0.dtd">
  <hibernate-mapping package="com.manning.hq.ch04">
    <class name="Location" table="locations">
        <id name="id" column="uid" type="long">
            <generator class="native"/>
```

```
        </id>
        <property name="name" type="string"/>
        <property name="address" type="string"/>
    </class>
</hibernate-mapping>
```

Note that in listing 4.3 you include a DTD declaration, which helps IDEs validate the document. The line `<class name="Location table="locations">` persists instances to the location's table.

Next, create a mapping file for your Event class (listing 4.4) and put it in the same directory.

Listing 4.4   The Event.hbm.xml mapping file, which makes Event persistent and links it to your Location class

```
<?xml version="1.0"?>
<!DOCTYPE hibernate-mapping PUBLIC
   "-//Hibernate/Hibernate Mapping DTD 3.0//EN"
   "http://hibernate.sourceforge.net/hibernate-mapping-3.0.dtd">
<hibernate-mapping package="com.manning.hq.ch04">
    <class name="Event" table="events">
        <id name="id" column="uid" type="long">
            <generator class="native"/>
        </id>
        <property name="name" type="string"/>
        <property name="startDate" column="start_date"
            type="date"/>
        <property name="duration" type="integer"/>
  <many-to-one name="location" column="location_id"
class="Location" />
    </class>
</hibernate-mapping>
```

The mapping element `<many-to-one class="Location" />` in listing 4.4 converts the Java field location into its SQL/relational-based representation. This element says that there should be a foreign key, `location_id`, in the `events` table, which links to the `locations` table. The `class` attribute defines which Java class handles the association.

At this point, you have created all the individual files for your persistent many-to-one classes, including Event.java, Event.hbm.xml, Location.java, and Location.hbm.xml. The next thing you need to do is actually configure your SessionFactory so that it can work with your two persistent classes. You will do that in the next section by creating a single configuration file that has all the information needed to connect to the database. You will also define which classes can be made persistent.

4.1.2 The central configuration file

The previous section defined the classes and the mapping files needed to make your many-to-one classes, Event and Location, persistent. The final step before you can start saving and finding your objects is to configure a SessionFactory. In this section you will do just that, by using a hibernate.cfg.xml file.

As we mentioned in section 3.1.1, there are a number of ways to configure the SessionFactory. For our sample application, you are going to use hibernate.cfg.xml as your single central configuration file. You'll configure it to make both Event and Location persistent classes.

As a quick reminder, the hibernate.cfg.xml file contains the properties to configure the database and declare the location of the mapping files. So create this file, called hibernate.cfg.xml, in the /work/calendar/src/ java directory. Open a text editor and add the code shown in listing 4.5.

Listing 4.5   The hibernate.cfg.xml file for Event and Location

```
<?xml version="1.0"?>
<!DOCTYPE hibernate-configuration PUBLIC
  "-//Hibernate/Hibernate Configuration DTD 3.0//EN"
  "http://hibernate.sourceforge.net/
  ➡ hibernate-configuration-3.0.dtd">
<hibernate-configuration>
    <session-factory>
        <property name="connection.username">root</property>
        <property name="connection.password"></property>
        <property name="connection.url">
```

```
            jdbc:mysql://localhost/events_calendar
        </property>
        <property name="connection.driver_class">
            com.mysql.jdbc.Driver
        </property>
        <property name="dialect">
            org.hibernate.dialect.MySQLDialect
        </property>
        <mapping resource="com/manning/hq/ch04/Event.hbm.xml"/>
        <mapping resource="com/manning/hq/ch04/Location.hbm.xml"/>
    </session-factory>
</hibernate-configuration>
```

We covered the details of the hibernate.cfg.xml file in listing 3.1, so only a quick review is needed here. Note that you have configured the database to point to your event_calendar database, which you will create and populate in sections 4.1.3 and 4.2. You connect to the database as the root user, using the MySQL Connector/J database driver. You have also defined the paths to your Event.hbm.xml and Location.hbm.xml files, which tell the SessionFactory where to find them.

At this point you have finished the configuration needed to get down to business and start persisting objects. In the next section, you will load some sample Events and Locations into the database using your freshly configured SessionFactory.

4.1.3 Defining sample data

To give you some sample data to play with, let's create a Java class that you will use to populate your database in section 4.2.3. Your event loader (shown in listing 4.6) will connect to the session factory, create some events and locations, and save them to the database.

Listing 4.6 EventLoader.java

```
package com.manning.hq.ch04;

import org.hibernate.*;
import org.hibernate.cfg.Configuration;
```

```
import java.util.*;
import com.manning.hq.ch04.Location;

public class EventLoader {                                    ❶ Creates a
    public static void main(String[] args) {                    Location and
        Location location = new Location();         ◁──────────  populates it
        location.setName("Hilton Convention Center");
        location.setAddress("950 North Stafford St.");

        Event event = new Event();        ◁─────────┐  Creates an
        event.setName("Annual Meeting");            │  Event and
        event.setDuration(60);                     ❷  populates it
        event.setStartDate(createDate(2004, 11, 1));
        event.setLocation(location);     ◁──────────┐  Associates the
                                                    │  Location and
        Session session = null;                    ❸  the Event
        Transaction tx = null;
        SessionFactory sessionFactory = null;
        try {
            Configuration configuration = new Configuration();
            // Configure from hibernate.cfg.xml
            // at root of classpath.
            configuration.configure();

            sessionFactory = configuration.buildSessionFactory();
            session = sessionFactory.openSession();
            tx = session.beginTransaction();

            session.save(location);  ◁────┐  Saves your
            session.save(event);          │  Location and
            session.flush();             ❹  Event
            tx.commit();
            System.out.println("Event and location saved!");
        } catch (HibernateException e) {  ◁─────┐  Performs necessary
                                                 │  exception handling
            try {                               ❺  and resource cleanup
                if(tx != null) {
                    tx.rollback();
                }
            } catch (HibernateException ignore) {
                // ignore
            }

            throw e; // Rethrow
```

```
        } finally {
            if (session != null) {
                try {
                    session.close();
                } catch (HibernateException ignore) {
                    // ignore
                }
            }
            if (sessionFactory != null) {
                try {
                    sessionFactory.close();
                } catch (HibernateException e) {
                    // ignore
                }
            }
        }
    }

    /**
     * @param year
     * @param month - This is 0-based:
     *     0 = January, 11 = December
     * @param day
     * @return
     */
    private static Date createDate(int year, int month, int day) {
        Calendar calendar = Calendar.getInstance();
        calendar.set(year, month, day);
        return calendar.getTime();
    }
}
```

A few lines in listing 4.6 warrant a bit more explanation:

❶ ❷ Here we are creating our Event and Location objects and populating them with some sample data. In a typical application, the user might create and populate these objects via a GUI or web interface. In any case, since you are just working with JavaBeans, the choice of how you get data into them is left to you, the application developer.

We also use a helper method to create a specific date, in this case December 1, 2004. Hiding the slightly complex creation of dates away in a helper method makes the main code easier to read.[3]

❸ Associating an `Event` and a `Location` is the point of the exercise, and isn't any harder than setting other simple properties in ❶ and ❷.

❹ Building the `SessionFactory` this way looks for a resource hibernate.cfg.xml at the root of the classpath. We save the location first, and then the event. As long as we save both before calling `session.flush()`, Hibernate will correctly associate them. Calling `flush()` and committing the transaction causes Hibernate to generate SQL that inserts an `Event` and a `Location` into the database.

❺ The final necessary step performs resource cleanup and exception handling. Here we roll back any changes we made, if a `HibernateException` was thrown while saving our objects. Last but not least, we clean up all the resources we opened, including the `Session` and `SessionFactory`.

If you run this code, you should have two new rows in your database. There will be one row in the `events` table and one in the `locations` table, linked by a foreign key, `location_id`. The only catch is that you don't have those tables in your `events_calendar` database yet. So before you can run your `EventLoader`, you need to create those tables. We'll do that next.

4.2 Building tables with Ant and SchemaExport

Adding tables is a common task when you are working with a database. It should be fairly trivial to issue a few CREATE TABLE statements against your database. However, beware of drifting along the dangerous path of duplication. You have already created your `Event` class,

---

[3] Java's `Calendar` and `Date` classes are notoriously non-user-friendly, especially for simple and common tasks like creating a specific date in time. The non-intuitiveness includes using 0-based months, which makes December month #11.

with its name field, and a mapping document, which again has a name field. Why should you have to create yet a third file with the SQL statement to create the events table? Considering that Hibernate is already generating SQL to do inserts, updates, and deletes, surely it can give you a hand here in creating tables as well. Thankfully, it can.

To that end, Hibernate includes an Ant task, SchemaExport, which will examine your mapping files, persistent classes, and hibernate.cfg.xml file, and generate the tables for you. Adding it to your build.xml file also means you can drop and re-create the database very easily. You are going to update the build.xml file you saw in chapters 2 and 3, and add a SchemaExport task to build your database quickly (listing 4.7). In addition, you will modify the file to run your EventLoader class.

Listing 4.7   The build4.xml file with a SchemaExport task that builds the tables Hibernate needs

```
<project name="build4.xml" default="build">
    <property name="src.java.dir" value="src/java"/>
    <property name="build.classes.dir" value="build/classes"/>
    <property name="hibernate.version" value="3.0"/>
    <property name="mysql.jdbc.version" value="3.1.7"/>
    <property name="applications.dir" location="/applications"/>
    <property name="hibernate.lib.dir"
      value="${applications.dir}/hibernate-${hibernate.version}"/>

        <property name="jdbc.driver.jar"
          value="${applications.dir}/mysql-connector-java-
    ${mysql.jdbc.version}/mysql-connector-java-
    ${mysql.jdbc.version}-bin.jar" />        ◀──┐  Specifies location of
                                                │  JAR with MySQL's
        <import file="hibernate-build.xml" />   ❶  database driver

        <path id="project.classpath">
            <pathelement location="${build.classes.dir}"/>
        </path>                                      ┌ Indicates new classpath with all the
        <path id="runtime.classpath">     ◀─────────┘ needed JARs and Hibernate files
            <path refid="project.classpath"/>   ◀──┐ Includes compiled
            <path refid="hibernate.lib.path"/>     │ .class files
```

```
        <pathelement location="${jdbc.driver.jar}"/>      ⟵
        <pathelement location="${src.java.dir}" />      ⟵
    </path>                          Adds mapping files to the classpath
    <target name="clean">
        <delete dir="${build.classes.dir}"/>
    </target>                           Includes MySQL
                                      driver specified above
    <target name="init">
         <mkdir dir="${build.classes.dir}"/>
    </target>
    <target name="compile" depends="init" >
        <javac
            srcdir="${src.java.dir}"
            destdir="${build.classes.dir}">
            <classpath refid="hibernate.lib.path"/>
        </javac>
    </target>
    <target name="build" depends="compile" >
        <java classname="com.manning.hq.ch04.EventLoader">      ⟵
            <classpath refid="runtime.classpath"/>
        </java>                          Runs EventLoader class,
    </target>                         using newly defined classpath

    <target name="schema-export" depends="compile" >
      <taskdef name="schemaexport"
        classname="org.hibernate.tool.hbm2ddl.SchemaExportTask">
            <classpath refid="runtime.classpath" />  ⟵ Defines
      </taskdef>                               SchemaExport task
        <schemaexport config="${src.java.dir}/hibernate.cfg.xml"/>   ⟵

    </target>                         Builds database schema
</project>
```

This is mostly the same as the previous chapter's build file, so let's focus on what has changed: You defined a new classpath, which you use in several places throughout the build file. One of the places it is used is the SchemaExport task, so you need to specify a few essential elements, including

- The compiled persistent classes, Event.class and Location.class files.
- The Hibernate library JAR files.

- The MySQL JDBC driver (since `SchemaExport` executes JDBC statements, it needs the driver). You will very likely need to modify ❶ above to make the `mysql.version` and `jdbc.driver.jar` properties match your configuration.

- The hibernate.cfg.xml and the hbm.xml files, including Event.hbm.xml and Location.hbm.xml files. For the sake of simplicity, we are storing the mapping files alongside their corresponding Java source files; this is why we add the ${src.java.dir} directory to the runtime classpath.

- The log4j.properties file (we haven't covered it yet, but it needs to be at the root of the classpath, right next to hibernate.cfg.xml).[4]

Also note that you are using a new Ant task, called `taskdef`, which allows you to define new tasks that you can invoke later in the Ant file. Here you define a new task, `SchemaExport`, and link it to the actual `SchemaExportTask`. You also use the runtime.classpath you defined earlier.

Finally, the `SchemaExport` task needs a few configuration details, such as which database to run against and the user/password information. You have already provided this information in the hibernate.cfg.xml file, and `SchemaExport` can use it if you provide its location.

With all this in place, you should be able to run the `SchemaExport` task and build the database. And you can—but there is one more piece that you should configure first: Hibernate's logging framework.

4.2.1 Logging with log4j and Commons Logging

Hibernate uses a logging framework, which can help new developers figure out just what it's doing under the covers. It uses the Apache Commons Logging framework, which is a simple API that allows users to substitute different logging implementations without recompiling. Developers can use the Java 1.4 java.util.logging framework or the

---

[4] If you can't handle the suspense, you can skip ahead to 4.2.1, where we discuss logging and what the log4j.properties file is used for.

popular open source log4j framework. So, just as JDBC is a database-neutral API that abstracts away the specific data, Commons Logging is a logging-neutral API.

By default, Hibernate is set up to use log4j, so the path of least resistance is to use that. Hibernate will work just fine without configuring logging, but it will nag you about it. So when you run the SchemaExport task, you will see something like this:

```
[schemaexport] log4j:WARN No appenders could be found for logger
(org.hibernate.cfg.Environment).
[schemaexport] log4j:WARN Please initialize the log4j
    system properly.
```

By putting a log4j.properties file into the root of the classpath, you stop the nagging and obtain information about Hibernate's internal steps. Use your text editor to create a new file called log4j.properties (listing 4.8) in the /work/calendar/src/java directory.

Listing 4.8 log4j.properties, which configures Hibernate to log information to the console

```
### direct log messages to stdout
log4j.appender.stdout=org.apache.log4j.ConsoleAppender
log4j.appender.stdout.Target=System.out
log4j.appender.stdout.layout=org.apache.log4j.PatternLayout
log4j.appender.stdout.layout.ConversionPattern=%d %5p %c{1}:%m%n

### set log levels - for more verbose logging change
###   'info' to 'debug'
log4j.rootLogger=warn, stdout

log4j.logger.org.hibernate=warn
```

The purpose of the logging file is to specify three main things:

- How much information to log, and how "noisy" the output is (via log levels)

- Where that information goes (via appenders)
- How the information is formatted (via patterns)

This listing includes a single appender, called `stdout`, which sends all of the output to the command line. It configures the global `root` logger (log4j.rootLogger) to log at the warn level. `warn` is "medium" noisy, `debug` is extremely detailed, and `fatal` will stay quiet unless something goes seriously wrong. In addition to the global logging, you can configure it on a per-package level, if you only want the gritty details from one particular package. You did so above, using `log4j.logger.org.hibernate=warn`. This is the package where all the Hibernate classes live. It allows you to set them to their loggers individually; for example, you can set them to `debug` but leave the `root` logger at `warn`.

Hibernate also comes with a more detailed log4j.properties file, which this one is based on. It contains a few more in-depth examples. Look in the /applications/hibernate-3.0/src for it. You should also visit the log4j and Commons Logging homepages, which can be found at http://logging.apache.org/log4j/docs and http://jakarta.apache.org/commons/logging, respectively, for more information and complete documentation for both of these projects. Now, with this final piece in place, you can go ahead and build the tables.

4.2.2 Running SchemaExport

With everything in place, you can now run the target that contains the `SchemaExport` task. Every time you run it, the task will drop all the tables and rebuild them. Let's go ahead and run it (listing 4.9).

Listing 4.9   Using Hibernate to build the database

```
$ ant -f build4.xml clean schema-export
Buildfile: build4.xml

clean:
   [delete] Deleting directory C:\work\calendar\build\classes

init:
    [mkdir] Created dir: C:\work\calendar\build\classes
```

```
compile:
    [javac] Compiling 3 source files
      to C:\work\calendar\build\classes

schema-export:
[schemaexport] drop table if exists events      ◁── Drops the old tables
[schemaexport] drop table if exists locations   ┃ Generates correct
[schemaexport] create table events (  ◁─────────┛ column types for MySQL
[schemaexport]     uid BIGINT NOT NULL AUTO_INCREMENT,
[schemaexport]     name VARCHAR(255),  ◁──── If unspecified,
[schemaexport]     start_date DATE,          strings turn into
[schemaexport]     duration INTEGER,         VARCHAR (255)
[schemaexport]     location_id BIGINT,
[schemaexport]     primary key (uid)
[schemaexport] )
[schemaexport] create table locations (
[schemaexport]     uid BIGINT NOT NULL AUTO_INCREMENT,
[schemaexport]     name VARCHAR(255),
[schemaexport]     address VARCHAR(255),
[schemaexport]     primary key (uid)
[schemaexport] )
[schemaexport] alter table events add index (location_id), add
  constraint FKB307E11920EBB9E5 foreign key (location_id) references

locations (uid)  ◁──┐ Generates index for the foreign key
                    ┃ between the two tables
BUILD SUCCESSFUL
Total time: 4 seconds
```

Here you can see the SQL that is being run against the database. SchemaExport has converted the generic types of integer, Long and String, that we specified in the mapping files into MySQL-specific column types, including VARCHARs and BIGINTs.

Even though we didn't specify column sizes, especially for strings, Hibernate uses reasonable defaults. For MySQL, it's using VARCHAR (255). Other databases may have slightly different defaults, but Hibernate's dialects know how to do the right thing.

In addition to building the tables, SchemaExport performs a few optimizations, based on the database. In this listing it builds indexes on the foreign keys, which should make joins perform better. This is nice, especially for developers who don't happen to be database administrators or who are just forgetful.[5]

As mentioned earlier, running this task will drop the database tables and rebuild them from scratch every time. This is great if you are deep in the "zone" of rapid development, but not so wonderful if you accidentally drop a production database. If you are really paranoid and don't want to accidentally drop the database, you can use the Schema-UpdateTask, which is discussed in chapter 7. It will "diff" your database and selectively adds columns rather than dropping and rebuilding the entire database.

4.2.3 Loading the Events

Since the tables are now in place, you can run your EventLoader and populate the database with some sample data. You are going to run the default Ant target, which will run the compiled EventLoader class:

```
Buildfile: build4.xml

init:

compile:

build:
     [java] Event and location saved!

BUILD SUCCESSFUL
Total time: 5 seconds
```

We ran only the default build task, and all of the classes were compiled already from running SchemaExport before, so the only task that's really doing anything is the java task. If you look back at listing 4.6, you'll note that it's configuring and building the SessionFactory, and

---

[5] Also, despite the fact that it's generating foreign key constraints, MySQL only supports foreign keys if you are using the InnoDB table types. So check the documentation for MySQL on which table types you are using.

persisting two objects. Building a `SessionFactory` is a reasonably expensive operation, so you generally don't want to do it too often. Usually it's constructed once when the application starts up.

While you have the success message, you should actually take a look at the database and see what you have. Go ahead and open a new command window and start up the MySQL console. Listing 4.10 shows how you check the database to see the new entries.

Listing 4.10 Inspecting the contents of the database

```
$ cd applications/mysql/bin

$ mysql -u root -p
Enter password:

mysql> use events_calendar;
Database changed
mysql> select * from events;
+-----+----------------+------------+----------+-------------+
| uid | name           | start_date | duration | location_id |
+-----+----------------+------------+----------+-------------+
|   1 | Annual Meeting | 2004-12-01 |       60 |           1 |
+-----+----------------+------------+----------+-------------+
1 row in set (0.00 sec)

mysql> select * from locations;
+-----+-------------------------+-------------------------+
| uid | name                    | address                 |
+-----+-------------------------+-------------------------+
|   1 | Hilton Convention Center | 950 North Stafford St. |
+-----+-------------------------+-------------------------+
1 row in set (0.00 sec)
```

Since we configured `Event` and `Location` to use native key generation, MySQL is using `auto_increment` fields for both uid columns. By associating the `Event` and `Location`, Hibernate knows to set the `location_id` to match the uid column of the new `Location`.

Alternatively, if you aren't a fan of the command line and you are using a more recent MySQL version (4.1.5+), you can also choose to use the optional download for the MySQL Query Browser, or other free SQL tools such as TOAD, SQuirreL, or DBVisualizer.

4.2.4 Refactoring

Looking back at listing 4.6, you might notice that there is a fair amount of exception handling and resource cleanup code. This was very necessary in 2.x versions of Hibernate since Hibernate classes threw checked exceptions, which you as a developer needed to handle. In Hibernate 3, HibernateException is unchecked, extending Runtime-Exception, so catching them is not strictly necessary. But because you are dealing with database connections, you can't leave it to the garbage collector to clean up after you. You must explicitly close sessions and end transactions manually. All this is necessary for older versions, but it certainly clutters up the example code.

Refactoring: Extract HibernateFactory utility class

In this section, you will refactor[6] the EventLoader class, with the intent of simplifying the resource cleanup code. As a nice effect, you should have a good reusable Hibernate utility class, which you can use in the remainder of our examples. Create a new class HibernateFactory and move the resource cleanup code from EventLoader into it. Listing 4.11 shows EventLoader2, which uses the refactored-out HibernateFactory. Listing 4.12 shows the HibernateFactory utility class.

Listing 4.11 Refactored EventLoader2, with all new reduced cleanup code

```
// package and import statements omitted
public class EventLoader2 {
    public static void main(String[] args) {
        // Event and Location population code omitted

        Session session = null;
        Transaction tx = null;
```

---

[6] Refactoring is improving the internal structure of code, without altering its existing outward behavior.

```
        try {

    HibernateFactory.buildSessionFactory();   ◁─┐  Factory builds and
            session = HibernateFactory.openSession();   stores the
                                                        SessionFactory
            tx = session.beginTransaction();

            session.save(event);
            session.save(location);

            session.flush();
            tx.commit();
            System.out.println("Event and location saved!");
        } catch (HibernateException e) {
            HibernateFactory.rollback(tx);
            throw e; // Rethrow
        } finally {
            HibernateFactory.close(session);
            HibernateFactory.closeFactory();
        }
    }
    // Omitted Date Helper method
}
```

Listing 4.12 HibernateFactory utility class

```
package com.manning.hq.ch04;

import org.hibernate.SessionFactory;
import org.hibernate.Session;
import org.hibernate.Transaction;
import org.hibernate.HibernateException;

import org.hibernate.cfg.Configuration;
import org.apache.commons.logging.LogFactory;
import org.apache.commons.logging.Log;


public class HibernateFactory {
    private static SessionFactory sessionFactory;
    private static Log log =
                                                    Allows you to
                                                    use logging
    LogFactory.getLog(HibernateFactory.class);   ◁─┘

    public static SessionFactory buildSessionFactory()
```

```
    throws HibernateException {          Configures and stores
    if(sessionFactory != null){          SessionFactory as a singleton
        closeFactory();
    }
    Configuration configuration = new Configuration();
    configuration.configure();
    sessionFactory = configuration.buildSessionFactory();
    return sessionFactory;
}

public static SessionFactory getSessionFactory() {
    return sessionFactory;                       Allows direct
}                                                access if needed

public static Session openSession() throws HibernateException {
    return sessionFactory.openSession();     Provides
}                                            convenience access
                                             for opening sessions
public static void closeFactory() {
    if (sessionFactory != null) {
        try {
            sessionFactory.close();
        } catch (HibernateException ignored) {
            log.error("Couldn't close SessionFactory",
                     ignored);
        }
    }
}
public static void close(Session session) {
    if (session != null) {
        try {                           Essentially ignores
            session.close();            exceptions
        } catch (HibernateException ignored) {
            log.error("Couldn't close Session", ignored);
        }
    }
}
public static void rollback(Transaction tx) {
    try {
        if (tx != null) {
            tx.rollback();
        }
    } catch (HibernateException ignored) {
```

```
            log.error("Couldn't rollback Transaction", ignored);
        }
    }
}
```

As you can see, you moved four responsibilities into your Hibernate-Factory class: configuring the SessionFactory, closing the SessionFactory, closing sessions, and rolling back transactions. The latter three operations need a bit of null checking and throw their own unchecked exceptions if they fail. Now you shouldn't too concerned if you fail to close a session, so you just log the exception and move on.

After configuring the SessionFactory, you store it in a static field, which functionally makes this a Singleton pattern. Only one Session-Factory will be created, and it can be used to open as many sessions as are needed. Looking back at the refactored EventLoader2, you can see that it's quite a bit less cluttered and exception handling no longer obscures the main point of the code.

Refactoring: Extract the SchemaExport task

Most Hibernate projects we have worked on use the SchemaExport task, which makes it a good candidate for reuse. Now that you have the SchemaExport task running correctly, let's go ahead and extract the schema-export target from our project build file into our reusable hibernate-build.xml file. We also want to rename a few properties and paths, so that the schema-export target is less coupled to our build.xml file. Go ahead and add the following code to the hibernate-build.xml:

```xml
<target name="schema-export">
  <taskdef name="schemaexport"
    classname="org.hibernate.tool.hbm2ddl.SchemaExportTask"
  >
      <classpath refid="hibernate.runtime.classpath"/>
  </taskdef>
  <schemaexport config="${hibernate.cfg.xml.file}" />
</target>
```

As you can see, you are mostly copying and pasting from the build.xml file. The biggest change is that hibernate-build.xml has a few new properties and paths that allow the importing build.xml to configure it. Making the cfg.xml file a property means that any build file can import it and make it work for its directory structure. Also, to keep naming conventions consistent, prefix the classpath with hibernate, as in hibernate.lib.path. Now rework your build.xml, as shown in listing 4.13.

Listing 4.13 build4.xml using the imported SchemaExport task

```
<project name="build4.xml" default="build">
    <!-Other Properties omitted -->
    <property
        name="hibernate.cfg.xml.file"
        value="${src.java.dir}/hibernate.cfg.xml"/>      <-- Adds property to
                                                              configure the location
    <import file="hibernate-build.xml"/>                      of the config file

    <path id="runtime.classpath">
        <path refid="project.classpath"/>
        <path refid="hibernate.lib.path"/>
        <pathelement location="${jdbc.driver.jar}"/>
        <pathelement location="${src.java.dir}"/>
    </path>                                              Adds new path
    <path id="hibernate.runtime.classpath"              that hibernate-
        refid="runtime.classpath"/>       <--           build.xml needs

    <!-- Other Targets omitted -->                      Overrides the imported
    <target name="schema-export"                          SchemaExport task
        depends="compile,hibernate-build.schema-export"/>   <--
</project>
```

Only the important changes from build.xml file are shown. You have to configure the property and classpath that the imported file needs. One of the changes requires a bit more explanation; as you can see in the line

```
<target name="schema-export"
    depends="compile,hibernate-build.schema-export"/>
```

there is still a SchemaExport task here, but didn't you move that? Here you are taking advantage of one of the import task's ability to override targets. When you run

```
$ ant schema-export
```

it will execute this target, which in turn runs the compile target and the imported schema-export target from the hibernate-build.xml file. Notice that the name of the target is hibernate-build.schema-export. Look at the hibernate-build.xml file and check out the <project> element:

```
<project name="hibernate-build">
```

You can reference an imported target by combining [project name].[target name]. The outward behavior of build.xml is the same. Run the schema-export target again and verify that it still builds the database exactly as before. And with that you now have a reusable schema-export target.

4.2.5 Finding Events

Storing linked objects is only half of the benefit of using a many-to-one association. The other half is that when you find Events, the location data will be pulled back into memory as well, through a join. Create a simple EventFinder (listing 4.14), which loads the Event, and verify that the location comes with it.

Listing 4.14 EventFinder, which loads a single Event by its primary key

```java
package com.manning.hq.ch04;

import org.hibernate.*;
import org.apache.commons.logging.*;

public class EventFinder {
    private static Log log = LogFactory.getLog(EventFinder.class);

    public static void main(String[] args)
        throws HibernateException {
        HibernateFactory.buildSessionFactory();
        Session session = HibernateFactory.openSession();
        Transaction tx = session.beginTransaction();
```

```
try {
    Event event = new Event("EventFinder");
    Location location = new Location("A Random Location");
    event.setLocation(location);
    session.save(location);
    session.save(event);
    session.flush();
    tx.commit();
    Event event2 = (Event) session.load(Event.class,
                            event.getId());

    log.warn("Event: " + event2.getName());

    log.warn("Location1: " +
            ➡    event2.getLocation().getName());
} finally {
    HibernateFactory.close(session);
    HibernateFactory.closeFactory();
}
    }
}
```

Loads a known event by its primary key

Uses logging to display property values

Verifies location that gets loaded along with event

Here you are inserting an Event into the database, and then looking it up again. Since Hibernate sets the id of an object when it saves it, you know the id of the Event. So you can retrieve it using the session.load() method. This method loads an Event and any associated objects, such as the Location. Then you use logging to display properties from both Event and Location.[7] Finally, you do what should be familiar cleanup code.

Next, go ahead and add another target to the build.xml file, which will run the EventFinder:

```
<target name="find" depends="compile">
    <java classname="com.manning.hq.ch04.EventFinder">
        <classpath refid="runtime.classpath"/>
```

---

[7] Why use Commons Logging instead of just System.out.println()? First, we have already configured it for Hibernate, so it might as well just piggyback onto it. Second, we think it's a good habit to get into; logging you put in for testing can be used later for debugging.

```
        </java>
    </target>
```

After adding this target to the build, you can run the `find` target from the command line:

```
$ ant -f build4.xml find
```

When the `find` target runs, you should see something like this:

```
find:
      [java] 15:42:43,947  WARN EventFinder: – Event: Annual Meeting
      [java] 15:42:43,947  WARN EventFinder: – Location: Hilton
            Convention Center
```

As you can see, both the `Event` and `Location` objects are loaded from the database and their properties are displayed.

4.2.6 Cascades

You can make one more refinement to your model. In section 3.2, we discussed collections and cascades. Since your location is just the opposite end of a collection, you can use cascading here as well.

Saving the object graph

In your `EventLoader`, you had to explicitly save both the `Event` and `Location` objects, even though you specifically set the `Location` object on `Event`. If you remove the `session.save(location)` line from the `EventLoader`, you will see an exception like this:

```
org.hibernate.TransientObjectException: object references
an unsaved transient instance – save the transient instance
before flushing: com.manning.hq.ch04.Location
```

Hibernate is telling you that you associated the `Event`, which is persistent, with a nonpersistent (or transient) `Location` object. So when the `session.flush()` method is called, inserting the `Event`, it balks at the `Location`, which wasn't made persistent. Needing to explicitly save one associated object, the location isn't too bad, but if Event had two or three associated objects (or more), it's just extra work for you. Hibernate can minimize this unnecessary work by allowing you to define cascading behavior relationships between your objects.

Location cascading

Cascading means that when you save, update, or delete an object, its associated objects can be affected as well. In our case, you want the Location to be saved when you save or update the Event. Modify the Event.hbm.xml file and add a new attribute to the <many-to-one> element, as shown here:

```
<many-to-one name="location" column="location_id"
    class="Location" cascade="save-update" />
```

You have defined the location relationship as save-update. This means any time you save a new event, the Location will be saved too. You can test this out by modifying the EventLoader class and commenting out the code that saves Location:

```
session.save(event);
// Use cascading to save the location
// session.save(location);
```

Rerun the build target and you should see that both Event and Location have been saved. Refer back to section 3.2 for a complete list of the possible cascades.

4.3 Components

Associations in Hibernate define relations between tables. In the previous example, you have two tables, events and locations, and two objects, Event and Location. So the general usage is one table equals one object. Sometimes it is useful to have a more granular relationship, where one table equals more than one object. Hibernate allows you to do this by using components. Components are not entities, like their containing object, and are bound by their parent. They also do not have an identity, and exist only if the parent entity does.

4.3.1 What's in a component?

Components allow you to take several columns and group them into a single object. Let's look back at our Location object. Currently it has an address field, which is a simple String. We just put in a single street, but you could certainly stuff a full address into that one field, like so:

```
location.setAddress("950 North Stafford St. Arlington, VA 22204");
```

This will work, but you can't do much with one amalgamated column of address data. You probably want to break it up into several columns, with street, city, state, and zip code. This would make your Location object look like this:

```
public class Location implements Serializable {
    private Long id;
    private String name;
    private String streetAddress;
    private String city;
    private String state;
    private String zipCode;

    // getters and setter omitted
}
```

This would certainly work. But you could also refactor this code to extract a component. Do this by grouping these new fields into a single logical object, Address, and have Hibernate handle it as a component. Figure 4.3 shows a UML diagram of what this would look like.

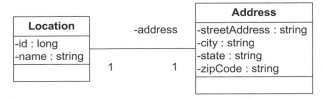

Figure 4.3 Location and Address component UML diagram

Next modify your Location class:

```
public class Location implements Serializable{
    private Long id;
    private String name;
    private Address address = new Address();

    // Other getter/setters omitted

    public Address getAddress() { return address; }
    public void setAddress(Address address) {
        this.address = address;
    }
}
```

This is quite a bit shorter; all we have done is moved the four address-related fields into a discrete Address class, shown in listing 4.15.

Listing 4.15 The Address object, our new component

```
package com.manning.hq.ch04;

public class Address {
    private String streetAddress;
    private String city;
    private String state;
    private String zipCode;

    public String getStreetAddress() { return streetAddress; }
    public void setStreetAddress(String streetAddress) {
        this.streetAddress = streetAddress;
    }

    public String getCity() { return city; }
    public void setCity(String city) {
        this.city = city;
    }

    public String getState() { return state; }
    public void setState(String state) {
        this.state = state;
    }
```

```
        public String getZipCode() { return zipCode; }
        public void setZipCode(String zipCode) {
            this.zipCode = zipCode;
        }
    }
}
```

As you can see, the address fields have been grouped together under that `Address` object. All you need to do now is map the columns from the `locations` table to the `Address` object.

4.3.2 Mapping a component

Since `Address` is not a separate entity like `Event` or `Location`, and is a component of `Location`, it has a strictly child-to-parent relationship to its `Location`. Its mapping goes in the Location.hbm.xml file. Go ahead and modify that file as shown in listing 4.16 and add the mapping information for the address field there.

Listing 4.16 Mapping an Address component

```xml
<hibernate-mapping package="com.manning.hq.ch04">
    <class name="Location" table="locations">
        <id name="id" column="uid" type="long">
            <generator class="native"/>
        </id>
        <property name="name" type="string"/>
        <component name="address" class="Address" >
            <property name="streetAddress"
                column="street_address" type="string"/>
            <property name="city" type="string"/>
            <property name="state" type="string"/>
            <property name="zipCode"
                column="zip_code" type="string"/>
        </component>
    </class>
</hibernate-mapping>
```

Notice that each field on the `Address` component is mapped to a column of its own. Also, you specified explicit column names for a few of the columns, rather than using the property name as the column name. Now since you have added a few columns, you need to update the database schema. Run the `schema-export` task again, and look for the rebuilding of the `locations` table:

```
$ ant -f build4.xml schema-export
```

Among other output, you should see this...

```
[schemaexport] create table locations (
[schemaexport]     uid BIGINT NOT NULL AUTO_INCREMENT,
[schemaexport]     name VARCHAR(255),
[schemaexport]     street_address VARCHAR(255),
[schemaexport]     city VARCHAR(255),
[schemaexport]     state VARCHAR(255),
[schemaexport]     zip_code VARCHAR(255),
[schemaexport]     primary key (uid)
[schemaexport] )
```

As you notice, four new columns have been added to the `locations` table; these are the four columns that the `Address` component uses. Now you can populate the `Location` object. Modify the `EventLoader` to populate the `Location` using the new `Address` object:

```
Location location = new Location();
location.setName("Hilton Convention Center");
location.getAddress().setStreetAddress("950 North Stafford St.");
location.getAddress().setCity("Arlington");
location.getAddress().setState("VA");
location.getAddress().setZipCode("22204");

Event event = new Event();
```

Populating the `Address` isn't much different from any of the other objects. None of the rest of the `EventLoader` needs to be changed. You can run the `build` target again and it should save `Event`, `Location`, and the new `Address` object together. When `Location` is loaded, Hibernate will populate the address fields just like the rest of the fields on `Location`.

4.3.3 Why use a component?

Just because you can split one table into a bunch of objects, why would you want to? In this case, it helps simplify the Location object by making the details of an address a separate object. But it's still yet another object. Components are best used if there is going to be more than one complex field or you want a place to put other address-specific methods or logic.

Multiple addresses

Consider the case of multiple addresses; perhaps Location needs both a mailing address and billing address. It's less duplication to add a second address field than it is to add four additional fields. An updated Location might look like this:

```
public class Location implements Serializable{
    private Long id;
    private String name;
    private Address mailingAddress = new Address();
    private Address billingAddress = new Address();

    // getters/setters omitted
}
```

We renamed the original address field to mailingAddress and added a second field. You will still need to update the Location.hbm.xml file to add the four additional columns, which map to the second field, billingAddress.

Grouping domain logic

Another good reason to use components is so that you can group related domain logic. For example, suppose you have a method that parses a string and splits it into multiple fields. It makes sense to keep that as close to the Address object as possible. Fine-grained objects are more easily reusable. So you could populate the address as follows:

```
Address address = location.getBillingAddress();
address.parse("950 North Stafford St. Arlington, VA 22204");
```

`Address`'s parse method could handle multiple different address formats, and generally evolve into a cohesive reusable object.

4.4 Summary

A single persistent object with no associations is a lonely one. The purpose of this chapter was to demonstrate how Hibernate can allow you to create flexible object models that can span multiple tables, or alternatively, create multiple objects for a single table.

You learned about the most basic object-relational association, the many-to-one, which maps two related tables via a foreign key to two Java objects. In the Java code, linking the objects is done just like any other basic JavaBeans. After making objects persistent, via a `session.save()` call, Hibernate will automatically manage the foreign keys for you under the covers. You can also set cascading associations for each field, which can automatically make an entire transient object graph persistent with a single `save()` or `update()`. Once objects are linked, you can pull back a web of objects from the database with a single `load()` call.

To cut down on tedious duplicative work, Hibernate provides the `SchemaExport` task, which creates the database schema for you. It reads the mapping files and persistent classes and generates the SQL commands to create the necessary tables. It is very handy for rapid development, because it keeps the database in sync with the persistent object model.

Finally, you learned how to create very fine-grained object models using components. Components allow you to turn one table into multiple objects. Components group several related columns into a single object, helping organize your model and making reuse easier.

5

Collections and custom types

This chapter covers

- *Persisting Java collections*
- *Creating custom Hibernate data types*
- *Converting components into custom types*

The Java Collections API has been part of the Java Foundation Classes (JFC) since the release of JDK 1.2. The Collections API was rapidly adopted by developers because of its flexibility and relative power. Most Java applications make use of at least a handful of the Collections classes, and domain models typically use collections to maintain multiple children for a parent object. For instance, our event management application makes use of multiple collections. One example of this is the collection of `Attendees` maintained by the `Event` class. If collections are used in the domain model, it's also logical that they would need to be persisted.

Hibernate provides support for the core Collections interfaces: `java.util.List`, `java.util.Map`, and `java.util.Set`. Since there is a great deal of variability in how collections can be used by the domain model, Hibernate offers a number of ways to persist collections. Additionally,

Hibernate supports persisting arrays of objects and primitive types. Persistent arrays are managed in a similar fashion to collections.

In the previous chapter we introduced components. You'll recall that components allow you to group several columns in a table and treat them as a single object. Custom value types might appear to be similar to components, but they offer quite a bit more power, as they allow you to dictate how Hibernate will persist an object. They are typically used when you want to persist data in a specific way, or provide support for a data type not handled by Hibernate.

Although Hibernate offers a rich set of data types, they may not meet every application requirement. If you need to, you can easily create a new data type that you can then reuse in your other applications. Custom value types provide another extension mechanism for Hibernate.

Chapter goals

This chapter examines two important concepts: persisting collections and arrays, and creating custom value types. As before, we'll present this information in the context of our event management application. Once this chapter is complete, we will have accomplished the following:

- Created mapping definitions for collections and custom value types
- Examined the different types of collection associations
- Converted the Address instance introduced in chapter 4 from a component to a custom value type

Assumptions

Since we're building on the lessons in the previous chapter, you should be able to

- Create a basic mapping document with properties, many-to-one associations, and components
- Use Ant to create and update the application database

5.1 Persisting collections and arrays

Persisting collections with Hibernate is straightforward, but some details can cause you problems if you're not aware of them. We start out this section discussing how Hibernate manages persistent collections, including the mapping definitions for one-to-many and many-to-many associations. After that, we'll give an example for each of the collection types and address some of the infrequently used components, such as idbags.

When a collection is persisted by Hibernate, it retains all of the semantics of the Java collection interface. For example, when a java.util.List is persisted, the index order of each element will also be persisted. The index order is persisted so that the list can be re-created when retrieved from the database.

Persisting the behavior of collections doesn't stop at the java.util.List interface. For instance, a persistent Set cannot contain duplicate elements, and is naturally unordered. In the case of a java.util.Map, the keys used must be unique.

Because Hibernate enforces the semantics of the collection class, how can you just store a collection of objects without worrying about the semantics of the underlying collection?

Hibernate supports another type of collection called a Bag. Bags are basically unordered and unindexed Lists that can contain duplicate elements. The notion of a Bag is Hibernate specific; there isn't a Java class or interface representing the Bag. In fact, there isn't even a specific class for a Bag collection. Persistent objects wishing to have a Bag collection can simply use a java.util.List. Hibernate handles the persistence details for you. We'll explain Bag usage later in the chapter.

To avoid confusing the Java collection classes with their Hibernate counterparts, table 5.1 summarizes the persistent collection types with their Java collection class.

Table 5.1 Hibernate persistent collections compared with Java collections

Hibernate collection type	Java collection type	Description
set	java.util.Set	Persists an unordered, unique collection of values or objects.
map	java.util.Map	Persists a collection of key/value pairs.
list	java.util.List	Persists an ordered, non-unique collection of values or objects.
bag	java.util.List	Persists an unordered, non-unique collection of values or objects.
array	N/A	Persists an indexed, non-unique collection of values or objects.
primitive-array	N/A	Persists an indexed, non-unique collection of primitive values.
idbag	java.util.List	Persists an unordered, non-unique, many-to-many collection using a surrogate key.

If you use a collection class that adds additional behavior to the implemented interface, like a LinkedList (LinkedList implements List), keep in mind that the additional behavior is not persisted. Behind the scenes, Hibernate uses its own implementation of the core Collections interfaces, primarily to support lazy collections. (We'll discuss lazy collections in section 5.1.4.) The custom interface implementations allow Hibernate to intercept calls to the persistent collection and populate it when needed.

5.1.1 Using interfaces

Hibernate's custom collection implementations have another impact on your persistent classes. When you're creating the accessor methods for the collection classes, it's important to declare the collection interface, from the java.util package, instead of having a class implement the interface. To illustrate, suppose you have a class with the following accessors:

```
public void setGroups(ArrayList groups) { … }
public ArrayList getGroups() { … }
```

Since your accessor uses a java.util.ArrayList, you'll have problems at runtime when Hibernate tries to populate the collection. Instead, you should use a java.util.List. This is because Hibernate provides its own implementation of the Collections interfaces, partially illustrated in figure 5.1.

By examining figure 5.1, you can see that Hibernate simply implements the Collections interfaces in the java.util package. When Hibernate populates a collection, such as a java.util.List, the implementing class is actually org.hibernate.collection.List.

We'll get started by looking at mapping definitions for a collection. For demonstration purposes, we'll use collections of type java.util.Set. Despite the different collection types supported by Hibernate, managing persistent collections is similar regardless of the underlying collection type. We'll point out some subtle configuration and usage differences as we encounter them.

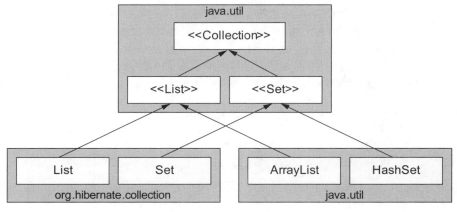

Figure 5.1 Hibernate collection implementations

5.1.2 Mapping persistent collections

Persistent collections are defined in the mapping definition for the class that contains them.

One-to-many associations

In chapter 3 we examined the mapping file for the Event class, which had two <set> definitions. Let's look at that portion of the mapping file again:

```xml
<hibernate-mapping package="com.manning.hq">
    <class name="Event" table="events">

        ...
        <set name="speakers">
            <key column="event_id"/>
            <one-to-many class="Speaker"/>
        </set>
        <set name="attendees">
            <key column="event_id"/>
            <one-to-many class="Attendee"/>
        </set>
        ...
    </class>
</hibernate-mapping>
```

Looking at the portion of the Event mapping definition, you can see that each <set> has a name attribute that corresponds to the property names in the Event class. The <set> definitions correspond to the properties and accessors in the Event class shown in listing 5.1.

Listing 5.1 Set accessors in the Event class

```java
public class Event {
    private Set speakers;
    private Set attendees;

    public void setSpeakers(Set speakers) {
        this.speakers = speakers;
    }

    public Set getSpeakers() {
        return this.speakers;
```

```
        }

        public void setAttendees(Set attendees) {
                this.attendees = attendees;
        }

        public Set getAttendees () {
                return this.attendees;
        }
        …

    }
```

The <key> element, with the column attribute, names the column storing the foreign key of the containing class. Earlier, we explained that foreign keys are used to link two tables. In this case, the purpose of the foreign key is to link the Attendee to its parent Event instance. The attendees table, used to store Attendee instances, has a column named event_id containing the id of the Event instance that the Attendee belongs to.

A one-to-many association links a single parent instance with multiple children. In our example, we're using Events and Attendees. We presented the mapping definition in the previous section; now let's take a look at the database schema for the association in figure 5.2.

We've defined the attendees set as one-to-many, meaning that one Event instance will be associated to multiple Attendee instances. Instead of a one-to-many collection association, we can define a many-to-many association if Attendees can attend multiple Events.

As you can see, basic one-to-many associations are straightforward. We'll cover some options for one-to-many associations later in the chapter. Many-to-many associations can be slightly more complicated, but are still quite manageable.

Figure 5.2 A one-to-many association from events to attendees

Many-to-many associations

Many-to-many associations are quite a bit more interesting than one-to-many associations. Instead of tables being directly linked through the use of foreign keys, many-to-many associations require a collection table storing the collection of object references.

Suppose `Attendees` can attend more than one `Event`. This is a natural many-to-many mapping for the set of `Attendees`:

```
<set name="attendees" table="event_attendees">
    <key column="event_id"/>
        <many-to-many column="attendee_id" class="Attendee"/>
</set>
```

Note two changes in the many-to-many mapping definition. First, the `<set>` element has a `table` attribute. This is the table used to store the event-to-attendee mappings, so we've named it `event_attendees`. You only use the `table` attribute for many-to-many associations, or when persisting value objects, which we discuss later. Figure 5.3 shows this table in relation to the `events` and `attendees` tables.

The other change we've made to the mapping definition is the `<many-to-many>` element. Unlike the `<one-to-many>` element, the `column` attribute is required. The column defined stores the id of the `Attendee`.

So far we've talked about many-to-many `Sets`, but what about the other available Collections classes? You can also use `Lists` and `Maps` for many-to-many collections. You'll still need to specify the `table` attribute that defines the name of the collection (or join) table, and `Lists` and `Maps` still need an index column defined.

There is one last collection type we haven't yet discussed: collections of values.

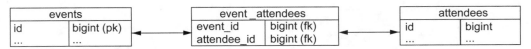

Figure 5.3 A many-to-many table schema for `Events` and `Attendees`

Persisting collections of values

Of course, you don't just deal with domain objects. You also work with collections of Strings and primitive values. Suppose you need to persist a collection of values, such as Strings or Integers, instead of a collection of persistent objects (also called entity objects). The mapping definition for a persistent set of Integers is straightforward:

```
<set name="ratings" table="event_ratings">
    <key column="event_id"/>
    <element column="rating" type="integer"/>
</set>
```

The table attribute defines the event_ratings table, which is used to store the values. Like other collection mappings we've examined, the <key> element is still required. If your collection is an array, list, or map, you still need to define the <index> element to maintain the order of the collection.

The <element> tag has two required attributes: column and type. Like other elements in the mapping definition, these attributes define the column used to store the value and the value's type, respectively.

5.1.3 Collection types

So far, we've looked at the plumbing that goes into creating persistent collections, concentrating on the Set interface. However, Hibernate supports all of the major Java Collections interfaces, each with special characteristics and capabilities. This section examines each collection type.

Sets

Since we've been using Sets in most of our examples, we don't need to spend much time with them here. In short, Sets in Hibernate retain the semantics of the Java interface: Sets are a collection of unique objects. A Set cannot contain duplicate elements, and Sets do not require an <index> element, since they are unordered.

Lists and Arrays

Unlike their Set counterparts, Lists can contain duplicate elements. Since Lists are indexed, meaning that contained elements are stored at a specific location in the List, you need to define a <list-index> element:

```
<list name="speakers">
    <list-index column="speaker_index"/>
    <key column="event_id"/>
    <one-to-many class="Speaker"/>
</list>
```

When a persistent list is retrieved from the database, the elements are ordered according to the index value. This also applies to Arrays:

```
<array name="speakers">
    <list-index column="speaker_index"/>
    <key column="event_id"/>
    <one-to-many class="Speaker"/>
</array>
```

The <list-index> element defines the column storing the object's index in the collection or array. The index column type is an integer for Lists and Arrays. An integer is used because it corresponds to the primitive type used to refer to a specific element in an Array or a List. For instance, the variable i is an integer in the code snippet shown here:

```
Object o = myObjectArray[i];
```

as well as this one:

```
Object o = myList.get(i);
```

Persistent arrays behave in the same manner as Lists. We've never had a reason to use a persistent array since Lists are much more flexible.

In addition to requiring an index column, Lists cannot be mapped inversely to the parent object. In sections 5.1.6 and 5.1.7, we explain this problem and show how to work around it with Bags.

Maps

Maps are probably the most distinctive of the persistent collections because they behave exactly like their Java counterparts. Maps store entries in key/value pairs, meaning that you retrieve the value by looking up the associated key. Maps are also called dictionaries and associative arrays. Let's look at two method signatures from the java.util.Map interface:

```
Object Map.get(Object key)
Object Map.put(Object key, Object value)
```

The get(…) method returns the value object for the given key, if any. The put(…) method stores the value in the map under the specified key. If an object is already stored under the specified key, it is returned. This means you can have only one value per key. The keys are stored in an index column.

Maps use the index column to store the key for an entry in the map. In Hibernate 3, indexes for Maps are defined using map-key elements. Since keys for a java.util.Map can be of any type, you can specify just about any type for the index value, including composite types. The only type that can't be used as a Map index is another collection.

To define a Map index, you'd use the type attribute to declare the map-key as a String:

```
<map-key column="attendee_index" type="string" length="20"/>
```

This snippet defines a VARCHAR(20) column for a Map. This assumes your map will use Strings for keys. Let's look at the full mapping definition that assumes the Event class stores Speaker instances in a Map instead of a List:

```
<map name="speakers">
    <map-key column="speakers_index" type="string" length="20"/>
    <key column="event_id"/>
    <one-to-many class="Speaker"/>
</map>
```

When inserting elements into the map, use a `String` for the key:

```
Map speakers = new HashMap();
speakers.put("speaker1", new Speaker());
speakers.put("speaker2", new Speaker());
Event event = new Event();
event.setSpeakers(speakers);
```

However, `Maps` provide another option to the standard `<index>` element. If your collection is a `Map`, you can also use an entity for the index. To do that, you need to use the `<map-key-many-to-many>` element instead of the `<index>` element:

```
<map-key-many-to-many column="entity_index_column"
        class="EntityClass"/>
```

You'll recall that when we refer to entity, we're talking about a persistent object with its own identity. We use the terms entity and persistent object interchangeably. (As far as we're concerned, there are entity types and value types. Value types, like a `String`, do not have their own identity.) While we're not going to be using `<map-key-many-to-many>` in the sample code, this element provides enough developer confusion to warrant an example.

Suppose your `Event` class has a map of `Speakers` instead of a list. To index the map, you want to use an entity object. For this example, create a simple entity object called `SpeakerKey`. The `SpeakerKey` object has two properties: an id and a string. Listing 5.2 shows the `SpeakerKey` class and the corresponding Hibernate mapping.

Listing 5.2 SpeakerKey and associated mapping document

```
public class SpeakerKey {

    private Long id;
    private String value;

    // ... accessors omitted
```

```
        }
        <hibernate-mapping package="com.manning.hq">
            <class name="SpeakerKey" table="speaker_keys">
                <id name="id" type="long">
                    <generator class="native"/>
                </id>
                <property name="value" type="string" length="20"/>
            </class>
        </hibernate-mapping>
```

Now you need to define the mapping for your collection of Speakers:

```
        <map name="speakers" table="event_speakers">
            <key column="event_id"/>
            <map-key-many-to-many column="speaker_key_id"
                class="SpeakerKey"/>
            <many-to-many column="speaker_id" class="Speaker"/>
        </map>
```

This mapping declares that instances of SpeakerKey will be used as the key when adding a Speaker to the map. With the details in place, let's take a look at the Hibernate-generated database schema shown in figure 5.4.

Using a persistent object as the key for your maps may not be the most common usage, but it's important to realize that it's an option if you need it.

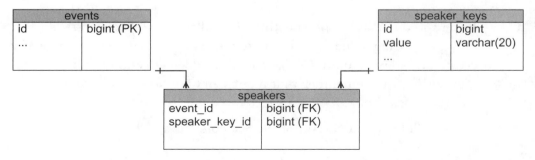

Figure 5.4 Table schema for a map-key-many-to-many mapping

Bags

Sometimes it's desirable to simply store a collection of objects without worrying about ordering or duplicate elements. This is where Bags come in.

When you declare a Bag in the mapping definition, it just corresponds to a java.util.List in the domain object. Let's look at a mapping snippet, followed by the source code:

```
<bag name="speakers">
    <key column="event_id"/>
    <one-to-many class="Speaker"/>
</bag>
```

You'll notice that our Bag definition resembles a Set. Now let's look at the code:

```
import java.util.List;
…
public class Event {
    private List speakers;
    …
    public void setSpeakers(List speakers)
      this.speakers = speakers;

    public List getSpeakers() { return this.speakers; }
    …
}
```

From the JavaBean's perspective, the collection of Speakers is a List. However, using a Bag for Hibernate means you don't need to explicitly create an index column. Of course, a Set doesn't require an index column either, but remember that a Set can't contain duplicate elements, whereas Bags can.

Next we'll look at a variant of the Bag collection: idbag.

idbags

idbags are a little difficult to explain, so we'll start off with an example. Suppose you have a many-to-many association between Events and Speakers. Speakers can belong to the same Event multiple times, so we can't use a Set. We also need to ensure fast and efficient access to the many-to-many table, event_speakers. We really need to be able to assign a primary key to the event_speakers table. This is where idbags come in.

An idbag allows you to assign a primary key to a row in a many-to-many join table. Let's look at the mapping definition:

```
<idbag name="speakers" table="event_speakers"
    lazy="true" cascade="all">
    <collection-id type="long" column="event_speakers_id">
        <generator-class="hilo"/>
    </collection-id>
    <key column="event_id"/>
    <many-to-many class="Speaker" column="speaker_id"/>
</idbag>
```

The above mapping definition results in the database schema shown in figure 5.5.

Since the join table has its own primary key, accessing the join table is very efficient. Specific rows can be updated, retrieved, and deleted

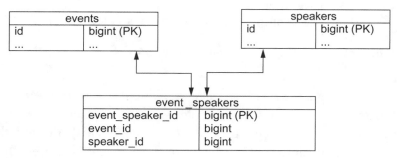

Figure 5.5 idbag schema

very quickly. idbags aren't used very often, but because of their support for a primary key, they are useful in isolated cases.

With all of the collection types under our belt, let's look at populating a lazy collection.

5.1.4 Lazy collections

We've mentioned lazy collections a few times without going into them in detail. A lazy collection is populated on demand. By "on demand," we mean that the collection of entity objects or values is populated only when the application accesses the collection. Populating the collection happens transparently when the collection is first accessed.

Why have lazy collections at all? A collection of objects can possibly contain hundreds or thousands of objects, and the application may not need to access the collection immediately, or at all. Loading hundreds of persistent objects for no reason will certainly impact application performance. It's better to populate the persistent collection only when it is needed.

To populate a lazy collection, the same Session instance used to retrieve the persistent object from the database must be open when the collection is populated. The following code incorrectly attempts to load the collection of attendees for an Event after the Session has been closed:

```
Session session = factory.openSession();
Event event = session.get(Event.class, eventId);
session.close();
Set attendees = event.getAttendees();
```

First, line 1 opens the Session instance. Then, the second line retrieves the Event instance, and line 3 closes the Session. Finally, line 4 attempts to access the collection of Attendees. This line will throw a LazyInitializationException because the Session is closed. If you're getting this exception in your code, it means that you're trying to access a lazy collection when the `Session` is closed. Here is the correct method to populate a lazy collection:

```
Session session = factory.openSession();
Event event = session.get(Event.class, eventId);
Set attendees = event.getAttendees();
session.close();
```

First, the code opens the `Session` instance and retrieves the `Event` instance. Then it accesses the collection of `Attendees` and closes the open `Session`.

Persistent collections are now lazy by default in Hibernate 3. For non-lazy collections, you must explicitly declare them as `lazy="false"` in the mapping definition. For example:

```
<set name="attendees" lazy="false">
    <key column="event_id"/>
    <one-to-many class="Attendee"/>
</set>
```

Any collection, including collections of values and arrays, can be declared not to be "lazy." The obvious problem with lazy collections is populating them in a multitier application, such as a web application, where keeping the `Session` open can be tricky. We present a few solutions to this problem in chapter 8.

In addition to being lazily populated, collections can be sorted. Sorted collections are the topic of the next section.

5.1.5 Sorted collections

A common requirement when dealing with collections is to sort them according to some criteria. The sorting criteria can be fixed or arbitrary, depending on application requirements. Hibernate supports sorting sets, maps, and bags. If you always want a collection returned in the same order, you can take advantage of the `order-by` attribute in the `<set>` element. For instance, to return all `Attendees` for an `Event` ordered by their last name, our mapping definition would be

```
<set name="attendees" order-by="last_name">
    <key column="event_id"/>
    <one-to-many class="Attendee"/>
</set>
```

The ordering value is the name of the SQL column, not the HQL property. The SQL column is given because the ordering takes place in the database. We can expand our ordering clause to sort by the first name as well:

```
order-by="last_name, first_name"
```

You can specify the type of sort, ascending or descending, by including the SQL keywords `asc` or `desc`, respectively, with `desc` as the default:

```
order-by="last_name, first_name asc"
```

Sorted collections use the `LinkedHashMap` or `LinkedHashSet` classes, which are only available in JDK 1.4 or later. If JDK 1.4 is not available in your environment, or you want to order the collections yourself, you may use the `sort` attribute to specify the type of sort to perform.

The `sort` attribute can take one of three values: `unsorted`, `natural`, or the name of a class implementing the `java.util.Comparator` interface. Unsorted results are returned in the order returned by the database. The natural sorting of elements is determined using the `compareTo(Object)` method in the `java.lang.Comparable` interface. A number of objects in the Java API, such as `String`, `Long`, and `Double`, implement `Comparable`. Here is an example of using `compareTo(Object)` with `Strings`:

```
String a = "a";
String b = "b";
System.out.println(a.compareTo(b));
```

This code prints –1, because "a" is less than "b". If you use the natural ordering of elements, they will typically be ordered from smallest to largest.

The last option, an implementation of the `Comparator` interface, allows custom sorting to be performed on the returned collection. A custom `Comparator` implementation allows the developer to apply business rules to sorting, or to enhance the natural ordering of a collection.

> **NOTE** Don't let the `Comparable` and `Comparator` interfaces confuse you. While they sound similar, they have different functions. `Comparable` is used to determine if two objects are the same or different. The `Comparator` interface is used to enforce ordering on a collection of objects.

The shortcoming of the two approaches that we've looked at, SQL ordering and `Comparator`, is that they are static. You can't change them at runtime. Hibernate gets around this by allowing you to apply a filter to a collection. Filters let you sort collections according to some arbitrary field. Suppose you wanted to sort the `Attendees` for an `Event` by their phone numbers:

```
Set sortedAttendees =
    session.filter(event.getAttendees(),
        "order by this.phoneNumber");
```

Since you're passing the `Set` of `Attendees`, you refer to the collection in the sort clause as `this`. Applying a filter to a lazy collection does not cause the collection to be initialized, so filters may be used efficiently with very large lazy collections.

Now that we've covered how to manage various types of persistent collections, let's discuss how to create and maintain associations between two persistent classes.

5.1.6 Bidirectional associations

The Event class allows you to easily navigate from a parent Event instance to a child Attendee instance. However, suppose you wanted to make the association bidirectional, allowing an Attendee to navigate to its parent Event? How would you go about implementing the bidirectional association?

You must first define the Event property in the Attendee class and provide a many-to-one definition in the Attendee mapping file. Next, the set in the Event must be defined as inverse. Setting the inverse attribute to true informs the Hibernate runtime that the association is bidirectional. The following snippet shows the relevant code from the Attendee class:

```java
public class Attendee {

    private Event event;
    ...
    public void setEvent(Event event) {
        this.event = event;
    }
    public Event getEvent() {
        return this.event;
    }
}
```

The following snippet shows the relevant code from the mapping file:

```xml
<hibernate-mapping package="com.manning.hq">
    <class name="Attendee" table="attendees">
        ...
        <many-to-one column="event_id" class="Event"/>
        ...
    </class>
</hibernate-mapping>
```

The inverse mapping from the Event class to the Attendee looks like this:

```
<set name="attendees" inverse="true">
<key column="event_id"/>
<one-to-many class="Attendee"/>
</set>
```

This mapping results in the relational schema shown in figure 5.6.

Following these three steps, you can now navigate from the Attendee instance to the parent Event instance. Remember that Hibernate only supports bidirectional one-to-many collections for sets and bags. Bidirectional lists, maps, and arrays are not supported, and Hibernate fails to report the error if you have the following in a mapping definition:

```
<list name="speakers" inverse="true">...</list>
```

If you try to map a list, map, or array as inverse, the index column of the collection will not be populated when it is persisted.[1] Hibernate won't tell you about this mistake—it will just fail silently.

Next, we'll take a look at mapping many-to-many bidirectional associations.

Many-to-many bidirectional associations

Many-to-many associations may also be bidirectional. In our earlier example, we presented a many-to-many association for Attendees and

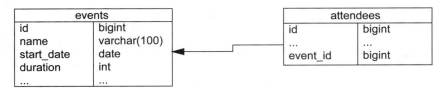

Figure 5.6 Bidirectional association for a one-to-many relationship

---

[1] Okay, if you really want to map an indexed collection as inverse, you can manage the index of the collection yourself. This is explained in detail at www.hibernate.org/116.html#A8.

Events. We'll revisit that example and convert it into a bidirectional association. Like the earlier bidirectional association, the `Attendee` class must have a collection property for the attended Events:

```
public class Attendee {

    private Set events;
    …
    public void setEvent(Event events) {
        this.events = events;
    }
    public Set getEvents() {
        return this.events;
    }
}
```

The set of Events replaces the Event property from listing 5.2. Also, you have to change the mapping document to contain a set of events:

```
<set name="events" table="event_attendees">
    <key column="attendee_id"/>
    <many-to-many class="Event"/>
</set>
```

You also need to update the Event mapping definition to reflect this bidirectional association:

```
<set name="attendees" inverse="true">
    <key column="event_id"/>
    <many-to-many class="Attendee"/>
</set>
```

Figure 5.7 shows the relational schema for your bidirectional mapping.

Note that only the Event end of the association is defined as inverse. For a many-to-many bidirectional association, one end of the

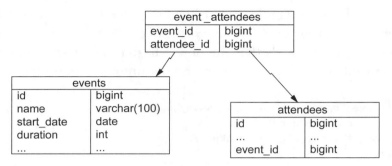

Figure 5.7 Bidirectional many-to-many association

association must be declared as inverse. The end declared as inverse is significant because the non-inverse end will control the join table that links the objects. Changes made to the inverse end of the association will not be persisted.

Before we end our discussion on collections, let's briefly cover how cascades impact collections.

5.1.7 Cascading collections

We touched on cascades and how they relate to child objects in chapter 3. Since cascades impact collections, we'll take a closer look in this section.

Suppose you create a new object, like our Event object, and add Speakers to it:

```
Event event = new Event();
Set speakers = new HashSet();
speakers.add(new Speaker());
speakers.add(new Speaker());
speakers.add(new Speaker());
event.setSpeakers(speakers);
```

When you try to persist this Event instance, you'll get an error because the Event references transient instances of the Speaker class. (Remember that transient means that the object hasn't been persisted yet.) To fix this problem, update your mapping definition for the set:

```
<set name="speakers" cascade="save-update">
    <key column="event_id"/>
    <one-to-many class="Speaker"/>
</set>
```

Notice the addition of the cascade attribute. By specifying save-update, you're specifying that save and update operations made to the parent Event should cascade to the Speakers. This way, Hibernate will handle the newly created Speakers correctly and save them to the database if necessary.

Another scenario is if you need to delete an Event. Since the speakers table references the events table, deleting an Event would cause a foreign key violation in the speakers table. There is another cascade you can use to ensure the child Speaker instances are deleted when the parent Event is deleted:

```
<set name="speakers" cascade="delete">
    <key column="event_id"/>
    <one-to-many class="Speaker"/>
</set>
```

When you delete the Event, the Hibernate service will cascade the delete to the child collection. Of course, since you want to cascade all of the operations to the child collection, you actually want to have the following mapping:

```
<set name="speakers" cascade="all">
    <key column="event_id"/>
    <one-to-many class="Speaker"/>
</set>
```

There is another cascade that fulfills a specific niche. Suppose you just remove a `Speaker` instance from the `Event`:

```
Session session = factory.openSession();
Transaction trans = session.beginTransaction();
Event event = (Event) session.load(Event.class, myEventId);
Set speakers = event.getSpeakers();
speakers.remove(mySpeaker);
session.saveOrUpdate(event);
```

The problem is you'll have an orphaned `Speaker`—a `Speaker` without a parent `Event`. It would be handy if Hibernate would delete the orphan since you don't need it anymore:

```
<set name="speakers" cascade="all-delete-orphan">
    <key column="event_id"/>
    <one-to-many class="Speaker"/>
</set>
```

The `all-delete-orphan` cascade cleans up objects that are orphaned by their parent. Hibernate caches the state of the original collection, so it knows when objects are orphaned and, therefore, which objects to delete.

In the next section, we examine extending the data types that Hibernate can persist through the use of custom types.

5.2 Implementing custom types

While Hibernate provides a fairly complete set of data types, it's impossible to expect the existing data types to support every use case. Because of this expected limitation, Hibernate allows developers to create custom data types using the `UserType` and `CompositeUserType` interfaces, both found in the `org.hibernate.usertype` package.

Custom user types allow you to tell Hibernate how to persist an object. The `UserType` and `CompositeUserType` interfaces provide a bridge that is used to persist another object. Most of the time, you can use a component instead of a custom user type. Typically, the only time you must use a custom user type is when you want to change how an object is persisted. This section discusses creating and using custom user types.

5.2.1 UserTypes

In chapter 4 we presented the Address class as a component. In this section, we'll convert the Address class into a reusable UserType implementation and then examine the advantages of UserTypes. Let's examine our existing Address class, as shown in listing 5.3.

Listing 5.3 The Address class as a component

```java
public class Address implements java.io.Serializable {
    private String streetAddress;
    private String city;
    private String state;
    private String zipCode;

    public String getStreetAddress() {
        return streetAddress;
    }
    public void setStreetAddress(String streetAddress) {
        this.streetAddress = streetAddress;
    }

    public String getCity() {
        return city;
    }
    public void setCity(String city) {
        this.city = city;
    }

    public String getState() {
        return state;
    }
    public void setState(String state) {
        this.state = state;
    }

    public String getZipCode() {
```

```
        return zipCode;
    }
    public void setZipCode(String zipCode) {
        this.zipCode = zipCode;
    }
}
```

As you can see, the Address class is a simple JavaBean. If we want to manage this class as a custom data type, we need to implement the UserType interface. Listing 5.4 shows the AddressType class.

Listing 5.4 AddressType class

```
package com.manning.hq.ch05;

import java.sql.PreparedStatement;
import java.sql.ResultSet;
import java.sql.SQLException;
import java.sql.Types;

import com.manning.hq.ch04.Address;

import org.hibernate.Hibernate;
import org.hibernate.HibernateException;
import org.hibernate.usertype.UserType;

public class AddressType implements UserType {

    private int[] types = {Types.VARCHAR, Types.VARCHAR,
                           Types.VARCHAR, Types.VARCHAR};

    public int[] sqlTypes() {
        return types;
    }

    public Class returnedClass() {
        return Address.class;
    }

    public boolean equals(Object a, Object b)
        throws HibernateException {

        return (a == b) ||
          ( (a != null) && (b != null) && (a.equals(b)) );
```

```
    }

    public Object nullSafeGet(ResultSet rs,
        String[] names, Object o)
        throws HibernateException, SQLException {

        Address addr = (Address) o;
        addr.setStreetAddress((String)
            Hibernate.STRING.nullSafeGet(rs, names[0]));
        addr.setCity((String)
            Hibernate.STRING.nullSafeGet(rs, names[1]));
        addr.setState((String)
            Hibernate.STRING.nullSafeGet(rs, names[2]));
        addr.setZipCode((String)
            Hibernate.STRING.nullSafeGet(rs, names[3]));
        return addr;
    }

    public void nullSafeSet(PreparedStatement ps, Object o, int i)
        throws HibernateException, SQLException {

        Address addr = (Address) o;
        Hibernate.STRING.nullSafeSet(ps,
            addr.getStreetAddress(), i);
        Hibernate.STRING.nullSafeSet(ps, addr.getCity(), i+1);
        Hibernate.STRING.nullSafeSet(ps, addr.getState(), i+2);
        Hibernate.STRING.nullSafeSet(ps, addr.getZipCode(), i+3);
    }

    public Object deepCopy(Object o) throws HibernateException {
        if (o == null) return null;
        Address origAddr = (Address) o;
        Address newAddr = new Address();
        String streetAddr =
            new String(origAddr.getStreetAddress());
        newAddr.setStreetAddress(streetAddr);
        newAddr.setCity(new String(origAddr.getCity()));
        newAddr.setState(new String(origAddr.getState()));
        newAddr.setZipCode(new String(origAddr.getZipCode()));
        return newAddr;
    }
```

```
    public boolean isMutable() {
        return true;
    }

}
```

You can see that the AddressType class wraps the Address class so it can be managed by Hibernate. Custom user types are not persisted to the database, but they provide information on how to persist another class to the database. (We have intentionally repeated that a few times. It's easy to lose sight of the actual purpose of custom types.) In our case, the AddressType class provides the bridge between our Address class and the Hibernate runtime. Notice that our Address class implements the java.io.Serializable interface. This is required if you want the class to be cached by a second-level caching service.

The AddressType class appears to be more complicated than you would expect, but it's really quite simple. Let's take a detailed look at the methods in the class.

The sqlTypes() method returns an array of java.sql.Types constants matching the property types of the Address class:

```
public int[] sqlTypes() {
    return new int[] {Types.VARCHAR, Types.VARCHAR,
        Types.VARCHAR, Types.VARCHAR};
}
```

Since the Address class has four properties of type java.lang.String, you use the Types.VARCHAR constant. Suppose the Address class had a timestamp storing the creation time of the address. In that case, you'd use the Types.TIMESTAMP constant for that property's SQL type.

The SQL types are used by the PreparedStatements in the nullSafeGet(…) and nullSafeSet(…) methods. The nullSafeSet(…) method populates an Address instance from the ResultSet object. As you've probably noticed, you're using an inner class of the Hibernate object: STRING. Since your Address object just contains Strings, you're going to use Hibernate's existing functionality rather than performing your own null checking. Once the object is populated, it is returned:

```
public Object nullSafeGet(ResultSet rs, String[] names, Object o)
    throws HibernateException, SQLException {

    Address addr = (Address) o;
    addr.setStreetAddress((String)
                    Hibernate.STRING.nullSafeGet(rs, names[0]));
    addr.setCity((String)
                    Hibernate.STRING.nullSafeGet(rs, names[1]));
    addr.setState((String)
                    Hibernate.STRING.nullSafeGet(rs, names[2]));
    addr.setZipCode((String)
                    Hibernate.STRING.nullSafeGet(rs, names[3]));
    return addr;
}
```

Next let's look at nullSafeGet(…), the partner method to nullSafeGet(…):

```
public void nullSafeSet(PreparedStatement ps, Object o, int i)
    throws HibernateException, SQLException {

    Address addr = (Address) o;
    Hibernate.STRING.nullSafeSet(ps, addr.getStreetAddress(), i);
    Hibernate.STRING.nullSafeSet(ps, addr.getCity(), i+1);
    Hibernate.STRING.nullSafeSet(ps, addr.getState(), i+2);
    Hibernate.STRING.nullSafeSet(ps, addr.getZipCode(), i+3);
}
```

Since the nullSafeGet(…) method populates an object from a ResultSet, it makes sense that the nullSafeSet(…) method performs the opposite task and populates a PreparedStatement from an Address instance. Here you've set four properties on the PreparedStatement, incrementing the index variable, i, each time. Again you're using the

Hibernate.STRING class to check for null values when populating the statement.

This leaves you with the deepCopy(Object) method:

```
public Object deepCopy(Object o) throws HibernateException {
    if (o == null) return null;
    Address origAddr = (Address) o;
    Address newAddr = new Address();
        String streetAddr =
            new String(origAddr.getStreetAddress());
        newAddr.setStreetAddress(streetAddr);
    newAddr.setCity(new String(origAddr.getCity()));
    newAddr.setState(new String(origAddr.getState()));
    newAddr.setZipCode(new String(origAddr.getZipCode()));
    return newAddr;
}
```

The deepCopy(Object) method returns a copy of the persistent state of the object. Persistent object associations and collections are not copied in this method; it copies only the persistent properties of the object. It is important to create a correct implementation of this method to avoid threading problems, with multiple objects referring to the same objects in memory.

When you create a deep copy of an object, not only do you copy the object, but you also copy all of the objects referred to by that object. This is different than the Object's clone() method, which only performs a shallow copy. A shallow copy does not create a new copy of the referred objects. Since object graphs can be quite large, creating a deep copy correctly can be difficult.

With your AddressType created, you need to update the mapping definition file to use it.

Using UserTypes

Now that you have the completed AddressType class, how do you use it? Like most things related to persistent classes and Hibernate, you edit the mapping definition to inform it of the UserType implementation:

```
<property name="address" type="AddressType"/>
```

And that's it. If your `UserType` maps to multiple database columns, you can use the `column` element to specify the columns to use in the relational table:

```
<property name="address" type="AddressType">
    <column name="street_address"/>
    <column name="city"/>
    <column name="state"/>
    <column name="zip_code"/>
</property>
```

Now that we've reviewed the `UserType` interface, let's examine a slightly more complicated, and interesting, interface: `CompositeUserType`.

5.2.2 Implementing CompositeUserTypes

There are two primary differences between `UserType` and `CompositeUserType`. First, the class bridged by the `CompositeUserType` does not need to implement the `java.io.Serializable` interface to be cachable by a caching service. Second, you are able to query on properties of the bridged class, allowing for a great deal of flexibility in HQL statements.

The more interesting feature of the `CompositeUserType` interface is the ability to query properties of the persisted object. Suppose we implemented the `CompositeUserType` interface for our `Address` class instead of `UserType`. Let's examine our new class, shown in listing 5.5. Note that we've omitted methods that are identical to the `AddressType`, shown in listing 5.4.

Listing 5.5 The CompositeAddressType class

```
package com.manning.hq.ch05;

import java.io.Serializable;
// .. AddressType imports omitted
import org.hibernate.usertype.CompositeUserType;
```

```java
import org.hibernate.engine.SessionImplementor;
import org.hibernate.type.Type;

public class CompositeAddressType implements CompositeUserType {

    // .. AddressType methods omitted

    private String[] propertyNames = {"streetAddress", "city",
                                      "state", "zipCode"};
    private Type[] propertyTypes = {Hibernate.STRING,
                                    Hibernate.STRING,
                                    Hibernate.STRING,
                                    Hibernate.STRING};

    public String[] getPropertyNames() {
        return propertyNames;
    }

    public Type[] getPropertyTypes() {
        return propertyTypes;
    }

    public Object getPropertyValue(Object component,
        int property) {
        Address addr = (Address) component;
        switch (property) {
            case 0:
                return addr.getStreetAddress();
            case 1:
                return addr.getState();
            case 2:
                return addr.getState();
            case 3:
                return addr.getZipCode();
        }
        throw new IllegalArgumentException(property +
            " is an invalid property index for class type " +
            component.getClass().getName());
    }

    public void setPropertyValue(Object component, int property,
        Object value) {

        Address addr = (Address) component;
        String propertyValue = (String) value;
```

```
        switch (property) {
            case 0:
                addr.setStreetAddress(propertyValue);
                return;
            case 1:
                addr.setState(propertyValue);
                return;
            case 2:
                addr.setState(propertyValue);
                return;
            case 3:
                addr.setZipCode(propertyValue);
                return;
        }
    }

    public Object assemble(Serializable cached,
        SessionImplementor session, Object owner)
        throws HibernateException {

        return deepCopy(cached);
    }

    public Serializable disassemble(Object value,
        SessionImplementor session)
        throws HibernateException {

        return (Serializable) deepCopy(value);
    }

    public Object nullSafeGet(ResultSet rs, String[] names,
        SessionImplementor session, Object o)
        throws HibernateException, SQLException {
            // TODO Auto-generated method stub
            return null;
        }

        public void nullSafeSet(PreparedStatement ps,
                    Object o, int i, SessionImplementor session
            throws HibernateException, SQLException {
            // TODO Auto-generated method stub
        }

    }
```

While the method signatures for the `CompositeUserType` look imposing at first glance, implementing them is fairly simple. The cost of the extra implementation time gives you the ability to query on properties of the `Address` class, something your `AddressType` class cannot do. Let's look at some HQL examples:

```
select l from Location l where l.address.streetAddress
    like '% Birch St.%'
```

This query returns all instances of the `Location` class located on "Birch St." Here's another example:

```
select l from Location l where l.address.city
    in ('Miami', 'London', 'Tokyo');
```

This time we're querying on `Location` instances located in Miami, London, or Tokyo. Don't worry if the HQL is somewhat confusing right now. We'll cover it in detail in the next chapter.

One requirement of the `UserType` interface is that the underlying class must implement the `Serializable` interface so that the class may be cached. This means that our `Address` class must implement `Serializable`. The `CompositeUserType` interface doesn't have this requirement. Instead, it provides two methods to manage interacting with the cache: `assemble(…)` and `disassemble(…)`. These methods are never called by the user; instead, they are used internally by Hibernate. Here are the method signatures for these two methods:

```
public Object assemble(Serializable cached,
    SessionImplementor session,
    Object owner)
    throws HibernateException

public Serializable disassemble(Object obj,
    SessionImplementor session)
    throws HibernateException
```

The `assemble(…)` method provides the opportunity to reconstruct the cached object from a `Serializable` representation. To perform the conversion to a persistent object, you should at least perform a deep copy using the cached instance. Creating a cachable instance of the persistent object is performed using the `disassemble(…)` method. Like the `assemble(…)` method, the developer should at least perform a deep copy of the object to be cached.

Implementing the `assemble(…)` and `disassemble(…)` methods is optional if the object being persisted implements the `Serializable` interface. In a typical application, the domain objects will have implemented the interface, so you shouldn't have any problems getting around this requirement.

Of course, you can also query individual properties of components. The two HQL examples will work just as well with components as with custom user types. Why go through the trouble of creating custom types at all?

Remember that the core purpose behind custom user types is not to support types that are already easily handled by Hibernate, but to support the unique cases where Hibernate doesn't have the data type that your application requires. A common use for a custom type is to represent phone numbers.

Phone numbers typically have four components: country code, area code, exchange, and line number, as shown in figure 5.8.

Depending on where you are in the world, phone numbers may have a different number of digits, but the basic scheme is consistent. You can

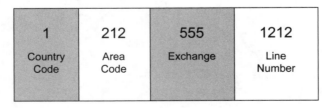

Figure 5.8 Phone number scheme

easily map the four parts of a phone number as a component, but if the scheme changes, you will need to update your mapping definitions. Using a custom type to persist the phone number, you can easily change how the phone number is persisted without changing how it is represented to the persistent classes.

While you will typically use components instead of custom value types, custom value types are an important extension mechanism for Hibernate. Developers often overlook them because of their apparent complexity, but appropriate use of custom types can greatly simplify persistence problems and make your application more portable.

5.3 Summary

This chapter presented two primary Hibernate features: persistent collections and custom data types. Persisting collections can be difficult when using JDBC or EJBs, but Hibernate makes it fairly simple.

Support is provided for the basic collection types: arrays, lists, maps, and sets. It's possible to store collections of persistent objects or basic types, like Strings or Dates. Persistent collections can also be lazily populated to improve performance of large collections.

Although Hibernate provides a large number of data types, you may need custom types for your application. The UserType and Composite-UserType interfaces provide the ability to create new data types to be managed by Hibernate. While both interfaces provide support persisting objects, CompositeUserTypes support querying on object parameters, unlike UserTypes.

It's important to remember that implementations of the custom type interfaces are not persisted. Instead, implementations provide the Hibernate runtime with additional information necessary to persist another object. For instance, our AddressType class managed the persistence of the Address class.

While similar to components, custom user types insulate your application from changes made to the persistent object. If a component changes, you are forced to update the mapping files using the component. If changes are made to a custom user type, you only need to update the implementing user type class.

Querying persistent objects

This chapter covers

- *Querying persistent objects using Hibernate*
- *The Hibernate Query Language*

With a solid grasp of Hibernate basics, we need to move on to querying our persistent objects. Instead of SQL, Hibernate has its own, object-oriented (OO) query language called Hibernate Query Language (HQL). HQL is intentionally similar to SQL so that it leverages existing developer knowledge and thus minimizes the learning curve. It supports the commonly used SQL features, wrapped into an OO query language. In some ways, HQL is easier to write than SQL because of its OO foundation.

Why do we need HQL? While SQL is more common and has been standardized, vendor-dependent features limit the portability of SQL statements between different databases. HQL provides an abstraction between the application and the database, and so improves portability. Another problem with SQL is that it is designed to work with relational tables, not objects. HQL is optimized to query object graphs.

This chapter introduces you to HQL gradually and quickly moves on to more complicated features and queries. First we'll cover the major concepts important to using HQL, such as executing queries using a few different classes. After the introductory material is covered, we'll spend the rest of the chapter with HQL examples. If you have a solid grasp of SQL, you shouldn't have any problem picking up the key concepts.

Chapter goals

We have three primary goals in this chapter:

- Exploring the basics of HQL, including two query mechanisms
- Identifying variations in HQL queries, including named and positional parameters
- Understanding how to query objects, associations, and collections

Assumptions

Since HQL is based on SQL, we anticipate that you

- Understand SQL basics, including knowledge of joins, subselects, and functions.
- Have a firm grasp of JDBC, including the `PreparedStatement` and `ResultSet` interfaces.

6.1 Using HQL

Hibernate queries are structured similar to their SQL counterparts, with SELECT, FROM, and WHERE clauses. HQL also supports subselects if they are supported by the underlying database. Let's jump in with the most basic query we can create:

```
from Event
```

This query will return all of the Event instances in the database, as well as the associated objects and non-lazy collections. (You'll recall from chapter 5 that, by default, persistent collections are populated only when initially accessed.) The first thing you probably noticed was the lack of the SELECT clause in front of the FROM clause. Because we want to return complete objects, the SELECT clause is implied and doesn't need to be explicitly stated.

How can we execute this query? Two methods are provided in the Hibernate API to execute queries. The Session interface has three find(…) methods that can be used for simple queries. The Query interface can be used for more complex queries.

6.1.1 session.find(...)

In Hibernate 2, the Session interface has three overloaded find(…) methods, two of which support parameter binding. Each of the methods returns a java.util.List with the query results. For instance, let's execute our earlier query:

```
List results = session.find("from Event");
```

The Session interface also has a set of methods, named iterate(…), which are similar to the find(…) methods. Although they appear to be the same, each of methods functions differently. The find methods return all of the query results in a List, which is what you'd expect. The objects in the list are populated when the query is executed. However, the iterate methods first select all of the object ids matching a query and populate the objects on demand as they are retrieved from the Iterator. Here's an example:

```
Iterator results = session.iterate("from Event");
while (results.hasNext()) {
    Event myEvent = (Event) results.next();
    // …
}
```

When the Iterator is returned, only the id values for the Event instances have been retrieved. Calling results.next() causes the next Event instance to be retrieved from the database. The iterate methods are typically less efficient than their find counterparts, except when dealing with objects stored in a second-level cache.

Hibernate stores objects in a second-level cache based on the object's class type and id. The iterate methods can be more efficient if the object is already cached, since only the matching object ids are returned on the initial query and the remainder of the object is retrieved from the cache.

The find methods in the `Session` interface are ideal for simple queries. However, most applications typically require at least a handful of complex queries. The `Query` interface provides a rich interface for retrieving persistent objects with complicated queries. If you're using Hibernate 3, you must use the `Query` interface since the find methods in the `Session` interface have been deprecated (although they have been moved and are still available in the `org.hibernate.class.Session` sub-interface). Hibernate 3 applications should use `createQuery()` and get `NamedQuery()` for all query execution.

6.1.2 The Query interface

Instances of the `Query` interface are created by the `Session`. The `Query` interface gives you more control over the returned objects, such as limiting the number of returned objects, setting a timeout for the query, and creating scrollable result sets. Let's execute our previous query using the `Query` interface:

```
Query q = session.createQuery("from Event");
List results = q.list();
```

If you want to set bounds on the number of `Event` objects to return, set the `maxResults` property:

```
Query q = session.createQuery("from Event");
q.setMaxResults(15);
List results = q.list();
```

The `Query` interface also provides an `iterate()` method, which behaves identically to `Session.iterate(…)`. Another feature of the `Query` interface is the ability to return query results as a `ScrollableResults` object. The `ScrollableResults` object allows you to move through the returned objects arbitrarily, and is typically useful for returning paged collections of objects, commonly found in web applications.

Of course, our static queries aren't very useful in real applications. Real applications need to populate query parameters dynamically. JDBC's `PreparedStatement` interface supports setting positional query parameters dynamically, but populating queries can be cumbersome.

Developers must know the type of each parameter in order to call the correct setter method in the interface. They also have to keep track of which positional parameter they are setting. Hibernate expands and improves on this notion by providing both positional and named query parameters.

Positional parameters

Positional parameters in Hibernate are very similar to their `Prepared-Statement` counterparts. The only significant difference is that the position index starts at 0 instead of 1, as in the `PreparedStatement`.

Suppose you want to return all of the `Event` instances with a certain name. Using a positional parameter, your code would look like

```
Query q = session.createQuery("from Event where name = ? ");
q.setParameter(0, "Opening Plenary");
List results = q.list();
```

Note that you didn't need to set the type of parameter; the `Query` object will attempt to determine the type using reflection. It's also possible to set a parameter to a specific type using the `org.hiber-nate.Hibernate` class:

```
q.setParameter(0, "Opening Plenary", Hibernate.STRING);
```

Named parameters are a more interesting, and more powerful, way to populate queries. Rather than using question marks for parameter placement, you can use distinctive names.

Named parameters

The easiest way to explain named parameters is with an example. Here's our earlier query with a named parameter:

```
from Event where name = :name
```

Instead of the ? to denote a parameter, you can use :name to populate the query:

```
Query q = session.createQuery("from Event where name = :name");
q.setParameter("name", "Opening Plenary");
List results = q.list();
```

With named parameters, you don't need to know the index position of each parameter. Named parameters may seem like a minor feature, but they can save time when populating a query—instead of counting question marks and making sure you're populating the query correctly, you simply match the named parameters with your code.

If your query has a named parameter that occurs more than once, it will be set in the query each time. For instance, if a query has the parameter startDate twice, it will be set to the same value:

```
Query q = session.createQuery("from Event where "+
    "startDate = :startDate or endDate < :startDate");
q.setParameter("startDate", eventStartDate);
List results = q.list();
```

We've covered the two styles of query parameters supported by Hibernate. For the purpose of our examples, we've been displaying the queries as hardcoded in application code. Anyone who's built an application will know that embedding your queries can quickly create a maintenance nightmare. Ideally, you would store the queries in a text file, and the most natural place to do that with Hibernate is in the mapping definition file.

Named queries

Named queries, not to be confused with named parameters, are queries that are embedded in the XML mapping definition. Typically, you put all of the queries for a given object into the same file. Centralizing your queries in this fashion makes maintenance quite a bit easier. Named queries are placed at the bottom of the mapping definition files:

```
<query name="Event.byName">
<![CDATA[from Event where name=?]]>
</query>
```

Note that here you wrap the actual query in a CDATA block to ensure that the XML parser skips the query text. This is necessary since some symbols, such as < and >, can cause XML parsing errors.

There is no limitation on the number of query elements you can have in a mapping file; just be sure that all of the query names are unique. You may name the queries anything you would like, although we have found that prefixing the name of the persistent class is helpful.

Accessing named queries is simple:

```
Query q = session.getNamedQuery("Event.byName");
...
List results = q.list();
```

You should take advantage of named queries when creating your mapping definitions. If you add or change a property name, you can also update all of the affected queries at the same time.

There is certainly no rule about storing your HQL queries in the mapping definition. You can just as easily put the queries into a resource bundle and provide your own mechanism to pass them to the query interfaces.

Now that you know how to query and some of the basics, what happens when you execute a query, using either the Session or Query interface?

First, the Hibernate runtime compiles the query into SQL, taking into account the database-specific SQL dialect. Next, a `PreparedStatement` is created and any query parameters are set. Finally, the runtime executes the `PreparedStatement` and converts the `ResultSet` into instances of the persistent objects. (It's a little more complicated than the three-sentence description, but I hope you get the idea.) When you retrieve persistent objects, you also need to retrieve the associated objects, such as many-to-ones and child collections.

6.1.3 Outer joins and HQL

Using SQL, the most natural way to retrieve data from multiple tables with a single query is to use a join. Joins work by linking associated tables using foreign keys. Hibernate uses an outer join to retrieve associated objects. When the HQL is compiled to SQL, Hibernate creates the outer join statements for the associated objects (assuming you've enabled outer joins—see chapter 3 for an explanation of the `max_fetch_depth` property). This results in one query returning all of the data necessary to reconstitute an `Event` instance. All of this happens behind the scenes in the Hibernate runtime. Compare this with writing the following SQL:

```
select e.*, l.* from events as e
    left outer join locations  as l on e.location_id = l.id
```

Clearly, HQL is much more concise than SQL. It's also possible to disable outer join fetching for a specific association by setting the `fetch` attribute in the mapping definition, as shown here:

```
<many-to-one name="location" fetch="select"/>
```

Alternatively, outer join fetching can be disabled globally by setting the `max_fetch_depth` property to 0 in the hibernate.cfg.xml file:

```
<property name="max_fetch_depth">0</property>
```

You will typically leave outer join fetching enabled, as it can greatly improve performance by reducing the number of trips to the database to retrieve an object. The `max_fetch_depth` property is just one configuration parameter that can impact queries. We'll look at two more: `show_sql` and `query_substitutions`.

6.1.4 Show SQL

While debugging HQL statements, you may find it useful to see the generated SQL to make sure the query is doing what you expect. Setting the `show_sql` property to `true` will result in the generated SQL being output to the console, or whatever you have `System.out` set to. Set the property in your hibernate.cfg.xml file:

```
<property name="show_sql">true</property>
```

You will want to turn off SQL output when deploying to production, especially in an application server. Application servers typically set `System.out` to a log file, and the SQL output can be overwhelming.

6.1.5 Query substitutions

Hibernate supports many different databases and SQL dialects, each with different names for similar functions. Using query substitutions, you can normalize function names and literal values, which simplifies porting to different databases. Query substitutions can be a confusing, so let's look at a few examples.

First, to configure query substitutions in the configuration file, use the following:

```
<property name="query.substitutions">
    convert CONV, true 1, false 0
</property>
```

This configuration setting performs three substitutions:

- The `CONV` function is now aliased to `convert`.
- Boolean `true` values are replaced with `1`.
- Boolean `false` values are replaced with `0`.

Query substitutions occur when the HQL is compiled into SQL. The substitutions for boolean values are useful if your database does not support boolean data types. This allows you to use true and false in your queries, which is clearer than using 1 and 0.

By substituting convert for the name of the CONV function, you can make your HQL statements more portable. For example, MySQL names the function CONV, while Oracle names the same function CON-VERT. If you port your application to Oracle, you only need to update the query substitution property instead of the HQL.

6.1.6 Query parser

Hibernate 3 introduces a new HQL abstract syntax tree (AST) query parser, which replaces the classic parser found in earlier releases. While the parser in use doesn't make much difference to you, we mention it because in some cases, particularly when migrating an application from Hibernate 2 to 3, you may want to use the classic parser. You'll likely want to use the classic parser if the AST parser complains about your existing HQL.

To switch from the AST parser (which is the default) to the classic parser, set the following property in your hibernate.properties file:

```
hibernate.query.factory_class=
    ➥ org.hibernate.hql.classic.ClassicQueryTranslatorFactory
```

If you're configuring Hibernate using the hibernate.cfg.xml property, use this:

```
<property name="query.factory_class">
org.hibernate.hql.classic.ClassicQueryTranslatorFactory
</property>
```

Ideally, you'll use the newer AST parser. When the SessionFactory is created, the AST parser validates all of the named HQL queries found in your mapping files, which can save you a lot of time when you're testing your application.

We've covered the introductory information necessary to use HQL in your applications. The remainder of the chapter will be spent discussing the features of the query language.

6.2 Querying objects with HQL

With a solid foundation in executing queries, you can concentrate on exploring the query language itself. If you have experience with SQL, you shouldn't have a problem getting a firm grasp of HQL.

This section doesn't have much Java code; instead, we provide a number of example queries and explanations. Although we've presented the occasional HQL statement at various points earlier in the book, this section examines features of HQL that we haven't used.

6.2.1 The FROM clause

The FROM clause allows you to specify the objects that will be queried. It also lets you create aliases for object names. Suppose you want to query all Event instances matching a given name. Your resulting query would be as follows:

```
from Event e where e.name='Opening Plenary'
```

This new query introduces a shorthand name, or alias, for the Event instance: e. This shorthand name can be used just like its SQL counterpart, except here you're using it to identify objects instead of tables. Unlike SQL, HQL does not allow the as keyword when defining the alias. For instance:

```
from Event as e where e.name='Opening Plenary'
```

The as in the previous query will cause an org.hibernate.QueryException when you attempt to execute the query. Since as is implied, there is no need to insert it in the query. You're also querying a property of the Event: the name. When querying properties, use the JavaBean property name instead of the column name in the table. You shouldn't be concerned with the underlying relational tables and columns when using HQL, but instead focus on the properties of the domain objects.

You will typically have one object in the FROM clause of the query, as in our examples to this point. Querying on one object type simplifies the results, since you're only going to get a List containing instances of the queried object. What happens if you need to query multiple associated objects? You could have multiple objects in the FROM clause, such as

```
from Event e, Attendee a where …
```

How do you know what object type the result list will contain? The result list will contain a Cartesian product of the queried objects, which probably isn't what you want. To query on associated objects, you'll need to join them in the FROM clause.

6.2.2 Joins

You're probably familiar with SQL joins, which return data from multiple tables with a single query. You can think of HQL joins in a similar way, only you're joining object properties and associations instead of tables. If we want to return all Events that a specific Attendee is going to be attending, join the attendee property to the Event in the query:

```
from Event e join e.attendees a where a.id=314
```

You can join all associations (many-to-one and one-to-one), as well as collections, to the query's base object. (We refer to the base object in a query as the object listed in the FROM clause. In this case, the base object is the Event.) As the previous query shows, you can also assign an alias to joined associations and query on properties in the joined object. The naming convention for HQL aliases is to use a lowercase word, similar to the Java variable naming convention.

Types of joins

HQL has different types of joins, all but one of them taken from SQL. We summarize the join types in table 6.1.

Table 6.1 Join types

Join Type	Rule
inner join	Unmatched objects on either side of the join are discarded.
left [outer] join	All objects from the left side of the join are returned. If the object on the left side of the join has no matching object on the right side of the join, it is still returned.
right [outer] join	All objects from the right side of the join are returned. If the object on the right side of the join has no matching object on the left side of the join, it is still returned.
full join	All objects from either side of the join are returned, regardless of matching objects on the opposite side of the join.
inner join fetch	Used to retrieve an associated object or a collection of objects regardless of the outer-join or lazy property on the association. This join does not have a SQL counterpart.

Unless you specify left, right, or full as the prefix to the join statement, the default is to use inner joins. All of the joins in table 6.1 behave like their SQL counterparts, except for inner join fetch. Joining a lazy collection with inner join fetch will cause the collection to be returned as populated. For example:

```
from Event e inner join fetch e.speakers
```

returns all of the Event instances with populated collections of Speakers. Let's look at joining an object associated to the base object as a many-to-one:

```
from Event e join e.location l where l.name = :name
```

Joining the Location instance to the Event allows querying on the Location properties, and results in a more efficient SQL query. Let's say you had the following query:

```
from Event e where e.location.name = :name and
    e.location.address.state = :state
```

Since you're walking the object graph twice, once for the Location name and again for the Location state, the query compiler will join the Location instance to the Event twice. Joining the Location to the Event in the FROM clause results in only one join and a more efficient query.

Joined objects can also be returned in the SELECT clause of the HQL statement. The HQL SELECT clause is discussed next.

6.2.3 Selects

The SELECT clause allows you to specify a list of return values to be returned from a query. If you recall from chapter 1, selecting specific columns of data returned from a query is called projection. Possible return values include entire objects, specific object properties, and derived values from a query. Derived values include the results from various functions, such as min(...), max(...), and count(...).

The SELECT clause does not force you to return entire objects. It's possible to return specific fields of objects, just as in SQL. Another interesting feature of HQL is the ability to return new objects from the selected values. We'll examine both features next.

Projection

Suppose that instead of returning the entire Event object in your queries, you only want to return the name of the Event. Retrieving the entire object just to get the name is pretty inefficient. Instead, your query will only retrieve the desired data:

```
select e.name from Event e
```

This query returns a list of String instances containing the Event names. If you want to return the Event start date in addition to the name, add another parameter to the SELECT clause:

```
select e.name, e.startDate from Event e
```

Each element in the returned list is an `Object[]` containing the specified values. The length of the `Object[]` array is equal to the number of columns retrieved. Listing 6.1 illustrates querying and processing multiple scalar values.

Listing 6.1 Multiple scalar values

```
Session session = factory.openSession();
String query = " select e.name, e.startDate from Event e ";
Query query = session.createQuery("query");
List results = query.list();
for (Iterator I = results.iterator(); i.hasNext();) {
    Object[] row = (Object[]) i.next();
    String name = (String) row[0];
    Date startDate = (Date) row[1];
    // …
}
```

Looking at listing 6.1, you'll notice the values in the `Object[]` array are in the same order given in the query. Also, since the array contains `Object instances`, no primitive values can be returned from a scalar query. This limitation is also present when querying a single scalar value, since a `List` cannot contain primitive values.[1]

A common use of scalar value queries is to populate summary objects containing a subset of the data in the persistent object. In our case, a summary object would consist of the `Event` name and start date. When iterating over the result list, you would need to create a separate list of summary objects. Fortunately, there's a better way to do this.

Returning new objects

The SELECT clause can be used to create new objects, populated from values in the query. Let's look at an example:

```
select new EventSummary(e.name, e.startDate) from Event e
```

---

[1] The contract for the `java.util.List` interface specifies that it can only store and return instances of `java.lang.Object`. Since primitive types (`int`, `long`, `boolean`, etc.) do not inherit from `java.lang.Object`, they cannot be stored in a `java.util.List`. For more information, refer to http://java.sun.com/docs/books/tutorial/collections/.

The result list will be populated with instances of the EventSummary class. Looking at the constructor used in the HQL statement, the EventSummary class must have a constructor matching the constructor used in the HQL statement: EventSummary(String, Date).

We have covered the major components of HQL queries. The following section presents the aggregate functions that are available in HQL and how they can be used in SELECT and WHERE clauses.

6.2.4 Using functions

Functions are special commands that return a computed value. In SQL, there are two types of functions: aggregate and scalar. Scalar functions typically operate on a single value and return a single value. There are also scalar functions that don't require arguments, such as now() or CURRENT_TIMESTAMP, which both return a timestamp. Aggregate functions operate on a collection of values and return a summary value.

Hibernate supports five of the most commonly used SQL aggregate functions: count, avg, min, max, and sum. The functions perform the same operations as their SQL counterparts, and each operates on an expression. The expression contains the values that the function operates on. Table 6.2 summarizes the five aggregate functions.

The count(...) function can also take advantage of the distinct and all keywords to filter the computed value. Let's look at some examples of using functions in HQL queries.

Table 6.2 Hibernate aggregate functions

Function	Usage
avg(expression)	Calculates the average value of the expression.
count(expression)	Counts the number of rows returned by the expression.
max(expression)	Returns the maximum value in the expression.
min(expression)	Returns the minimum value in the expression.
sum(expression)	Returns the sum of column values in the expression.

```
select count(e) from Event e
```

This example returns the number of Events persisted in the database. To count the number of distinct Events, use the distinct keyword:

```
select count(distinct e) from Event e
```

All of the aggregate functions return an Integer. The easiest way to retrieve the result is to get the first element in the result list:

```
Integer count =
    (Integer) session.find("select count(distinct e) from "+
                           "Event e").get(0);
```

You may also use functions in scalar value queries:

```
select e.name, count(e) from Event e
```

Suppose you want to get the collection of Attendees for a given Event. With what you know so far, you would have to retrieve the Event and then get the collection of Attendees. The code for this is as follows:

```
String query = "from Event e inner join fetch e.attendees "+
               "where e.name = :name";
Query q = session.createQuery(query);
q.setParameter("name", "Opening Plenary");
Event event = (Event) q.list().get(0);
Set attendees = event.getAttendees();
session.close();
```

While this takes six lines of code, there is a much shorter way to obtain a child collection. Hibernate provides the elements(…) function to return the elements of a collection:

```
select elements(e.attendees) from Event e where name = :name
```

This query returns a List of Attendee instances for a given Event. If you join the collection in the FROM clause, you can just use the join alias. For example, the next query is the same as our previous query:

```
select elements(a) from Event e
join e.attendees a
where name = :name
```

Functions can also be used in the WHERE clause, which we cover later in this chapter. HQL properties, or attributes available for objects in a query, are presented next.

6.2.5 HQL properties

HQL supports two object properties: `id` and `class`. The `id` property gives you access to the primary key value of a persistent object. Regardless of what you name the `id` property in the object and mapping definition, using `id` in HQL queries will still return the primary key value. For instance, if you have a class with an `id` property named `objectId`, you would still use the `id` property in HQL:

```
from MyObject m where m.id > 50
```

This query selects all instances of MyObject where the `objectId` property value is greater than 50. You can still use the `objectId` property if you prefer. Think of HQL's `id` property as shorthand for the primary key value. The `class` property provides a similar function.

The `class` property provides access to the full Java class name of persistent objects in an HQL query. This is typically useful when you have mapped a persistent class hierarchy and only want to return classes of a certain type. We'll look at an example to see how the `class` property can be used.

Let's say the `Attendee` class has an association to the `Payment` class. The `Payment` class specifies how the `Attendee` will pay for the `Events`. `Payment` has two subclasses: `CreditCardPayment` and `CashPayment`. You want to retrieve all `Attendees` who have paid with cash:

```
from Attendee a join a.payment p where p.class =
    com.manning.hq.ch06.CashPayment
```

As with the `id` property, you can also return the `class` property in the SELECT statement:

```
select p.id, p.class from Payment p;
```

This query returns all of the ids and classes for `Payment` as a `List` of `Object[]`s. However, the `class` property is not returned as an instance of `java.lang.Class`. Instead, the `class` property is a `java.lang.String`, which has the same value as the discriminator specified in the mapping definition.

The `class` property is only available on object hierarchies—in other words, objects mapped with a discriminator value. If you try to query the `class` property of an object without a discriminator value, you'll receive a `QueryException` stating that the query parser couldn't resolve the `class` property.

The `id` and `class` properties can be used in SELECT and WHERE clauses. Expressions that can occur in the WHERE clause are covered in the next section.

6.2.6 Using expressions

Expressions are used to query object properties for desired criteria. Occurring in the WHERE clause of an HQL query, expressions support most of the common SQL operators that you're probably accustomed to using. We won't explain each available expression but instead give a number of examples demonstrating expressions in HQL.

A number of available expressions are designed to query child collections or attributes of objects contained within a collection. The simplest function is `size(...)`, which returns the number of elements in a collection:

```
from Event e where size(e.attendees) > 0
```

The size of a collection can also be accessed as a property, like `id` and `class`:

```
from Event e where e.attendees.size > 0
```

Which form you choose is entirely up to you; the result is the same. If you are using an indexed collection (array, list, or map), you can take advantage of the functions shown in table 6.3.

Table 6.3 Functions for indexed collections

Function	Description
elements(expression)	Returns the elements of a collection.
indices(expression)	Returns the set of indices in a collection. May be used in a SELECT clause.
maxElement(expression)	Returns the maximum element in a collection containing basic types.
minElement(expression)	Returns the minimum element in a collection containing basic types.
maxIndex(expression)	Returns the maximum index in a collection.
minIndex(expression)	Returns the minimum index in a collection.

All of the functions in table 6.3 can only be used with databases that support subselects. Additionally, the functions can only be used in the WHERE clause of an HQL statement. We looked at the elements(…) function earlier, but its usage changes slightly when used in a WHERE clause. Like the size property, the maximum and minimum functions can also be used as properties. Let's look at a few examples. First:

```
from Speaker s where maxIndex(s.eventSessions) > 10
```

or in its property form:

```
from Speaker s where s.eventSessions.maxIndex > 10
```

The maxElement and minElement functions only work with basic data types, such as numbers (ints, longs, etc.), Strings, and Dates. These functions do not work with persistent objects, like Speakers or Attendees. For example, to select all Events with more than 10 available rooms:

```
from Event e where maxElement(e.availableRooms) > 10
```

Indexed collections can also be accessed by their index. For example:

```
from Speaker s where s.eventSessions[3].name = :name
```

The above HQL queries the fourth EventSession object in the collection and returns the associated Speaker instance. (Remember that collection indexes start at 0, not 1.) Let's look at another, more complicated example:

```
from Speaker s where
    s.eventSessions[ size(s.eventSessions) - 1 ].name = :name
```

You can get creative within the brackets—for instance, passing in an expression to compare properties of the last collection element. Here's another example of querying on indexed collections using an expression within brackets.

```
select e from EventSession e, Speaker s where
    s.eventSessions[ maxIndex(e.eventSessions) ] != e
```

You'll notice that at the end of the previous query, you just referenced the EventSession as e instead of using the id property of the EventSession. This demonstrates that you can use a persistent entity in a query. Let's look at a simple example:

```
Session sess = factory.openSession();
Query q = sess.createQuery("from EventSession e where e=?");
q.setEntity(1, myOtherEventSession);
List l = q.list();
sess.close();
```

When you call Query.setEntity(…), the generated SQL doesn't match on all fields of the entity object—only on the id value. The generated SQL for our query looks like

```
select e_.id, e_.name from event_sessions as e_ where (e_id=?)
```

Only the id of the passed entity is used, so it's perfectly acceptable to use entity instances in your query objects without worrying about overhead.

HQL also supports various operators, including logical and comparison operators. Logical operators include and, any, between, exists, in, like, not, or, and some. The comparison operators include =, >, <, >=, <=, and <>.

Grouping and ordering

The GROUP BY clause is used when returning multiple scalar values from a SELECT clause, with at least one of them the result of an aggregate function. For instance, you need a GROUP BY clause for the following HQL statement:

```
select e.name, count(elements(a)) from Event e
    join e.attendees a group by e.name
```

The GROUP BY clause is necessary so that the count function groups the correct Events together. Like most other things in relational theory, queries returning both scalar values and values from aggregate functions have a name: vector aggregates. The query shown here is a vector aggregate.

On the other hand, queries returning a single value are referred to as scalar aggregates. Scalar aggregate queries do not require a GROUP BY clause, but vector aggregate queries do. Let's look at a scalar aggregate query:

```
select count(a) from Event e join e.attendees a
```

Since there is nothing to group by in the SELECT clause, no GROUP BY clause is required.

The GROUP BY clause can be used with the HAVING clause to place search criteria on the results of GROUP BY. Using the HAVING clause does not impact the aggregates; instead, it impacts the objects returned by the query. You can use the HAVING clause as you would a WHERE clause since the same expressions are available:

```
select e.name, count(a) from Event e
    join e.attendees a group by e.name
    having length(e.name) > 10
```

This query returns the Event name and number of Attendees if the Event name has more than 10 characters. You can also be more creative in the HAVING clause:

```
select e.name, count(a) from Event e
    join e.attendees a group by e.name
    having size(a) > 10
```

This time you're getting the Event name and Attendee count for all Events with more than 10 Attendees. Of course, now that you have your Event names, you'll probably want to order them.

We've seen the ORDER BY clause in a few queries before this point, and its usage is very straightforward. The ORDER BY clause allows you to sort the result objects in a desired order. You may sort the objects in ascending or descending order, with ascending as the default. Build on the example by adding an ORDER BY clause:

```
select e.name, count(a) from Event e
    join e.attendees a, join e.location l group by e.name
    having size(a) > 10 order by e.name, l.name
```

This query returns the same objects with the same criteria, only now the returned objects are sorted according to the Event and Location names.

HQL provides a powerful mechanism to query persistent objects. The problem with HQL is that it is static and cannot easily be changed at runtime. Creating queries dynamically with string concatenation is a possibility, but that solution is tedious and cumbersome. Hibernate provides a simple API that can be used to create queries at runtime.

6.3 Criteria queries

The Criteria API provides an alternative method to query persistent objects. It allows you to build queries dynamically, using a simple API. Criteria queries are generally used when the number of search parameters can vary.

Despite their relative usefulness, Criteria queries are somewhat limited. Navigating associations is cumbersome, requiring you to create another Criteria, rather than using the dot notation found in HQL. Additionally, the Criteria API does not support the equivalent of count(…), or other aggregate functions. Finally, you can only retrieve complete objects from Criteria queries.

However, the Criteria API can be excellent for certain use cases—for instance, in an advanced search screen where the user can select the field to search on as well as the search value. Let's look at a few examples of using Criteria queries:

```
Criteria criteria = session.createCriteria(Event.class);
criteria.add(Restrictions.between("duration",
    new Integer(60), new Integer(90) );
criteria.add( Restrictions.like("name", "Presen%") );
criteria.addOrder( Order.asc("name") );
List results = criteria.list();
```

The Criteria query is essentially the same as the following HQL:

```
from Event e where (e.duration between 60 and 90) and
    (e.name like 'Presen%') order by e.name
```

The methods in the Criteria class always return the current Criteria instance, allowing you to create queries in a more concise manner:

```
List results = session.createCriteria(Event.class).
    .add( Restrictions.between("duration", new Integer(60),
        new Integer(90) )
    .add( Restrictions.like("name", "Presen%") )
    .addOrder( Order.asc("name") )
    .list();
```

The result is the same, but the code is arguably cleaner and more concise.

The Criteria API isn't as fully featured as HQL, but the ability to generate a query programmatically using a simple API can lend a great deal of power to your applications.

6.4 Stored procedures

A shortcoming in earlier releases of Hibernate was the lack of support for stored procedures. Thankfully, Hibernate 3 addresses this problem. Stored procedures are defined in the mapping document and declare the name of the stored procedure as well as the return parameters. Let's look at an example.

Suppose we have the following Oracle stored procedure:

```
CREATE FUNCTION selectEvents RETURN SYS_REFCURSOR
AS
    sp_cursor SYS_REFCURSOR;
BEGIN
    OPEN st_cursor FOR
        SELECT id, event_name, start_date, duration
        FROM events;
    RETURN  sp_cursor;
END;
```

You can see that the stored procedure retrieves four columns from the events table, which is used to populate an Event instance. Before you can use it, however, you have to declare the stored procedure in the mapping file for the Event class:

```
<sql-query name="selectEvents_SP" callable="true">
    <return alias="ev" class="Event">
        <return-property name="id" column="id"/>
        <return-property name="name" column="event_name"/>
        <return-property name="startDate" column="start_date"/>
        <return-property name="duration" column="duration"/>
    </return>
    { ? = call selectEvents() }
</sql-query>
```

Executing the stored procedure is the same as using a named HQL query:

```
Query query = session.getNamedQuery("selectEvents_SP");
List results = query.list();
```

If your stored procedures take parameters, you can set them using the `Query.setParameter(int, Object)` method. Your stored procedures must return a result set to be usable by Hibernate. If you have legacy procedures that don't meet this requirement, you can execute them using the JDBC `Connection`, accessed by `session.connection()`.

Stored procedures are an interesting addition to Hibernate and are useful in organizations that prefer to perform the majority of their database queries as procedures.

6.5 Hibern8IDE

One of the problems with HQL is testing the query to make sure it works. This is typically a problem when you're new to HQL or trying out new features. Hibern8IDE provides a simple interface to your mapping definitions and an HQL console for executing queries interactively. (Of course, you'll also want to add unit tests to your code base for repeatability.)

Hibern8IDE loads the Hibernate configuration file (either hibernate.cfg.xml or hibernate.properties) and the mapping definitions for your persistent objects. Once you have loaded the configuration file and mapping definitions, you can enter HQL queries in the HQL Commander tab. Hibern8IDE also supports executing named queries defined in the mapping documents. After you execute a query, the results are presented in a table that you can browse to ensure the correct objects and properties are returned.

Hibern8IDE is designed to be used from the command line, but you can also start it from an Ant build file:

```
<target name="hibern8" description="Starts Hibern8IDE.">
    <java classname="net.sf.hibern8ide.Hibern8IDE"
        classpathref="project.class.path" fork="true"/>
</target>
```

Hibern8IDE is a useful tool for exploring the query language, especially when you're first starting out with HQL. It is relatively easy to use and provides all of the necessary features for querying your objects.

Hibern8IDE only works with Hibernate 2. The project has been rebranded as HibernateConsole for Hibernate 3. HibernateConsole is a plug-in for the Eclipse IDE.

6.6 Summary

The Hibernate Query Language abstracts queries from the underlying database. While the language is similar to SQL, HQL is object oriented and has features to support querying object graphs.

There are two common methods used to execute an HQL statement. The Session interface provides an overloaded find method that can execute queries and return the results. The Query interface also offers the ability to execute queries, but it provides more fine-grained control of the query, such as limiting the number of returned objects.

Both the Query and Session interfaces allow results to be returned as a List or as an Iterator. The key difference between the two is that the Iterator actually retrieves objects when the next() method is called. When a List is returned, all of the contained objects are populated when the query is executed.

Like JDBC PreparedStatements, HQL queries can take positional parameters, denoted with a question mark. However, HQL also supports the concept of named parameters.

The Criteria class is used to create queries programmatically. It's handy when you don't know what the exact query will be, as in an advanced search function where the user can query on various fields. Criterias have some limitations, such as limited object graph navigation and an inability to retrieve specific fields from objects.

When you're first starting out with HQL or a query has you stumped, Hibern8IDE is a great tool. While it doesn't replace a unit test suite, it can save you time when crafting and optimizing queries, or if you just want to explore the syntax or new functionality.

7

Organizing with Spring and data access objects

This chapter covers

- Creating an abstraction layer using the DAO pattern
- Using the Layer Supertype pattern to simplify resource cleanup code
- Organizing your project with Spring

Understanding the basics of Hibernate will take you a long way toward using it productively on your projects. But beyond the foundations of the Hibernate library, like the SessionFactory, the Session, the mapping files, and Hibernate Query Language (HQL), it isn't always clear how to organize an application at a higher level. You can apply a number of patterns and best practices to your project. Some of these best practices come from the experiences of the community; others are adaptations of Java enterprise patterns as applied to persistence. This chapter is all about strategies for bringing order to your applications.

Programming is bit like building a tower from children's alphabet blocks. If you are building a small tower, you don't need to be all that careful about how you stack them. But to build a really big tower, perhaps one that goes all the way up to the ceiling fan, you need a slightly different set of techniques. A bit more planning, a more organized stacking technique, and possibly some super adhesive glue all might be useful.

Using better tools and techniques applies to both creating toy towers and writing software. So this chapter is about building the big towers. We will discuss a few common patterns: the Data Access Object (DAO) and the Layer Supertype patterns. Another popular open source project, Spring, also provides an organizational tool for simplifying your code. To wrap things up, this chapter will give a brief overview of this tool and how it can simplify your Hibernate projects.

Chapter goals

In this chapter, you'll accomplish the following:

- Create an abstraction layer, using the DAO pattern to keep queries together and thus simplifying client object usage.
- Improve the DAO objects with the Layer Supertype pattern, reducing the resource cleanup code.
- Use Spring to further organize and simplify your DAO code.

Assumptions

This chapter assumes that

- You are familiar with the concept of patterns.
- You understand how sessions and transactions work, specifically how persistent objects are linked to an open session.
- You are looking for techniques to organize a larger application. This means more investment up front for better-structured code as the project increases in size.

7.1   The ubiquitous DAO pattern

Odds are fair to even that most Java/J2EE developers will have some passing familiarity with the Data Access Object (DAO) pattern. It is one of the core patterns that Sun highlights in its Java Blueprints, and is mentioned often in many Java books. It's first and foremost a pattern for any application that uses a persistent data store. Most commonly used in applications that use SQL, it applies equally well to applications that use Hibernate.

7.1.1 Keeping the HQL together

The purpose of the DAO pattern is to answer one simple question: where to put your data access code? If you haven't experienced the pain of working with a legacy application where SQL code is shotgun-scattered everywhere, let me tell you it's not fun. Need to rename a column in that table? Be prepared to hunt through the entire application to be sure you haven't broken an SQL statement.

The DAO pattern encourages developers to keep all SQL together. And what's good for SQL is good for HQL. An application that keeps all HQL in a single place is far easier to maintain and modify. New developers don't have to decide where to put new HQL as well; they just put it into the DAO. Figure 7.1 shows how Event and EventDao interact with the database.

As you have seen throughout the previous chapters, the power of querying for objects comes with the responsibility of managing exception handling, transactions, and resource cleanup. It's far better to keep those details hidden from the rest the application. Such an approach decouples the rest of application from Hibernate, making it easier to change object/relational mapping (ORM) implementations (i.e., to JDO).[1] More important, this strategy simplifies how client objects

Figure 7.1 A diagram of Event and EventDao as they interact with the database

---

[1] But Hibernate is so cool, why would you want do that? In all seriousness, switching ORM implementations isn't trivial, and DAOs are leaky enough abstractions that doing so probably won't completely hide Hibernate from the application. So don't invest too much energy in an airtight DAO layer, solely for the purpose of "maybe" switching ORM implementations later.

interact with the persistence layer; they don't need to know about sessions, transaction boundaries, or cleaning up after themselves.

DAOs have style too

You can use one of two basic styles of DAO:

- DAO per application: A central DAO creates, updates, finds, and deletes all entity objects in the application.
- DAO per class: Each entity class has its own DAO, which creates, finds, updates, and deletes instances of that object only. An Event object has a corresponding EventDao class.

You could apply other minor variations, such as using one DAO per module, but ultimately which approach you choose depends mostly on how many persistent objects you have. With a large number of classes, we favor the DAO-per-class strategy. The DAO-per-application strategy can turn into a bit of a "bloatware" class. Second, there is also a nice naming symmetry to the DAO-per-class approach that is easy to remember; if you need to find Event objects, you can easily remember that its DAO is EventDao. Finally, it follows the open-closed principle, which states that classes should be open for extension but closed for modifications. You can add new persistent classes without having to modify the central uber-DAO. So with that in mind, let's use the DAO-per-class style for our examples.

A simple DAO

Listing 7.1 shows a simple DAO that handles the basic CRUD (create, read, update, and delete) operation that almost all entities need. In addition to these functions, it has a few responsibilities so its client objects don't have to worry about them:

- Includes one session per operation; each find, update, and delete method is handled in a single session.
- Provides a single transaction per operation. Client objects don't need to worry about starting or committing a transaction.
- In Hibernate 2.x, handles catching and handling the checked exceptions that Hibernate throws, turning them into unchecked exceptions, which won't clutter up client code. If you use Hibernate 3.x,

you can just let the unchecked HibernateExceptions go without rethrowing.

○ Features strongly typed and explicit DAOs; the EventDao only works with Events, meaning client code doesn't have to perform manual casting.

Listing 7.1 A simple EventDao, with create, read, update, and delete methods

```
package com.manning.hq.ch07;

import org.hibernate.HibernateException;
import org.hibernate.Session;
import org.hibernate.Transaction;
import org.apache.commons.logging.Log;
import org.apache.commons.logging.LogFactory;

import com.manning.hq.ch07.Event;
import com.manning.hq.ch07.HibernateFactory;

import java.util.List;

/**
 * The Data Access Object for managing the persistent Events.
 */
public class SimpleEventDao {
    Log log = LogFactory.getLog(SimpleEventDao.class);
    private Session session;
    private Transaction tx;

    public SimpleEventDao() {
        HibernateFactory.buildIfNeeded();        ◁── Initializes the
    }                                                SessionFactory, if it
                                                     hasn't been yet
    public void create(Event event)
        throws DataAccessLayerException {
        try {                              Opens a Session and
            startOperation();        ◁──── starts the transaction
            session.save(event);     ◁──── Saves the
            tx.commit();                    event
        } catch (HibernateException e) {
            handleException(e);      ◁──── Rolls back and throws an
        } finally {                        unchecked exception
            HibernateFactory.close(session);
```

```
        }
    }

    public void delete(Event event)
        throws DataAccessLayerException {
        try {
            startOperation();
            session.delete(event);
            tx.commit();
        } catch (HibernateException e) {
            handleException(e);
        } finally {
            HibernateFactory.close(session);
        }
    }

    public Event find(Long id) throws DataAccessLayerException {
        Event event = null;
        try {
            startOperation();
            event = (Event) session.load(Event.class, id);
            tx.commit();
        } catch (HibernateException e) {
            handleException(e);
        } finally {
            HibernateFactory.close(session);
        }
        return event;
    }

    public void update(Event event)
        throws DataAccessLayerException {
        try {
            startOperation();
            session.update(event);
            tx.commit();
        } catch (HibernateException e) {
            handleException(e);
        } finally {
            HibernateFactory.close(session);
        }
    }

    private void handleException(HibernateException e)
```

```
        throws DataAccessLayerException {
        HibernateFactory.rollback(tx);
        throw new DataAccessLayerException(e);
        // Alternatively, you could just rethrow, like so…
        // throw e;
    }

    private void startOperation() throws HibernateException {
        session = HibernateFactory.openSession();
        tx = session.beginTransaction();
    }
}
package com.manning.hq.ch07;
public class DataAccessLayerException extends RuntimeException {
    // Other Constructors omitted
    public DataAccessLayerException(Throwable cause) {
        super(cause);
    }
}
```

The SimpleEventDao is an extremely simple implementation of a DAO, with the four main methods that create, read, update, and delete instances of Events. Each method handles its operation within a single transaction, and opens and closes a single session. It is explicit, meaning that it works exclusively with Events, so clients' classes don't need to handle casting. While this implementation is simple (perhaps overly so, as we will explore here later), it greatly shortens the client code that works with events. So creating and finding an event can look as simple as this:

```
Event event = new Event();
event.setName("A new Event");

EventDao eventDao = new EventDao();
eventDao.create(event);

Event foundEvent = eventDao.find(event.getId());
```

As you can see, no messy exception handling is needed, nor is there a need to handle resource cleanup. Now let's talk a little more about some of the problems this implementation has, and what we can do to improve it.

7.2 Analyzing the DAO

The simple DAO implementation we examined in the previous section has a few problems, some of which you may already have already picked up on. Let's take a look.

7.2.1 Boilerplate code

Listing 7.1 includes lots of resource management and exception-handling code. Each method has to open a session, start a transaction, do its business operation, commit a transaction, handle rollbacks, and finally close the session. Each of the methods looks basically like this:

```
try {
    startOperation();
    session.save(event);
    tx.commit();
} catch (HibernateException e) {
    handleException(e);
} finally {
    HibernateFactory.close(session);
}
```

The line `session.save(event);` is essentially the only one that changes between methods. Even refactoring out a few convenience methods, such as `startOperation()` and `handleException()`, doesn't completely rid you of boilerplate code. One potential solution is the Layer Supertype pattern, discussed in section 7.3.

7.2.2 Potential duplication

Adding new DAOs could easily become a rat's nest of copy-and-paste reuse. If we need another DAO, say `LocationDao`, we would have to copy and paste `EventDao` and change a relatively few lines of code in each method. Since we know duplication is the root of all programming evil, clearly something must be done. This too can be helped by the Layer Supertype pattern.

7.2.3 Detached objects only

Since each method is working with a single session and transaction, all of the Events the DAO works with are strictly detached objects. This behavior might be fine, but it doesn't take advantage of Hibernate's automatic dirty object checking or the session-level object cache. For example, suppose a client writes the following:

```
Event foundEvent = eventDao.find(event.getId());
foundEvent.setDuration(30);
eventDao.update(foundEvent);
```

Here the find() occurs in one session and the update() occurs in another. This will certainly work, but it would be really nice if the find and update methods could somehow share a single session. Also, it would be preferable to avoid cluttering up the method signatures passing around a session. While this works, it's ugly, so we don't want to see something like this:

```
Session session = HibernateFactory.openSession();
Event foundEvent = eventDao.find(event.getId(), session);
    foundEvent.setDuration(30);
eventDao.update(foundEvent, session);
```

Adding Session parameters to the methods forces the responsibility, management, and sharing of sessions onto the client code, which increases coupling, complexity, and potential for errors.

One of the potential solutions to this problem is a pattern known as the Thread Local Session. This pattern is covered in chapter 8 so we aren't going to directly cover it here. Instead, in a moment, we examine another framework, Spring, which uses the Thread Local Session pattern under the covers.

7.3 The Layer Supertype pattern

Conventional J2EE wisdom says that an application should be divided into layers. Which layers your application is supposed to have does, of course, depend on which book you are reading. Some popular choices for layers are as follows:

- The Presentation layer, where all user interaction and presentation code goes
- The Domain layer, where all the "business" logic goes
- The Persistence layer, where our data storage access code goes

Regardless of which layers your application has, it's very common that each object in that layer have some common code that could be consolidated into a single class. This notion gives rise to the Layer Supertype pattern, where each layer has "a type that acts as the supertype for all types in its layer."[2] You can use the Layer Supertype pattern to simplify your DAO.

The sample hierarchy in figure 7.2 shows the layer supertype AbstractDao, which provides the protected methods that the subclasses override and make public.

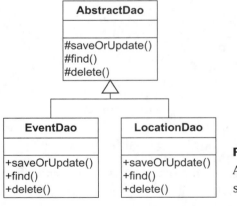

Figure 7.2

A diagram of the layer supertype AbstractDao

---

[2] From *Patterns of Enterprise Application Architecture*, by Martin Fowler (Addison-Wesley Professional, 2003).

The next step is to actually create the AbstractDao, which you'll do in the next section.

7.3.1 Creating an AbstractDao

The first step to creating your supertype is writing an AbstractDao, which all the DAOs will ultimately extend. Listing 7.2 shows how that class might look.

Listing 7.2 A layer supertype implementation, AbstractDao, which has the common operations all DAOs need

```
package com.manning.hq.ch07;
import org.hibernate.HibernateException;
import org.hibernate.Query;
import org.hibernate.Session;
import org.hibernate.Transaction;
import java.util.List;

/**
 * A layer supertype that handles the common operations for all
 * Data Access Objects.
 */
public abstract class AbstractDao {
    private Session session;
    private Transaction tx;

    public AbstractDao() {
        HibernateFactory.buildIfNeeded();
    }

    protected void saveOrUpdate(Object obj) {      ◁─┐ Works with
        try {                                            generic rather
            startOperation();                            than specific
            session.saveOrUpdate(obj);                   domain objects
            tx.commit();
        } catch (HibernateException e) {
            handleException(e);
        } finally {
            HibernateFactory.close(session);
        }
    }
```

```
protected void delete(Object obj) {
    try {
        startOperation();
        session.delete(obj);
        tx.commit();
    } catch (HibernateException e) {
        handleException(e);
    } finally {
        HibernateFactory.close(session);
    }
}

protected Object find(Class clazz, Long id) {
    Object obj = null;
    try {
        startOperation();
        obj = session.load(clazz, id);
        tx.commit();
    } catch (HibernateException e) {
        handleException(e);
    } finally {
        HibernateFactory.close(session);
    }
    return obj;
}

protected List findAll(Class clazz) {
    List objects = null;
    try {
        startOperation();
        Query query = session.createQuery(
            "from " + clazz.getName());
        objects = query.list();
        tx.commit();
    } catch (HibernateException e) {
        handleException(e);
    } finally {
        HibernateFactory.close(session);
    }
    return objects;
}

protected void handleException(HibernateException e)
```

Finds a single persistent
object based on class and id

```
        throws DataAccessLayerException {
        HibernateFactory.rollback(tx);
        throw new DataAccessLayerException(e);
    }

    protected void startOperation()
        throws HibernateException {
        session = HibernateFactory.openSession();
        tx = session.beginTransaction();
    }
}
```

In this listing, you see the common CRUD methods, including save, find, and delete methods that have been pulled up into the AbstractDao class. They have been made generic and protected so that only subclasses can call them. This greatly simplifies what your EventDao would look like. Here's a sample of some of the simplified methods:

```
public class ImprovedEventDao extends AbstractDao {
    // Other methods omitted
    public void create(Event event)
        throws DataAccessLayerException {
        saveOrUpdate(event);
    }

    public Event find(Long id) throws DataAccessLayerException {
        return (Event) find(Event.class, id);
    }
}
```

The only responsibilities that the ImprovedEventDao has to perform are casts and delegate calls to the superclass. The dual problems of boilerplate code and potential duplication have been fixed. As we add new entity objects, such as Locations or Speakers, it's very quick to add a new DAO, using AbstractDao as the layer supertype:

```
public class ImprovedLocationDao extends AbstractDao {
    // Other methods omitted
    public void create(Location location)
```

```
        throws DataAccessLayerException {
        saveOrUpdate(location);
    }

    public Location find(Long id)
        throws DataAccessLayerException {
        return (Location) find(Location.class, id);
    }
}
```

So with the introduction of the layer supertype, the remaining issue to solve is that the DAO is only working with detached objects. We want to be able to share sessions between our methods, even across different DAOs. To do that, we will next explore the popular new framework, Spring.

7.4 The Spring Framework

Some of the flaws we have identified in our DAO implementation have been taken care of. Duplicate resource management code and the use of one session per operation make the solution we laid out a bit more complex than it needs to be and not as flexible as we would like. We could certainly write a better and more robust solution. Fortunately, we don't need to bother—an excellent open source solution, the Spring Framework, has provided it for us.

The Spring Framework solves several more problems than just helping us out with Hibernate. It is, in fact, "a lightweight container which allows developers to wire up business objects, DAOs, and resources like JDBC DataSources and Hibernate SessionFactories."[3] It uses a central XML configuration file to manage the resources and even has its own web Model-View-Controller (MVC) framework. Spring is a general framework, which means it can be useful in quite a few different

---

[3] From an online article, "Data Access with Spring Framework," by Juergen Hoeller, July 2003; http://hibernate.bluemars.net/110.html.

situations. If you aren't familiar with Spring, you might be wondering how you can use it, and you might be concerned that it's just a framework you are "supposed" to use to maintain proper buzzword compliance. As we will demonstrate here, it delivers on its mandate.

Spring has been deliberately divided into tightly focused multiple modules, including the MVC web framework we mentioned earlier, JDBC support, aspect-oriented programming (AOP), and the ORM module. This allows you to use the one you need without having to learn or worry about the rest. For our purpose here, we will just focus on how it can simplify your Hibernate code, which is the ORM module. And the best place to start is with templates.

First, you will need to get a copy the Spring Framework, which you can find at www.springframework.org. Unzip it alongside Hibernate under the applications directory. Spring has a number of packaged options, but for simplicity's sake, the only JAR you need to worry about for now is the applications\spring-framework-1.2-rc2\dist\spring.jar file. Add it to the classpath by adding the following to your build.xml file:

```xml
<property name="spring.version" value="1.2-rc2"/>
<property name="spring.lib.dir"
  value="${applications.dir}/spring-framework-${spring.version}"/>
<path id="spring.lib.path">
    <fileset dir="${spring.lib.dir}\dist">
        <include name="**/spring.jar"/>
    </fileset>
</path>
<path id="runtime.classpath">
    // Other paths omitted.
    <path refid="spring.lib.path"/>
</path>
```

This code configures Spring so that it can be used in our example project. Since Hibernate 3 is a recent release (at the time of printing), other supporting projects such as Spring are catching up. Here we use the newest release of it. In addition, since Spring has to support both Hibernate 2 and 3, a new package, `org.springframework.orm.` `hibernate3`, has been added to support Hibernate 3 projects. Next, let's see how Spring can be used to simplify our example project.

7.4.1 What's in a template?

The basic way Spring helps out is by providing templates for Hibernate operations. So what's a template and why do we need it? The answer comes from looking back at the original `create()` method from our `SimpleEventDao`:

```
protected void create(Event event) {
    try {
        startOperation();
        session.save (event);
        tx.commit();
    } catch (HibernateException e) {
        handleException(e);
    } finally {
        HibernateFactory.close(session);
    }
}
```

If you notice, only one method call really matters here: the actual `save()` call. Every other line is what we like to call excise. Excise is the extra stuff you have to do to get the job done, things that aren't really of direct importance. It's like when you drive to work, the actual act of driving is the important stuff; opening the garage door and backing out of the driveway are excise tasks, which could, all else being equal, be skipped or automated.

In programming, excise is the code you have to write to satisfy the needs of the framework or language. One great example of excise that Java eliminates is memory management. Spring can eliminate part of the resource management excise that Hibernate and the underlying JDBC require.

Normally, when you have duplicate code, you can refactor out a method or class. Here, because the duplicate code is resource cleanup that surrounds the business method, it's a little more complicated. This is where templates come in. The important class that Spring provides is `org.springframework.orm.hibernate3.HibernateTemplate`. It wraps up all of the resource-handling code so that you only have to write the one important method. Our `create()` method can be rewritten to look like the following:

```
import org.hibernate.Hibernate;
import org.hibernate.SessionFactory;
import org.springframework.orm.hibernate3.HibernateTemplate;

protected void create(Event event) {
    SessionFactory sf = HibernateFactory.getSessionFactory();
    HibernateTemplate template = new HibernateTemplate(sf);
    template.saveOrUpdate(event);
}
```

Notice what we aren't doing anymore:

- Obtaining the session from the `SessionFactory`
- Beginning the transaction.
- Catching the checked exceptions and converting the exceptions into unchecked exceptions (not necessary for version 3.x, but is for 2.x)
- Committing the transaction
- Flushing changes to the database
- Closing the session

That's quite a few things that we don't need to worry about because the `HibernateTemplate` is taking care of them. As you may notice, the `HibernateTemplate` seems to be mainly a wrapper around `Session`. In fact, think of it as a "smart" `Session`, which knows how to open, close, and clean up after itself. By default, it follows the same single transaction per method model used before. This is pretty simple, but as you will see later you also have the opportunity to change the scope of transactions. There are two basic ways to interact with the Hibernate-Template: through convenience methods and via callbacks.

Convenience methods

Simple things should be easy. In many cases, what you want to do with a Session is pretty straightforward: execute a quick save, update a detached object, or run a HQL query. None of these should require much ceremony to get accomplished. The HibernateTemplate class provides basic methods so simple operations can be called with one line of code. Here's a quick sample of some of the methods:

```java
import com.manning.hq.ch07.Event;
import com.manning.hq.ch07.HibernateFactory;
import org.springframework.orm.hibernate3.HibernateTemplate;
import java.util.List;

SessionFactory sessionFactory =
    HibernateFactory.getSessionFactory();          // Creates a
HibernateTemplate template =                       // template that
new HibernateTemplate(sessionFactory);             // connects to the
                                                   // SessionFactory
Event event1 = new Event();
event1.setName("Event 1");
Event event2 = new Event();
event2.setName("Event 2");
try {                                              // Saves an event
    template.save (event1);                        // in a single
    template.save (event2);                        // transaction
    Event obj = (Event) template.load(Event.class, // Loads a
                event1.getId());                    // single event
    System.out.println("Loaded the event" + obj.getName());

    List events = (List) template.find("from Event");  // Finds all
    System.out.println("# of Events " + events.size()); // events
} finally {                                        // Deletes a
    template.delete(event1);                        // single event
    template.delete(event2);
}
```

The convenience methods are typically named exactly the same as the methods on the Session. They can be used as a one-for-one replacement for direct session calls, without all the hassle of messy resource cleanup code.

Callbacks

Complex things should be possible as well. Not all operations can easily be reduced to a single query in a single transaction. For these operations, Spring provides the Callback interface. It allows you to write a callback method that will be executed within the template. For example, you can use it if you want to build a complex query, update some data, and then save the changes, all within a single operation:

```java
import org.hibernate.HibernateException;
import org.springframework.orm.hibernate3.HibernateCallback;
import java.sql.SQLException;
import org.hibernate.Query;
import java.util.List;
import java.util.Iterator;
import com.manning.hq.ch07.Event;

template.execute(new HibernateCallback() {
    public Object doInHibernate(Session session)
        throws HibernateException, SQLException {
        Query query = session.createQuery("from Event");
        query.setMaxResults(2);

        List events = query.list();
        for (Iterator it = events.iterator(); it.hasNext();) {
            Event event = (Event) it.next();
            event.setDuration(60);
        }
        return null;
    }
});
```

Here, the Callback interface uses an anonymous inner class, the HibernateCallback, which defines only a single method, doInHibernate(). You will always write the body of the method, and then pass the HibernateCallback object to the template, which then executes it. The template handles the resource-management code, leaving you only the task of writing the query logic.

7.4.2 Beans and their factories

You have seen how Spring can be used programmatically to reduce resource cleanup code. In addition, it can be used to better organize the project architecturally. Spring's traditional claim to fame is that it is a lightweight container. It excels at working with and configuring simple JavaBeans. Essentially its role is to act as a factory for building and configuring beans for your application. This means it can be used to configure most existing architectures and libraries, including Hibernate.

A central configuration file

Up to this point, you have configured Hibernate through the combined use of the hibernate.cfg.xml file (declaratively) and some programmatic activities, such as using the HibernateFactory. Spring can provide an alternative way to configure Hibernate entirely declaratively. The biggest benefit of using Spring is that you can reduce or eliminate the need for programmatic configuration.

Spring reads an XML file, written in a generic configuration format. The XML file specifies how to wire together the various objects, including the DataSource, SessionFactory, and all of your DAOs. Once you configure the file, you can use it as the central clearinghouse to look up the DAOs. To illustrate, create at the root of the classpath a file called applicationContext.xml, which should look like the one shown in listing 7.3.

Listing 7.3 ApplicationContext.xml, which defines a data source, session factory, and DAO

```xml
<?xml version="1.0" encoding="UTF-8"?>
<!DOCTYPE beans PUBLIC
    "-//SPRING//DTD BEAN//EN"
    "http://www.springframework.org/dtd/spring-beans.dtd">
<beans>
    <bean id="dataSource"
        class="org.apache.commons.dbcp.BasicDataSource"
        destroy-method="close">       ❶
```

```
        <property name="driverClassName">
            <value>com.mysql.jdbc.Driver</value>
        </property>
        <property name="url">
            <value>jdbc:mysql://localhost/events_calendar</value>
        </property>
        <property name="username">
            <value>root</value>
        </property>
        <property name="password">
            <value></value>
        </property>
    </bean>
    <bean id="factory"
        class=
    "org.springframework.orm.hibernate3.LocalSessionFactoryBean">
        <property name="mappingResources">
            <list>
                <value>com/manning/hq/ch07/Event.hbm.xml</value>
                <value>com/manning/hq/ch07/Location.hbm.xml</value>
            </list>
        </property>
        <property name="hibernateProperties">
            <props>
                <prop key="hibernate.dialect">
                    org.hibernate.dialect.MySQLDialect
                </prop>
                <prop key="hibernate.show_sql">false</prop>
            </props>
        </property>
        <property name="dataSource">
            <ref bean="dataSource"/>
        </property>
    </bean>
    <bean id="eventDao"
        class="com.manning.hq.ch07.EventSpringDao">
        <property name="sessionFactory">
            <ref bean="factory" />
        </property>
    </bean>
</beans>
```

Some of the lines in listing 7.3 require a bit of explanation:

❶ Configures a basic data source, using the Apache Commons database connection pool (DBCP), which is distributed with Hibernate.

❷ Configures a SessionFactory, using the built-in Spring SessionFactory wrapper, LocalSessionFactoryBean. It builds a SessionFactory when Spring reads this file. The SessionFactory is stored under the key factory.

❸ Links the SessionFactory to the data source.

❹ Configures your EventSpringDao and names it eventDao.

❺ Connects the DAO to the session factory. This allows the DAO to open sessions and issue queries.

The configuration XML file in listing 7.3 holds all the details, things that can and do often change. It accomplishes a lot of the same things the hibernate.cfg.xml file does, but also handles building the SessionFactory for you, as you'll see in the next section.

Building the ApplicationContext

The applicationContext.xml you just created holds the details for how to build the session factory. It essentially takes the place of the hibernate.cfg.xml file that you have seen the HibernateFactory use, serving as a one-for-one replacement. It defines the properties and mapping files that would normally be in the hibernate.cfg.xml. In our previous code examples, you needed to build the SessionFactory, or have your EventDao object locate and connect to the SessionFactory. Spring inverts that concept. Instead, Spring builds the EventDao for you, and you need to ask it for a reference to an EventDao, like so:

```
import
org.springframework.context.support.ClassPathXmlApplicationContext;
import com.manning.hq.ch07.Event;

ClassPathXmlApplicationContext ctx = new
    ClassPathXmlApplicationContext("applicationContext.xml");
EventSpringDao eventDao =
```

```
    (EventSpringDao) ctx.getBean("eventDao", EventSpringDao.class);
Event event = new Event();
eventDao.saveOrUpdate(event);
```

The `ClasspathXmlApplicationContext` looks in the classpath for the name of the configuration file provided in the instructions. In this case, the applicationContext.xml file is at the root of the classpath. You can then request beans by name from the application context. The `get-Bean()` method takes two parameters: the name of the bean you want (eventDao), and the type of class you expect back (`EventSpringDao`).

Under the covers, Spring is building the `SessionFactory` and connecting all the beans together. We mentioned earlier that Spring works with JavaBeans. All of the <bean> elements in the applicationContext.xml file need to be JavaBeans. This includes the `EventSpringDao`, which looks something like this:

```
public class EventSpringDao extends AbstractSpringDao{
    public EventSpringDao(){}

    public Event find(Long id){
        return (Event) super.find(Event.class, id);
    }

    // Other methods excluded
}
```

In addition to other benefits mentioned earlier, Spring provides `org.springframework.orm.hibernate3.support.HibernateDaoSupport`, a layer supertype for application DAOs. It manages the `SessionFactory` field and provides helpful methods to deal with `Sessions`, logging, and the `HibernateTemplate`. Here's a sample of a few of its methods:

```
public abstract class HibernateDaoSupport
    implements InitializingBean {
    protected final Log logger;
    private HibernateTemplate hibernateTemplate;
```

```
public final void
    setSessionFactory(SessionFactory sessionFactory);
public final SessionFactory getSessionFactory();

public final void
    setHibernateTemplate(HibernateTemplate hibernateTemplate);
public final HibernateTemplate getHibernateTemplate();

protected final Session getSession()
    throws DataAccessResourceFailureException,
    IllegalStateException;
protected final void closeSessionIfNecessary(Session session);
}
```

It provides some basic methods, but let's choose to override the Hibernate DaoSupport object in order to provide a few more convenience methods. Listing 7.4 shows what your class should look like.

Listing 7.4 Layer supertype for your application DAOs

```
package com.manning.hq.ch07;

import java.util.List;
import
  org.springframework.orm.hibernate3.support.HibernateDaoSupport;

public abstract class AbstractSpringDao
    extends HibernateDaoSupport{

public AbstractSpringDao() { }

protected void saveOrUpdate(Object obj) {
    getHibernateTemplate().saveOrUpdate(obj);
}

protected void delete(Object obj) {
    getHibernateTemplate().delete(obj);
}

protected Object find(Class clazz, Long id) {
    return getHibernateTemplate().load(clazz, id);
}
```

```
protected List findAll(Class clazz) {
    return getHibernateTemplate().find(
        "from " + clazz.getName());
}
}
```

The key thing to note is that the AbstractSpringDao uses its parent's sessionFactory field. HibernateDaoSupport provides getters and setters, and Spring uses these setter methods to connect the SessionFactory. Recall these lines from the applicationContext.xml file:

```
<bean id="eventDao" class="com.manning.hq.ch07.EventSpringDao>
    <property name="sessionFactory">
        <ref bean="factory" />
    </property>
</bean>
```

This snippet calls setSessionFactory(), passing in the SessionFactory we configured, which we named factory. As you can see from the AbstractSpringDao, which is an evolution of AbstractDao, you have completely removed most of the resource-management code from the find() method. Everything is being handled by the HibernateTemplate and HibernateDaoSupport instead.

Creating a registry

Our final refinement is to bring all of this together and create a central registry, which developers can use to get references to the DAOs or the SessionFactory directly. By having a single class, CalendarRegistry, you ensure that future developers have an explicit, single, strongly typed class they can use, without having to know the details going on underneath. Figure 7.3 shows how everything will fit together.

Using Spring, you get the benefits of configuration, allowing you to easily swap data sources, databases, and add new domain objects. Listing 7.5 shows CalendarRegistry.

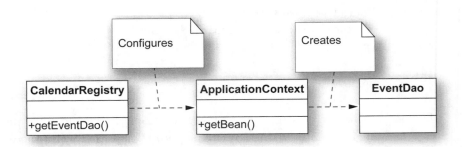

Figure 7.3 A diagram of `CalendarRegistry`, obtaining a reference to `EventDao`

Listing 7.5 CalendarRegistry, a central class for organizing the DAOs

```
package com.manning.hq.ch07;

import org.springframework.context.ApplicationContext;
import
org.springframework.context.support.ClassPathXmlApplicationContext;
import org.hibernate.SessionFactory;

public class CalendarRegistry {
    private static ApplicationContext ctx;

    static {
        ctx = new ClassPathXmlApplicationContext(
                "applicationContext.xml");
    }

    private CalendarRegistry() {
    }

    public static SessionFactory getSessionFactory() {
        return (SessionFactory) ctx.getBean(
                "factory", SessionFactory.class);
    }

    public static EventSpringDao getEventDao() {
        return (EventSpringDao)ctx.getBean(
                "eventDao", EventSpringDao.class);
    }
}
```

As you can see in listing 7.5, `CalendarRegistry` is a Singleton, but because it's backed by Spring, you can easily swap out the underlying implementation. It loads a single static `ApplicationContext` from the classpath, and then uses it to give out references. Now client objects can get a reference to the `EventDao` anywhere in the project, without needing to know anything about Spring:

```
EventSpringDao eventDao = CalendarRegistry.getEventDao();
eventDao.saveOrUpdate(event);
```

More Spring tools

As you have seen, using Spring can greatly simplify much of the Hibernate resource-management code. We have shown two levels of involvement you can use. The `HibernateTemplate` can be used programmatically inside your DAOs, or you can use Spring's lightweight container to manage the DAOs themselves.

Spring is a fairly straightforward framework, but we haven't scratched the surface of what it can do here. Spring also provides a Transaction API management framework, an AOP framework, and a Runtime-Exception framework that can inspect the fairly obtuse `SQLException` that most databases issue and convert them into more obvious and catchable exceptions. For more information, see the Spring documentation, which is pretty solid overall.

7.5 Summary

The focus of this chapter has been on improving the organization of your application code. We have looked at ways to keep your HQL code together, using the DAO pattern. We have further improved our initial implementation by adding another pattern, the Layer Supertype, which allows addition of more DAOs without excessive code duplication as new domain objects are added to your projects.

This chapter also explored how to use Spring, another popular open source project, to help manage the boilerplate resource-management code that Hibernate needs. Spring provides both a programmatic option, the `HibernateTemplate`, and a pluggable, configurable one, the `ApplicationContext`. Adding a central `CalendarRegistry` provides a way to use Spring to give out references within the project, without having to include a monolithic Singleton.

8

Web frameworks: WebWork, Struts, and Tapestry

This chapter covers

- A brief overview of MVC
- Session management in the web environment
- Web frameworks and Hibernate

The Java programming language, with its accompanying specifications, is a popular choice for building web applications. The J2EE architecture that Sun has developed, specifically the Servlet API, has given Java developers the ability to create reliable, interactive web applications. As fundamentally useful as the Servlet API has been, it has proved to be a bit cumbersome. It provides little help toward organizing a large-scale project, and adding new functionality can be messy.

In absence of early guidance from Sun, enterprising Java developers have invented their own web frameworks. A dizzying array of open source and some commercial frameworks have arisen to fill the void. While all of them utilize the Servlet API, each is slightly different and has its own idiosyncrasies. The goal of this chapter is to learn how to integrate Hibernate with a few of the more popular open source frameworks. The frameworks we are going to cover are Struts, the reigning king of the

Model-View-Controller (MVC) frameworks; WebWork 2, an evolutionary refinement on the Struts model; and Tapestry, a component-oriented framework that is a very different way to skin the web application cat.

To that end, you are going to build a sample calendar web application, which allows a user to browse through the months and quickly see what events are scheduled for each month. The application will be fairly simple — only a single page — but should provide an opportunity to see how Hibernate can be integrated with the various frameworks.

Before we get started with the example applications, we'll spend some time discussing the MVC pattern, as well as other common patterns we'll use in the example applications. Then we'll turn our attention to decoupling Hibernate from the web framework, a common topic when developers are just getting started with web applications.

Chapter goals

In this chapter, you'll accomplish the following:

- Know the basics of what a J2EE MVC pattern looks like.
- Create an Event Calendar web application using WebWork.
- Rewrite the application using Struts.
- Rewrite the application with Tapestry.
- Outline the general principle of using Hibernate in a web application.

Assumptions

Since it is impractical to explore three different web frameworks completely in a single chapter, we assume that you have some familiarity with at least one of the frameworks and just want to know how Hibernate fits in with it. We have used the same core persistence architecture, which is fleshed out in the WebWork section (8.4), then reused again in the Struts section (8.5), and again for Tapestry (8.6). This arrangement allows you to skip ahead to see how your framework fits together with Hibernate.

We also assume you are familiar with servlet containers, like Tomcat, Resin, or Jetty. Since the examples in the chapter are packaged as web application archives (WARs), you'll need to get a servlet container in order to run the examples.

8.1 Defining the application

Before we delve into the details of each web framework, let's talk about what your new web application is going to do. As we mentioned, it's going to be a fairly simple one-page application. The basic idea is that you'll have a bunch of events every month that you want publicize to your web readers. Here's the list of features your calendar should have:

1 Create a visual monthly calendar similar to one you might see in Microsoft Outlook. It should display a single month at time.

2 Each day that has events scheduled should list the names of those events.

3 Include navigation controls so the user can page back and forth between the months.

4 By default, the current month's events should be displayed.

To give you a sneak preview, figure 8.1 shows what your page will look like.

As you see, the current month's events are displayed in a table-based calendar. Back and Next links allow users to go back and forth among the months. Note that the URL is from the WebWork application, but the basic display will be the same for all of the applications.

8.2 A quick overview of MVC

Hibernate is commonly used as the persistence service in web applications. This section provides a brief overview of a common web application design pattern and discusses how Hibernate fits into it. Of course, the design we present isn't the only way to build web applications, but

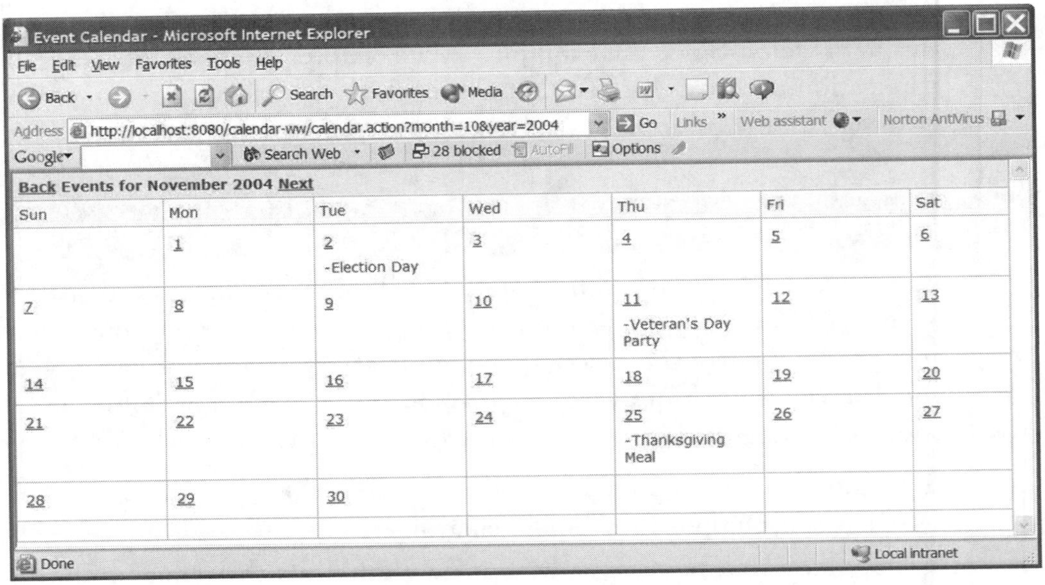

Figure 8.1 The Event Calendar application in action, showing events for November 2004

some variation on the theme is fairly common. Later, we discuss how to use Hibernate with specific web application frameworks. We have chosen three popular web application frameworks: WebWork, Struts, and Tapestry. Before we delve into each framework, let's review the common pattern they all share: Model-View-Controller.

The MVC architecture, also called Model 2, is a design pattern commonly used to separate an application into three primary concerns:

- The representation of the data
- The business logic, or rules, of an application
- The view the user has of the data representation

The MVC pattern isn't limited to web applications. In fact, MVC is used throughout the Swing library. Figure 8.2 shows a diagram of the basic MVC pattern.

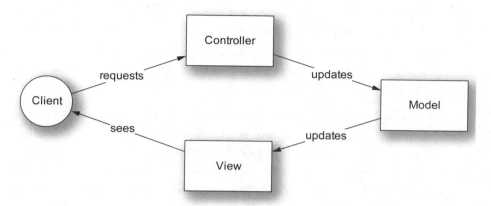

Figure 8.2 A diagram of the Model-View-Controller pattern

The MVC pattern can be described by examining the lifecycle of a user request. Your client, defined as a user interacting with a web browser, submits a request to the Controller. The Controller resides on the servlet container and defines the behavior of the application. Application behavior means how the application reacts to user requests. Typically, the Controller performs some update on the state of the Model. Once the Model has been updated, the user is presented with an updated View of the Model. Let's look at the responsibilities of each component in the MVC pattern:

The Model does the following:

- Stores the application state
- Returns the results of queries to the application state
- Informs the View of changes to the application state

The View is responsible for

- Displaying, or rendering, the Model to the user
- Sending user responses from the Controller

The Controller handles the following:

- Performs application behavior

- Updates the Model on behalf of user requests
- Determines the View that should be displayed to the user

Suppose your events management application is web based, and a user wants to make a change to a specific Event instance. Figure 8.3 displays the lifecycle of the user request.

As displayed in figure 8.3, the user submits a request to the controller servlet. The user request contains the changes made to the state of the Event instance. Assume that the user changed the name of the Event. The controller servlet passes the request off to the EventManager class to retrieve the appropriate Event instance and update its name property. Once this task is complete, the controller servlet sends the user a response notifying him or her that the request has been processed successfully.

Why did we use the EventManager class to update the state of the Event? Why didn't the servlet simply update the Event instance itself instead of delegating to the manager class? You'll find out in the next section.

8.2.1 Service Layer pattern

Two primary problems can occur when the controller component (like the servlet we just described) accesses business objects, such as

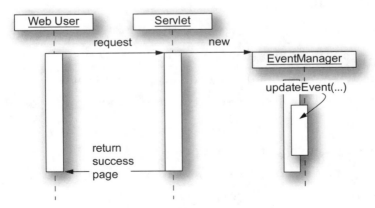

Figure 8.3 An application sequence diagram

an Event instance, in the domain model directly. First, the controller is directly dependent on the domain model. Any changes to the domain model will require changes to the controllers that interact with the model.

Second, since there is no consistent way to interact with the domain model, it's easy for controller components to misuse the business objects. For example, if you have numerous controllers interacting with Event instances, you must somehow ensure that all of the necessary error handling and validation is performed.

To get around these two problems, you can use the Service Layer pattern, also called the Business Delegate pattern, to provide a consistent interface to classes in the domain model. In this example, the Service Layer pattern is implemented by the EventManager class. Internally, the EventManager delegates persistence calls to an EventDao instance, while performing business operations itself. (You'll recall that we discussed the DAO pattern in the previous chapter.)

The EventManager class is shown in listing 8.1.

Listing 8.1 EventManager class

```
package com.manning.hq.ch08;

import com.manning.hq.ch08.Event;
import com.manning.hq.ch08.EventDao;

public class EventManager {

    public EventManager() {
    }

    public void save(Event e) throws ServiceLayerException {
        new EventDao().save(e);
    }

    public void delete(Event e) throws ServiceLayerException {
        new EventDao().delete(e);
    }

    public void delete(Long id) throws ServiceLayerException {
```

```
        Event e = new Event();
        e.setId(id);
        this.delete(e);
    }

    public Event get(Long id) throws ServiceLayerException {
        return new EventDao().find(id);
    }
}
```

The version of the EventManager class in listing 8.1 just delegates all calls to the EventDao, like the non-Spring version we worked on in section 7.3. As the application grows and becomes more complex, additional business logic can be placed in the EventManager. Let's look at an example of adding a delegated method call to the EventManager.

We'll examine two examples of the kinds of methods you might find in the EventManager class. One is pretty simple and just compares two Events. The second example utilizes our DAO class to associate an Attendee with an Event instance. First, we'll look at the comparator.

Suppose you need to compare two Event instances. Start out by creating an EventComparator class, which implements the java.util.Comparator interface. The methods from this comparator are shown in listing 8.2.

Listing 8.2 EventComparator

```
package com.manning.hq.ch08;

import java.util.Comparator;
import com.manning.hq.ch08.Event;

public class EventComparator implements Comparator {

    public int compare(Object a, Object b) {
        if ( (a == null) || !(a instanceof Event) ) {
            throw new RuntimeException("First object is null or"+
                " not an instance of Event");
        } else if ( (b == null) || !(b instanceof Event) ) {
            throw new RuntimeException("Second object is null or"+
```

```
                    " not an instance of Event");
        }

        Event e0 = (Event) a;
        Event e1 = (Event) b;
        // just do a simple comparison
        return e0.getId().compareTo(e1.getId());
    }

    public boolean equals(Object o) {
        if (o == null) {
            return false;

        } else {
            // this isn't a robust equality check,
            // but it works for our purposes.
            return (o instanceof EventComparator);
        }
    }

}
```

With the `EventComparator` done, add the delegate method call to `Event-Manager`:

```
public int compare(Event a, Event b) {
        return new EventComparator().compare(a, b);
}
```

The controller servlet then calls the `compare(Object, Object)` method in the `EventManager` class. Some software developers don't like moving all of the business logic into the service layer. Instead, they prefer to stick with a pure object-oriented design and have all of the business logic operations reside in the domain object. While we agree with this philosophy in principle, it's often more convenient to create a service layer containing the business logic when building web applications.

Our comparator example is a bit contrived. In most cases, you'd probably find a method comparing domain objects in the domain objects themselves. Next, let's look at the `EventManager` method that assigns an

Attendee to an Event. This example is slightly more complicated since you'll be using two DAO classes. The code is shown in listing 8.3.

Listing 8.3 Assigning an Attendee to an Event

```java
public class EventManager {
    public void addAttendeeToEvent(Long eventId, Long attendeeId) {
        AttendeeDao attendeeDao = new AttendeeDao();
        Attendee attendee =
        attendeeDao.find(Attendee.class, attendeeId);

        EventDao eventDao = new EventDao();
        Event event =
            eventDao.find(Event.class, eventId);

        event.getAttendees().add(attendee);
        eventDao.save(event);
        eventDao.getSession().close();
    }
    ...
}
```

Suppose you're building a relatively simple application, with about 5–10 objects in your domain model. Should you go through the extra work of creating a service layer? It really depends on the application. Probably the most useful advice is to start out building your application without a service layer component. If it later makes sense to introduce a service layer, refactor the application code.

For instance, you may want to start the application with a service layer if you plan on having multiple application clients, like a web client and a standalone application accessing the same data. Figure 8.4 shows an example.

Instead of duplicating the business logic in the web and standalone clients, the service layer allows you to centralize the business logic in the application.

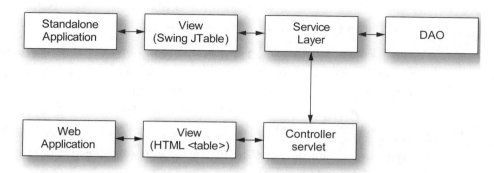

Figure 8.4 Multiple application clients using the same service layer

Now that you understand the basic web application architecture, let's look at the common problems developers run into when building web applications with Hibernate.

8.3 Decoupling Hibernate from the web layer

Applications are typically broken up into concerns. A concern is made up of a specific unit of functionality, like security or, in the case of Hibernate, persistence. Most concerns are only accessed by one other concern in the application, but some, like logging, are used by all concerns within an application.

Developers typically have difficulty decoupling Hibernate from the web tier in three areas, which we describe in this section. Later, we'll examine how to address these pitfalls using some of the popular web application frameworks.

8.3.1 Working with detached objects

Suppose a user wants to edit an object. In a web application, this typically means that the user makes a request to the server, which retrieves the object from the database and presents it to the user in an editable format, such as an HTML form. The user makes changes and submits the form. The application typically validates the input data and then stores the updated object in the database.

As you know by now, you always access persistent object using the Session interface. Up to this point, you've persisted and updated objects using one Session instance. Next we're going to talk about how updates to an object can span multiple Sessions.

Suppose you want to make changes to an object that has already been persisted. In a single Session scenario, you retrieve the desired object from the Session, make changes, and save it:

```
Session s = factory.openSession();
Transaction t = s.beginTransaction();
Event e = (Event) s.get(Event.class, myEventId);
e.setName("New Event Name");
s.saveOrUpdate(e);
t.commit();
s.close();
```

This becomes slightly more complicated in a web application; you have to first retrieve the object and send it to the user:

```
Session s = factory.openSession();
Event e = (Event) s.get(Event.class, myEventId);
s.close();
// send the object to the web application user
```

By closing the Session instance, you're detaching the Event instance from the Session that loaded it. When the user submits the changes to the object, you have to open a new Session and reassociate the Event instance with a Session:

```
Session s = factory.openSession();
Transaction t = s.beginTransaction();
// update our Event instance
s.saveOrUpdate(e);
```

```
t.commit();
s.close();
```

How you associate a detached object with a Session can depend on the web application framework you use. Managing detached objects also impacts another decision you have to make when building your Hibernate web application: the scope of the Session object.

8.3.2 Session scope

You'll recall from chapter 3 that Session objects are meant to be short-lived, generally used for a single database operation or transaction. In the context of web applications, a single database operation would be, for instance, retrieving an object for display in the view tier. Typically, a Session exists for the duration of a user request, and is then discarded. This is referred to as request-scoped Sessions.

An alternative is to disconnect the Session from the JDBC connection that it maintains and store the Hibernate Session in the user's javax.servlet.http.HttpSession. (You guessed it: session-scoped Sessions.) When the user submits the changes, call Session.reconnect() to obtain a new JDBC connection and commit your changes. An example of this process is shown in listing 8.4, using a hypothetical servlet.

Listing 8.4 Disconnecting a Session from the JDBC connection

```
public void service(HttpServletRequest req,
    HttpServletResponse res) {
    // … obtain the SessionFactory instance
    Session s = factory.openSession();
    if (!s.isConnected()) {
        s.reconnect();
    }
    // … perform some unit of work, like retrieving an object
    s.disconnect();
    HttpSession session = req.getSession();
    session.setAttribute("hibernate.session", session);
}
```

While listing 8.4 is a fairly contrived example, there is still a drawback with this approach. There's no guarantee that the user will ever submit the form, leaving the Session in the user's HttpSession until the latter expires. Hibernate Sessions are small, but it's still unnecessary overhead. Because of that, you're going to create a new Session object for each incoming request. With that decided, let's determine how you'll be getting Sessions in the first place.

8.3.3 Accessing the Session from the Controller

Let's look at two different scenarios for obtaining Sessions. In the first, assume the web application is relatively simple and that the Controller uses Hibernate Sessions directly. Next, we'll see what happens when we use the Service layer architecture with our web application.

If your Controller interacts with the Session directly, you'll need to determine the best way to obtain the Session from the SessionFactory. Also, you'll have to close the Session when you've finished with it. The first solution, using an initialization servlet, addresses part of the problem.

An initialization servlet creates the SessionFactory and places it into the ServletContext scope. Once there, the Controller servlets can obtain the SessionFactory to get Sessions. It is then up to the servlet to close the Session object. Listing 8.5 shows the initialization servlet.

Listing 8.5 Initialization servlet

```
package com.manning.hq.ch08;

import java.io.IOException;

import javax.servlet.GenericServlet;
import javax.servlet.ServletConfig;
import javax.servlet.ServletException;
import javax.servlet.ServletRequest;
import javax.servlet.ServletResponse;

import org.hibernate.HibernateException;
import org.hibernate.SessionFactory;
```

```
import org.hibernate.cfg.Configuration;

public class SessionFactoryInitServlet extends GenericServlet {
    public void init(ServletConfig cfg) throws ServletException {
        super.init(cfg);
        SessionFactory f = null;

        try {
            f = new Configuration().
                configure().buildSessionFactory();
        } catch(HibernateException e) {
            e.printStackTrace();
        }

        getServletContext().setAttribute("session.factory", f);
    }
    public void service(ServletRequest req,
        ServletResponse res) throws ServletException,
        IOException {
    }

}
```

Creates the SessionFactory using the hibernate.cfg.xml file

Inserts the SessionFactory into the ServletContext

Next, you need to tell the web server to start your initialization servlet before any others. To do so, edit the web.xml file as shown here:

```
<servlet>
  <servlet-name>initServlet</servlet-name>
  <display-name>initServlet</display-name>
  <servlet-class>
    com.manning.hq.ch08.SessionFactoryInitServlet
  </servlet-class>
  <load-on-startup>1</load-on-startup>
</servlet>
```

Finally, your controller servlets need to obtain and close Session instances. Listing 8.6 displays the relevant methods.

Listing 8.6 Obtaining and closing sessions

```
package com.manning.hq.ch08;

import javax.servlet.http.HttpServlet;

import org.hibernate.HibernateException;
import org.hibernate.Session;
import org.hibernate.SessionFactory;

public class ControllerServlet extends HttpServlet {

    public Session getSession() {
        Session session = null;
        SessionFactory f =
            (SessionFactory)getServletContext().
            getAttribute("session.factory");

        try {
            session = f.openSession();
        } catch(HibernateException e) {
          e.printStackTrace();
        }         return session;
    }

    public void closeSession(Session session) {
        try {
            session.close();
        } catch(HibernateException e) {
            e.printStackTrace();
        }
    }
}
```

The problem with using the initialization servlet is that you are forced
to close the Session instance, which can be easily forgotten. To
improve upon this method, you'll use a relatively new feature of servlets: filters.

Servlet filters

Servlet filters intercept requests and responses, allowing you to manip-
ulate or transform the contained information. While we're not going to
delve into filters in great detail, the following example should give you

an initial idea of what filters can do. The filter class shown in listing 8.7 has two responsibilities. First, it places a Session instance into the servlet request scope. The controller servlet retrieves the Session and uses it. Second, the filter has to close the Session instance.

Listing 8.7 Session management filter

```
package com.manning.hq.ch08;

import javax.servlet.Filter;
import javax.servlet.FilterChain;
import javax.servlet.FilterConfig;
import javax.servlet.ServletException;
import javax.servlet.ServletRequest;
import javax.servlet.ServletResponse;

import org.hibernate.SessionFactory;

public class SessionFilter implements Filter {

    private SessionFactory factory;

    public void init(FilterConfig cfg) throws ServletException {
        factory =
            new Configuration().configure().buildSessionFactory();
    }

    public void doFilter(ServletRequest req, ServletResponse res,
        FilterChain chain) throws ServletException {
        Session session = factory.openSession();
        req.setAttribute("hibernate.session", session);
        try {
            chain.doFilter(req, res);
        }
        finally {
            if ((session != null) && (session.isOpen())) {
                session.close();
            }
        }
    }

    public void destroy() {}
}
```

Annotations:
- **Initializes the SessionFactory** → `new Configuration().configure().buildSessionFactory();`
- **Opens a new Session** → `Session session = factory.openSession();`
- **Places the Session into the request scope** → `req.setAttribute("hibernate.session", session);`
- **Calls the next item in the filter chain, which is your servlet** → `chain.doFilter(req, res);`
- **After the servlet returns, closes the Session** → `if ((session != null) && (session.isOpen())) {`

Once the filter is created, you need to edit the web.xml file to configure it. Configuring the filter consists of telling the application server which requests should pass through the filter. Listing 8.8 shows the filter configuration.

Listing 8.8 Filter configuration

```
<filter>  ⊲— Declares the filter
  <filter-name>smFilter</filter-name>
  <filter-class>com.manning.hq.ch08.SessionFilter</filter-class>
</filter>                          Maps the filter to the
<filter-mapping>  ⊲—┘ desired servlet
  <filter-name>Session Management Filter Mapping</filter-name>
  <servlet-name>myControllerServlet</servlet-name>
</filter-mapping>
<servlet>  ⊲— Declares the servlet
  <servlet-name>myControllerServlet</servlet-name>
  <servlet-class>
    com.manning.hq.ch08.ControllerServlet
  </servlet-class>
</servlet>                         Maps the servlet to
<servlet-mapping>  ⊲—┘ a URL pattern
  <servlet-name>myControllerServlet</servlet-name>
  <url-pattern>/controller</url-pattern>
</servlet-mapping>
```

Using the configuration in listing 8.8, your filter will always be called before myControllerServlet is executed. The filter guarantees that you will always have a valid Hibernate Session before the request reaches the servlet and that the Session will be properly cleaned up when the request has finished with it.

Of course, if you have multiple controller servlets in the application, you need to intercept each of them. If there is a common naming scheme for all servlets, you can simply use a URL pattern instead of a servlet name, for example:

```
<filter-mapping>
  <filter-name>Session Management Filter Mapping</filter-name>
```

```
    <url-pattern>*Servlet</url-pattern>
  </filter-mapping>
```

Making the Hibernate Session available to the Controller is fairly straightforward using either of the two methods detailed above. If you're using a web framework, such as Struts, you have other options for making Sessions available. We'll look at the options for each framework in the next section.

8.3.4 Accessing the Session from the Service layer

Since the Service layer is encapsulated from the web application, you can't easily pass the Session instance to the relevant classes from the web layer. Instead, one component of the Service layer, the DAO, needs to obtain Sessions. A preferred pattern for this is the Thread Local Session.

The Thread Local Session pattern makes use of the java.lang.Thread-Local class to create a Session that is accessible from a single application thread. This is particularly convenient in multithreaded applications, such as web applications. The core of the pattern is defined in one class, shown in listing 8.9.

Listing 8.9 Thread Local Session provider

```
package com.manning.hq.ch08;

import org.hibernate.HibernateException;
import org.hibernate.Session;
import org.hibernate.SessionFactory;
import org.hibernate.cfg.Configuration;

public class ServiceLocator {
    private static final ThreadLocal t = new ThreadLocal();
    private static SessionFactory factory;

    static {
        try {
            factory =                                    Builds the SessionFactory
              new Configuration().configure().buildSessionFactory();
        } catch (HibernateException e) {
```

```
                    e.printStackTrace();
        }
    }
    public static Session getSession()
        throws HibernateException {
        Session s = (Session) t.get();
        if (s == null) {
            s = factory.openSession();
            t.set(s);
        }
        return s;
    }

    public void closeSession() {
        Session s = (Session) t.get();
        if (s != null) {
            try {
                s.close();
            } catch (HibernateException e) {
                e.printStackTrace();
            }
        }
        t.set(null);
    }

}
```

Retrieves the Session from the ThreadLocal instance → `Session s = (Session) t.get();`

If the returned Session is null, opens a new Session → `if (s == null) {`

Sets it as the current Session for the ThreadLocal instance → `t.set(s);`

Sets the contained Session to null → `t.set(null);`

If there is any magic to the ServiceLocator class, it's in how the ThreadLocal class behaves. By storing the initialized Session instance in the ThreadLocal variable, you are ensured that only one Session is created per request thread. When the Session is retrieved the first time, a new Session is opened by the SessionFactory and set in the ThreadLocal instance. Subsequent calls to getSession() return the same Session instance as long as the Session hasn't been closed with a call to closeSession().

Why is this valuable? DAOs frequently need to access the same Session object over multiple method calls, and the Thread Local Session pattern guarantees that behavior. Reusing the same Session during the life of an application thread also provides better performance compared with needlessly creating multiple Sessions.

Next, let's look at how you'll use the ServiceLocator class with the Service Layer pattern. In chapter 7, we introduced the EventDao class, which extends the AbstractDao class. AbstractDao retrieves the Hibernate Session from the HibernateFactory class, which we also introduced in chapter 7. The problem with HibernateFactory is that it is not thread safe. In this example, you'll extend AbstractDao so that it takes advantage of the ServiceLocator class. Listing 8.10 shows the new AbstractServiceLocatorDao implementation.

Listing 8.10 **AbstractServiceLocatorDao** using the **ServiceLocator** class

```
package com.manning.hq.ch08;

import org.hibernate.HibernateException;
import org.hibernate.Session;
import org.hibernate.Transaction;

import com.manning.hq.ch08.AbstractDao;

public abstract class AbstractServiceLocatorDao
  extends AbstractDao {
    private Session session;
    private Transaction tx;

    public AbstractServiceLocatorDao() {
    }

    protected void startOperation() throws HibernateException {
        session = ServiceLocator.getSession();
        tx = session.beginTransaction();
    }
}
```

You only needed to override startOperation() to use the ServiceLocator class instead of HibernateFactory. This small change allows you to consistently access the same Session instance throughout the lifetime of an application thread. Another option for accessing Sessions is to use the excellent Spring Framework, discussed in chapter 7. The next section discusses WebWork, as well as Spring.

8.4 WebWork

WebWork 2.0 is a Java web application framework. To quote the project website, it is "built specifically with developer productivity and code simplicity in mind."[1] It is, at its heart, a refined evolutionary version of the Model-View-Controller pattern that Struts pioneered and popularized for Java web applications.[2] Like Struts, there is a controller, which is a Java class. The controller handles the request, and then forwards control over to a view that handles the display.

Before we can proceed, you need to get a copy of WebWork 2.0. Do this by going to www.opensymphony.com/webwork/ and clicking on the Download link at the right. As of this writing, the current version is 2.1.7. Extract this to the applications directory where Hibernate is installed.

8.4.1 WebWork fundamentals

The core class, or interface in WebWork's case, is `com.opensymphony.xwork.Action`. It defines a very simple execute method, which the developer will implement to do something interesting. It looks like this:

```
public String execute() throws Exception;
```

The execute method will typically handle the request and make the results available as a getter field on the action. WebWork automatically stores the action where the view, typically a JSP, can access the result. The `String` value that `execute()` returns determines which view (JSP) will be used to generate the HTML.

---

[1] www.opensymphony.com/webwork

[2] For the sake of completeness, the original MVC pattern originated with Smalltalk, and was modified for stateless web use by Struts.

One of the basic responsibilities of any Java web application is converting URLs into method calls on a Java object. Like Struts, Web-Work uses a central XML configuration file that maps the URL to an individual `Action`. That file is the xwork.xml file.[3] Here's what a sample `Action` mapping might look like:

```
<action name="calendar" class="com.manning.hq.ch08.CalendarAction">
    <result name="success"
        type="dispatcher">/calendar-ww.jsp</result>
</action>
```

This code maps the URL /calendar.action to the class `CalendarAction`. When a user requests that URL, the `CalendarAction.execute()` method will be called, and then control will be forwarded to the /calendar-ww.jsp to display the results.

"`*`.action" is WebWork's commonly accepted mapping extension pattern that allows the web application to know that the URL is handled by WebWork in general. This is roughly equivalent to Struts' /do/* or *.do pattern mappings. For both frameworks, you would specify the pattern matching in the web.xml to tell the Servlet API how to redirect requests to the framework.

8.4.2 Creating controllers

Having covered the basic interaction of WebWork, let's go ahead and create the `CalendarAction` and the `/calendar.jsp` page. The main responsibility of the `CalendarAction` is to load all the events for a given month and put them into the view (see listing 8.11).

---

[3] What is this XWork that we keep mentioning? XWork is actually a separate, derivative project from WebWork, but since WebWork doesn't function without it, for the sake of simplicity, we are just going to refer to it all as WebWork for now.

Listing 8.11 CalendarAction, which loads the Event data into the page

```
package com.manning.hq.ch08;

import java.util.Calendar;
import java.util.List;

import com.manning.hq.ch08.EventDao;
import com.opensymphony.webwork.ServletActionContext;
import com.opensymphony.xwork.ActionSupport;

public class CalendarAction extends ActionSupport
    implements EventDaoAware {
    private EventDao eventDao;
    private int month = 0;
    private int year = 0;

    private CalendarModel calendar;
    private Integer nextMonth = null;
    private Integer nextYear = null;
    private Integer previousMonth = null;
    private Integer previousYear = null;              ❶ Sets the default month/
                                                         year to this month
    public CalendarAction() {
        Calendar thisMonth = Calendar.getInstance();
        month = thisMonth.get(Calendar.MONTH);
        year = thisMonth.get(Calendar.YEAR);
    }                                                    ❷ Sets via Inversion
                                                            of Control
    public void setEventDao(EventDao eventDao) {
        this.eventDao = eventDao;                  Provides properties for ❸
                                                       Webwork to bind
    }                                                HttpParameters to

    public void setMonth(int month) { this.month = month; }   ◄
    public void setYear(int year) { this.year = year; }

                                           Exposes parameters for JSP view ❹

    public Integer getNextMonth() { return nextMonth; }   ◄
    public Integer getNextYear() { return nextYear; }
    public Integer getPreviousMonth() { return previousMonth; }
    public Integer getPreviousYear() { return previousYear; }
                                           Creates a View Helper for ❺
                                              the chosen month/year
    public String execute() throws Exception {
        calendar = new CalendarModel(month, year);   ◄
        List events = eventDao.findEventsFor(month, year);
```

```
calendar.setEvents(events);
ServletActionContext.getRequest().
    setAttribute("calendar", calendar);

// Compute and Store next and
// previous months for navigation
Calendar next =
    DateUtils.createCalendarMonth(
        month + 1, 1, this.year);
nextMonth = new Integer(next.get(Calendar.MONTH));
nextYear = new Integer(next.get(Calendar.YEAR));

Calendar previous =
    DateUtils.createCalendarMonth(
        month - 1, 1, year);
previousMonth = new Integer(previous.get(Calendar.MONTH));
previousYear = new Integer(previous.get(Calendar.YEAR));

    return SUCCESS;
    }

}
```

6 Finds events and loads them into view helper

7 Shows how to expose objects in HttpServletRequest

8 Stores previous and next months/years for page navigation

As you see, this Action has a lot going on; it has even delegated some responsibility to a View Helper, CalendarModel and a data access object, EventDao. Let's walk through what it is doing step by step:

1 Since the default is the current month and year, in the constructor you set these values from a Calendar object.

2 This code uses WebWork's Inversion of Control (IoC) to get a reference to an EventDao. For now, just consider it magic; we will investigate how it works a bit later.

3 By providing setter methods, WebWork will automatically bind Http-Parameters to the Action. In this case, month = 10 and year = 2004, so setMonth(10) and setYear(2004) will be called prior to the execute() method being called.

4 These four methods allow the Webwork JSP to access the fields on this action.

⑤ The `CalendarModel` is a View Helper, which organizes the list of events into a simplified grid so the JSP can display them.

⑥ This code finds all the events for the given month/year and stores them in the `CalendarModel`, which sorts them.

⑦ Normally, WebWork exposes variables and objects to the JSP view using getter and setter methods. Alternatively, you should know how to access `HttpServletRequest`, where you store your `CalendarModel` so that you can access it using the JSP Standard Tag Library (JSTL) in the view.

⑧ Knowing the current month/year, calculate the last and next months and store the values so the JSP can build the navigation links.

Data access object

The next class we are going to examine is the `EventDao`. This class is built off the basic `AbstractDao`, which you built in chapter 7. In this case, you are just going to look at the `findEventsFor()` method:

```java
import java.util.Date;
// … Other statements omitted

/**
 * Find all events in the given month and year.
 * @param month – 0–11 (0 = January)
 * @param year
 */
public List findEventsFor(int month, int year) {
    List events = null;
    try {
        startOperation();
        Date firstDay = DateUtils.newDate(month, 1, year);
        Date lastDay = DateUtils.newDate(month + 1, 1, year);
        String q =
            "from Event event where "+
            "event.startDate >= :firstDay and "+
            "event.startDate < :lastDay";
        Query query = getSession().createQuery(q);
        query.setParameter("firstDay", firstDay);
```

```
        query.setParameter("lastDay", lastDay);
        events =  query.list();
        getTx().commit();
    } catch (HibernateException e) {
        handleException(e);
    } finally {
        HibernateFactory.close(getSession());
    }
    return events;
}
```

Here you construct two `java.util.Date` objects, which form the bounds of the given month. Your query then uses these two dates and finds all Events with a `startDate` field in between them. Note that the month is 0 (zero-based) because, for some unexplained, inane design reason, `java.util.Calendar` months are 0 (zero-based). So just play nicely with it.

Date manipulations are often a bit of a pain due the cumbersome nature of `java.util.Calendar`. You often find yourself with a `Factory` object, such as the `DateUtils` object, which can create `Dates` for queries like this:

```
package com.manning.hq.ch08;

import java.util.Calendar;
import java.util.Date;

public class DateUtils {
    /**
     * Creates a Date, at 00:00:00 on the given day.
     *
     * @param month 0-11 (0 = January)
     * @param date
     * @param year
     */
    public static Date newDate(int month, int date, int year){
        Calendar inst = Calendar.getInstance();
        inst.clear();
        inst.set(year, month, date);
```

```
        return inst.getTime();
    }
}
```

Calendar models

Show any two developers an architecture, and tell them to pick out which classes are part of the Controller and/or Model and you are likely to get two different answers. Nonetheless, here, our "model" (as we call it) consists of several classes, including our domain model, the Event. However, to avoid complicating the view, let's add a few more classes to the model, as shown in listing 8.12.

Listing 8.12 CalendarModel, which builds a 7x6 grid of calendar days that can hold events

```
package com.manning.hq.ch08;

import java.util.ArrayList;
import java.util.Calendar;
import java.util.Date;
import java.util.Iterator;
import java.util.List;

import com.manning.hq.ch08.Event;

public class CalendarModel {
    private Date date;
    private List rows = new ArrayList();
    /**
     * Creates a Model for the given month and year. Builds a 7x6
     * grid that is full of empty days.
     * @param month 0-11 (0 = January)
     * @param year
     */
    public CalendarModel(int month, int year){         ◁── Creates an
        Calendar m = Calendar.getInstance();                empty month
        m.set(year, month,  1);
        date = m.getTime();
        int dayOfWeek = m.get(Calendar.DAY_OF_WEEK);
        int offsets = 0;
```

```
        int currentDay = 0;
        boolean done = false;
        for(int i = 0; i < 6; i++){
            ArrayList row = new ArrayList();
            for(int j = 0; j < 7; j++){
                offsets++;
                if(offsets >= dayOfWeek && !done){
                    currentDay++;
                }
                row.add(new CalendarDay(currentDay));
                if(m.get(Calendar.MONTH) > month){
                    currentDay = 0;
                    done = true;
                }else {
                    m.add(Calendar.DATE, 1);
                }
            }
            rows.add(row);
        }
    }

    public Date getDate() { return date; }
    public void setDate(Date date) { this.date = date; }

    /**
     * Sorts a list of Events into their proper days.
     * @param events
     */
    public void setEvents(List events) {        ⟵  Sorts events
        Calendar date = Calendar.getInstance();        into the days
        date.clear();
        // Put each event into the correct day.
        for (Iterator it = events.iterator(); it.hasNext();) {
            Event ev = (Event) it.next();
            date.setTime(ev.getStartDate());
            int weekOfMonth = date.get(Calendar.WEEK_OF_MONTH) - 1;
            int dayOfWeek = date.get(Calendar.DAY_OF_WEEK) - 1;
            List row = getRow(weekOfMonth);
            CalendarDay day = (CalendarDay) row.get(dayOfWeek);
            day.addEvent(ev);
        }
    }
```

```
/**
 * Iterated over by the JSP.
 * @return
 */
public List getRows() { return rows; }

/**
 * Get row at the given index.
 * @param rowNumber
 * @return
 */
private List getRow(int rowNumber){
    return (List) rows.get(rowNumber);
}
}
```

The class in listing 8.12 seems a bit complex, but the net result is to greatly simplify the JSP presentation logic. One of the bigger challenges of displaying information in a useful, attractive fashion in an HTML page is that essentially everything has to be either a table or a list. By using a View Helper pattern, like `CalendarModel`, the JSP just has to iterate over rows and columns to build a table. All of the complicated sorting code can be left as a Java class (where it can very easily be tested by JUnit).

The three important methods to examine are the constructor, which builds the empty grid; `setEvent()`, which sorts; and `getRows()`, which is what the JSP will use to iterate over. The ugly details of sorting and grid building are kept private in `CalendarModel`, where no doubt an enterprising developer can streamline them without having to worry about changing either the JSP or `CalendarAction`. The final piece of the model is the `CalendarDay`, a simple value object that holds the event and the number to display on the page (see listing 8.13). Each `CalendarDay` represents a single grid square in your calendar table.

Listing 8.13 CalendarDay, a simple value object that holds events and the day

```java
package com.manning.hq.ch08;

import java.util.ArrayList;
import java.util.List;

import com.manning.hq.ch08.Event;

public class CalendarDay {
    private List events = new ArrayList();
    private int day;

    public CalendarDay(int currentDay) {  day = currentDay;  }
    public void addEvent(Event event){
        events.add(event);
    }
    public int getDayOfMonth() { return day; }
    public List getEvents() { return events; }

    public boolean isNotEmpty() {
        return day != 0;
    }
}
```

Now that we have defined both the Model and Controller, the final piece of the puzzle is the JSP view (see listing 8.14), which is used to display your CalendarModel. In the view layer here, you will use a mixture of both WebWork's tag libraries and JSTL. Most J2EE web frameworks have their own tag libraries, which handle some of the basics such as iteration and the display of values and URLs. WebWork is no exception. WebWork's form processing and presentation tag libraries are excellent and well worth using, though we won't see them in action here. We recommend you check out *WebWork in Action* (Manning, forthcoming) for more details on WebWork's tag library.

However, it is often far easier to just use JSTL, which works identically in any JSP-based web framework, like Struts, WebWork, or Spring MVC. If you work on as many different projects as we do, you might see how knowing one set of tag libraries beats learning three or four.

Listing 8.14 calendar-ww.jsp, the view for your Action

```
<%@ taglib prefix="c" uri="http://java.sun.com/jstl/core" %>
<%@ taglib prefix="fmt" uri="http://java.sun.com/jstl/fmt" %>
<%@ taglib prefix="ww" uri="webwork" %>
<HTML><HEAD><TITLE>Event Calendar</TITLE>                          ┐ Uses WebWork's
<LINK href="<ww:url value="'style.css'" />"                       │ url tag to import
    type="text/css" rel="stylesheet" /></HEAD>  ◁────────────────┘ a .css sheet
<BODY>
<TABLE class=border cellSpacing=0
    cellPadding=4 width="100%" border=0>                          ┐ Uses WebWork's
  <TR><TD class=thBorder colSpan=7>                               │ url tag to create
    <a href="<ww:url value="/calendar.action">  ◁────────────────┘ navigation
      <ww:param name="'month'" value="previousMonth" />  ◁───────┐
      <ww:param name="'year'" value="previousYear" />
    </ww:url>">Back</a>                  Calls getPreviousMonth() on action │
    Events for <fmt:formatDate value="${calendar.date}"
        pattern="MMMM yyyy"/>  ◁──────────────────────────┐ Displays the
    <a href="<ww:url value="/calendar.action">            │ current month
      <ww:param name="'month'" value="nextMonth"/> │      │ and year
      <ww:param name="'year'" value="nextYear"/>
    </ww:url>">Next</a>
    </TD></TR>
  <TR>
    <TD class=td2>Sun</TD>
    <TD class=td2>Mon</TD>
    <TD class=td2>Tue</TD>
    <TD class=td2>Wed</TD>
    <TD class=td2>Thu</TD>
    <TD class=td2>Fri</TD>
    <TD class=td2>Sat</TD>
  </TR>                                                   ┐ Iterates over
<c:forEach items="${calendar.rows}" var="row">  ◁────────┘ each row
    <TR>                                                 ┐ Iterates over each
    <c:forEach items="${row}" var="day">  ◁─────────────┘ column in a row
    <TD class=td1 vAlign=top width="15%">
      <TABLE>
```

```
        <TR>
          <TD colSpan=2><c:if test="${day.notEmpty}">
<U><c:out value="${day.dayOfMonth}"/></U></c:if>
          </TD>
          <TR>
          <c:forEach items="${day.events}" var="event">
          <TR><TD>-<c:out value="${event.name}"/></TD></TR>
          </c:forEach>
          </TR>
        </TABLE>
      </TD>
      </c:forEach></TR>
    </c:forEach>
    </TABLE></BODY></HTML>
```

Displays the number for the day, if day is populated

Iterates over each event in a day

Displays the name of the event

The calendar-ww.jsp in listing 8.14 is doing several important things. Let's take a look.

Builds the navigation

Using the <ww:url /> and <ww:param /> tags, calendar-ww.jsp creates the links for forward and backward navigation to scroll back and forth between the months. The only tricky thing you might not understand is the syntax. When you see this:

```
<ww:param name="'year'" value="nextYear"/>
```

the tag is creating a parameter year and looking up the value of nextYear from WebWork's ValueStack. How the value stack works is outside the scope of this book, but it ultimately calls getNextYear() on your CalendarAction. Using the single quotes means that year is string literal and isn't looked up, as nextYear is.

Builds the Calendar table

Using the <c:forEach /> and <c:out /> JSTL tags, calendar-ww.jsp iterates over the calendar model object to display the contents of each grid square. This is where your CalendarModel pays dividends as the iteration code is pretty simple to understand.

Displays the day

The final iteration is over the Event in each day. With no events, nothing is displayed. You also do a quick <c:if /> to test that a day is notEmpty, and if not, you display an underlined number. Many of the CalendarDay objects are empty, to represent the blank cells, so you have to check here for that.

Applies some style

Since style matters, you use the <ww:url /> tag to import a Cascading Style Sheet, style.css, to make your table look a bit nicer. For more information on CSS, check out *Cascading Style Sheets: The Definitive Guide*, 2nd edition, by Eric Meyer (O'Reilly, 2004).

IoC components

One piece that we left out was how the EventDao was actually "bound" to the CalendarAction; we just called it "magic." Now let's look behind the magician's curtain to see how it works. Enabling components involves a few steps. First, you need to add a few lines to web.xml, which should look like the one in listing 8.15, in its entirety.

Listing 8.15 web.xml for WebWork

```
<web-app>
    <filter>
        <filter-name>container</filter-name>
        <filter-class>
com.opensymphony.webwork.lifecycle.RequestLifecycleFilter
        </filter-class>
    </filter>
    <filter-mapping>
        <filter-name>container</filter-name>
        <url-pattern>/*</url-pattern>
    </filter-mapping>
    <listener>
        <listener-class>
com.opensymphony.webwork.lifecycle.ApplicationLifecycleListener
        </listener-class>
    </listener>
    <listener>
```

```
        <listener-class>
com.opensymphony.webwork.lifecycle.SessionLifecycleListener
        </listener-class>
    </listener>
    <servlet>
        <servlet-name>webwork</servlet-name>
        <servlet-class>
com.opensymphony.webwork.dispatcher.ServletDispatcher
        </servlet-class>        ◁──┐  Defines WebWork servlet
    </servlet>                      │  that handles all the requests
    <servlet-mapping>
        <servlet-name>webwork</servlet-name>
        <url-pattern>*.action</url-pattern>   ◁──┐  Maps all requests that
    </servlet-mapping>                            │  look like *.action to be
    <taglib>                                      │  handled by WebWork
        <taglib-uri>webwork</taglib-uri>   ◁──┐  Lets JSP use the
        <taglib-location>                      │  WebWork tag library
            /WEB-INF/lib/webwork-2.1.5.jar
        </taglib-location>
    </taglib>
</web-app>
```

All of the filters and listeners in listing 8.15 are needed so that components will be correctly bound. In addition, you need to create a /WEB-
INF/classes/components.xml file, which defines the components. It
should look like this:

```
<components>
    <component>
        <scope>request</scope>
    <class>com.manning.hq.ch08.EventDao</class>
        <enabler>
            com.manning.hq.ch08.webwork.EventDaoAware
        </enabler>
    </component>
</components>
```

If you look back at CalendarAction, you will see that it implements
EventDaoAware, which is how WebWork knows to give it an instance of

EventDao. WebWork allows you to specify the scope of the component, which can be request, session, or application. Here, you state that a new EventDao should be created for every request and given to an action that implements EventDaoAware, which looks like this:

```
package com.manning.hq.ch08;

import com.manning.hq.ch08.EventDao;

public interface EventDaoAware {
    public void setEventDao(EventDao eventDao);
}
```

Finally, the xwork.xml file needs a bit of modification to identify which actions should have components bound to them. Here's what the completed xwork.xml file looks like:

```
<xwork>
    <include file="webwork-default.xml"/>
    <package name="default" extends="webwork-default">
        <interceptors>
            <interceptor-stack name="componentStack">
                <interceptor-ref name="component"/>
                <interceptor-ref name="defaultStack"/>
            </interceptor-stack>
        </interceptors>
        <default-interceptor-ref name="componentStack"/>
        <action name="calendar"
        class="com.manning.hq.ch08.webwork.CalendarAction">
            <result name="success"
              type="dispatcher" >/calendar-ww.jsp</result>
        </action>
    </package>
</xwork>
```

A lot is going on here, but the important thing is that each action has a stack of interceptors. Think of interceptors as "things that happen before execute() is called." In addition to binding parameters to the action, you need to configure the components that should be bound to the action. By defining the componentStack, and stating it as the default, you ensure that all actions will use components. By using the <include /> statement, which pulls the webwork-default.xml from webwork.jar file, you can use the component and defaultStack interceptors that are specified in webwork-default.xml.

To sum up, WebWork's IoC framework can be useful, even it it's not as well developed or robust as Spring at the moment. In particular, we have found that when we use Spring on projects, we tend not to use WebWork's IoC.

8.5 Struts

Struts is a popular MVC web application framework, closely tied to the Servlet and JavaServer Pages specifications. Struts utilizes a centralized controller servlet to preprocess user requests and distribute them to special action classes. Action classes, written by the developer, determine the business logic that should be executed, and then forward the user to the next view component. The view components may be JSP pages, but other view technologies, such as Velocity and Extensible Stylesheet Language Transformations (XSLT), are also supported. Struts also provides internationalization and a validation framework.

Struts is an open source project sponsored by the Apache Software Foundation and is released under the Apache License. You can download the latest release of Struts from http://struts.apache.org/acquiring.html. The latest version at the time of this writing is 1.2.4. To use the example application, extract the downloaded bundle to the applications directory used throughout the book.

This section uses the same business classes as the WebWork section, with some minor differences. The duplication is intentional, since we want to demonstrate that it doesn't really matter which web application framework you choose—the Hibernate code stays the same.

8.5.1 Struts fundamentals

For the developer, the primary class is `org.apache.struts.Action`. The `Action` class provides a method for processing user requests and redirecting or forwarding them to a view component. All `Actions` in a Struts application must subclass the `Action` class, or one of its ancestors. Let's look at the `execute(...)` method:

```
public ActionForward execute(ActionMapping mapping,
    ActionForm form, HttpServletRequest req,
    HttpServletResponse res)
    throws ServletException, IOException {...}
```

The `execute(...)` method has four arguments. The `ActionMapping` represents the mapping of an incoming user request to a specific `Action` class. It is passed to the `Action` class in case the `Action` needs to perform some utility operation, such as accessing the application configuration or looking up a view location. All of the action mappings for an application are defined in the Struts configuration file, struts-config.xml. An example action mapping is shown here:

```
<action-mappings>
    <action name="calendarForm" path="/calendar"
        type="com.manning.hq.ch08.struts.StrutsCalendarAction">
        <forward name="success" path="calendar-struts.jsp"/>
    </action>
</action-mappings>
```

The `ActionForm` parameter represents the input parameters from the user request. An `ActionForm` is a simple JavaBean that is associated with one or more action mappings. `ActionForms` are also defined in the struts-config.xml:

```
<form-beans>
    <form-bean name="calendarForm"
        type="com.manning.hq.ch08.struts.StrutsCalendarForm"/>
</form-beans>
```

Notice that the name of the form bean, calendarForm, is also used as the value in the action mapping configuration. This is so the ActionMapping class knows which form to use when processing a user's input request.

When a user clicks on a link or submits a form on a web page, the submitted parameters are bound to the properties in the ActionForm. For example, let's say the user submits a form with two parameters: month and year. Retrieving the parameters from the HttpServletRequest object looks like this:

```
int month = Integer.parseInt(req.getParameter("month"));
int year = Integer..parseInt(req.getParameter("year"));
```

Performing this type of conversion for each input parameter is tedious and error-prone. Note that we didn't check for null values or NumberFormatExceptions. With our ActionForm, the conversion from String to int is performed for us:

```
int month = calendarForm.getMonth();
int year = calendarForm.getYear();
```

Converting the user's request to the ActionForm instance is performed for us. ActionForms can also be reused for different actions, thus reducing the number of classes needed in an application. Another advantage of ActionForms is that they can be validated using the Jakarta Commons Validator.

The Commons Validator package provides a mechanism that validates user input and returns error messages if validation fails. Although the Commons Validator can be extremely difficult to learn, it's well worth the flexibility and power that it can provide.

The remaining parameters to the execute(...) method are the standard HttpServletRequest and HttpServletResponse objects from the Servlet API. They are passed in case the Action class needs to do custom processing, such as streaming a PDF to the user instead of sending him or her to another view.

Assuming the user is to be sent to a view or another Action class, the ActionForward class represents the resource the user will be sent to.

Since Struts uses a single controller servlet to dispatch requests to the appropriate Action classes, we need to configure the servlet to process all incoming requests with a given extension. The standard extension is *.do, and is reflected in the web.xml configuration shown in listing 8.16.

Listing 8.16 web.xml Struts configuration

```
<web-app>
<servlet>
  <servlet-name>action</servlet-name>
  <servlet-class>                                        ⟵  Defines the
      org.apache.struts.action.ActionServlet     ⟵         servlet class
  </servlet-class>
  <init-param>                                               Defines the
    <param-name>config</param-name>                          location of the
    <param-value>/WEB-INF/struts-config.xml</param-value>  ⟵ configuration file
  </init-param>
  <load-on-startup>1</load-on-startup>
</servlet>
<servlet-mapping>
  <servlet-name>action</servlet-name>
  <url-pattern>*.do</url-pattern>   ⟵  Maps the servlet to the URL
</servlet-mapping>
</web-app>
```

This web.xml will force all URLs ending in *.do to pass through the Struts controller servlet so that your Action classes can process the requests. Next, we'll look at creating our Action class for the calendar example.

8.5.2 Building Struts Actions

The Action class is the basic unit of work in a Struts application. For the example application, you have one Action class, StrutsCalendar-Action. It is responsible for placing Event objects for the current month and year into the HttpServletRequest scope for display to the user. The code for this Action class is displayed in listing 8.17.

Listing 8.17 StrutsCalendarAction class

```java
package com.manning.hq.ch08.struts;

import java.io.IOException;
import java.util.List;

import javax.servlet.ServletException;
import javax.servlet.http.HttpServletRequest;
import javax.servlet.http.HttpServletResponse;

import org.apache.struts.action.Action;
import org.apache.struts.action.ActionForm;
import org.apache.struts.action.ActionForward;
import org.apache.struts.action.ActionMapping;

public class StrutsCalendarAction extends Action {

    public ActionForward execute(ActionMapping mapping,
        ActionForm form, HttpServletRequest req,
        HttpServletResponse res)
        throws ServletException, IOException {

        StrutsCalendarForm calendarForm =      ⦗ Casts the ActionForm to
            (StrutsCalendarForm) form;   ◁──┘   the appropriate subclass
        EventServiceLocatorDao dao =            ⦗ Creates the
            new EventServiceLocatorDao();        EventServiceLocatorDao
        int month = calendarForm.getMonth();
        int year = calendarForm.getYear();
                                    Creates a new    ⦗ Retrieves a
        StrutsCalendarModel calendar = StrutsCalendarModel  list of
            new StrutsCalendarModel(month, year);  ◁──┘ events for a
                                                         given month
        List events = dao.findEventsFor(month, year);  ◁─┘ and year
        calendar.setEvents(events);  ◁───────────────┐
        req.setAttribute("calendar", calendar);  ◁─┐ │ Sets the events
                          Sets the model in the    │   in the model
                          request scope │
        return mapping.findForward("success");  ◁─┐ Forwards the user
    }                                               to the forward
}                                                   defined in the
                                                    action mapping
```

The StrutsCalendarAction class is pretty simple. Once you get the request parameters, you use them to query the database and put the search results in your StrutsCalendarModel. In the previous section, you created a subclass of the CalendarModel to simplify your presentation logic.

Struts calendar model

The StrutsCalendarModel class (listing 8.18) extends the Calendar-Model introduced in the WebWork section. It provides some additional getters for display assistance in the JSP.

Listing 8.18 StrutsCalendarModel class

```
package com.manning.hq.ch08.struts;

import java.util.Calendar;

import com.manning.hq.ch08.CalendarModel;
import com.manning.hq.ch08.DateUtils;

public class StrutsCalendarModel extends CalendarModel {

    private Integer nextMonth;
    private Integer nextYear;
    private Integer previousMonth;
    private Integer previousYear;

        public StrutsCalendarModel(int month, int year) {
            super(month, year);
            initNavigationDates();
    }

        protected void initNavigationDates() {
            Calendar next = DateUtils.createCalendarMonth(
                month + 1, 1, this.year);
            nextMonth = new Integer(next.get(Calendar.MONTH));
            nextYear = new Integer(next.get(Calendar.YEAR));
            Calendar previous = DateUtils.createCalendarMonth(
                month - 1, 1, this.year);
            previousMonth = newInteger(
                previous.get(Calendar.MONTH));
            previousYear = new Integer(
                previous.get(Calendar.YEAR));
    }
```

```
        // getters omitted
    }
```

Since Struts actions cannot be referenced from the JSP in the way the WebWork actions can, we've moved the presentation assistance to the StrutsCalendarModel class. Once the model has been populated and placed into the request, the user is sent to the JSP page.

Viewing events

The JSP page used to display events is based on the previous Web-Work example. It is shown in listing 8.19.

Listing 8.19 calendar-struts.jsp

```jsp
<%@ taglib prefix="c" uri="http://java.sun.com/jstl/core" %>
<%@ taglib prefix="fmt" uri="http://java.sun.com/jstl/fmt" %>
<HTML>
<HEAD><TITLE>Event Calendar</TITLE>
<c:url var="css" value="style.css"/>
<LINK href="<c:out value="${css}"/>"
  type="text/css" rel="stylesheet"/>
</HEAD>
<BODY>
<TABLE class="border" cellSpacing="0" cellPadding="4"
  width="100%" border="0">
  <TR>
    <TD class="thBorder" colSpan=7>
    <c:url var="previous" value="/calendar.do">
        <c:param name="month" value="${calendar.previousMonth}"/>
        <c:param name="year" value="${calendar.previousYear}"/>
    </c:url>
    <a href="<c:out value="${previous}"/>">Previous</a>
    Events for
    <fmt:formatDate value="${calendar.date}" pattern="MMMM yyyy"/>
    <c:url var="next" value="/calendar.do">
        <c:param name="month" value="${calendar.nextMonth}"/>
        <c:param name="year" value="${calendar.nextYear}"/>
    </c:url>
    <a href="<c:out value="${next}"/>">Next</a>
    </TD></TR>
  <TR>
    <TD class=td2>Sun</TD>
```

```
        <TD class=td2>Mon</TD>
        <TD class=td2>Tue</TD>
        <TD class=td2>Wed</TD>
        <TD class=td2>Thu</TD>
        <TD class=td2>Fri</TD>
        <TD class=td2>Sat</TD>
    </TR>
  <c:forEach items="${calendar.rows}" var="row">
      <TR>
      <c:forEach items="${row}" var="day">
      <TD class=td1 vAlign=top width="15%">
         <TABLE>
             <TR>
               <TD colSpan=2>
                 <c:if test="${day.notEmpty}">
                   <U>
                   <c:out value="${day.dayOfMonth}"/>
                   </U>
                 </c:if></TD>
             <TR>
             <c:forEach items="${day.events}" var="event">
             <TR><TD>-<c:out value="${event.name}"/></TD></TR>
             </c:forEach>
             </TR>
         </TABLE>
      </TD>
      </c:forEach>
      </TR>
  </c:forEach>
  </TABLE>
  </BODY>
  </HTML>
```

The JSP used to display the Event instances for the Struts application
is remarkably similar to the WebWork JSP. The only difference is that
you are able to omit the Struts tag libraries completely while achieving
the same display result.

In the Struts version of the application, you use the Service Locator
pattern instead of the Spring Framework. Spring can also be used with

Struts, although here we chose to illustrate a different method with the Struts version of the application.

Next we present Hibernate integration with our third and final web framework: Tapestry.

8.6 Tapestry

Tapestry is yet another open source framework, but it's cut from a different mold than the previous two frameworks, Struts and WebWork. Instead of following the conventional Model 2 framework, with a Servlet-like action forwarding to a JSP or Velocity view, Tapestry is a component-based framework. Every page is a component, and can contain other components. Instead of a JSP page, Tapestry has its own HTML template that parses and uses the components to render HTML dynamically. Due to its component-based nature, it's easy to break down complicated pages into smaller bite-sized chunks.

8.6.1 Getting started

Before we get started, you will need to get a copy of Tapestry. Go to http://jakarta.apache.org/tapestry/ and click on the binary download at the left. Unzip it to the applications directory next to where you installed Hibernate. Because of Apache license restrictions, two important Java libraries, javassist.jar and ognl.jar, are not distributed with it. We have included them as part of our source code, but you can also find them at http://prdownloads.sourceforge.net and www.ognl.org/, respectively.

8.6.2 Tapestry fundamentals

Tapestry, like all frameworks, has its own set of core objects and concepts. Central to it are the HTML templates, which make up the view; page objects, which are the Controllers; and page specification files, which wire the controllers and views together. At its simplest, a single-page Tapestry application consists of one template, one page specification, and a single class.

Like a straight Model 2 framework, such as WebWork and Struts, there is a central object you as a developer implement: `org.apache.tapestry.html.BasePage`. Unlike with those frameworks, there is no central `execute()` method you need to implement.[4] Instead, you can "call back" into the page object from your template. This may sound a bit confusing, but it highlights the different approach that Tapestry offers, especially if you are already used to the Model 2 style. Let's work through an example that should make everything clear.

8.6.3 HTML views

With Tapestry's focus on the HTML template, we will start in the front and work our way to the back. As previously mentioned, Tapestry doesn't use JSPs; instead it uses its own template language, which is designed to be HTML editor friendly. Unlike a JSP using tag libraries or Java code, which is typically not viewable in an HTML editor, Tapestry templates use HTML constructs, which are parsed out and replaced dynamically with the HTML. Perhaps it's easier to demonstrate than it is to explain, so let's take a look at a sample template. Since we are re-implementing our Event Calendar using Tapestry, the template shown in listing 8.20 does the same thing as the previous two we have seen.

Listing 8.20 Home.html: a Tapestry template for the main Event Calendar page

```
<HTML>
<HEAD><TITLE>Event Calendar</TITLE>
<LINK href="style.css" type="text/css" rel="stylesheet" />
</HEAD>
<BODY>
```

---

[4] Note that this isn't strictly true with WebWork, as you can name your `execute()` method differently. But Tapestry isn't as focused on a "central" controller method.

```
<TABLE class="border" cellSpacing="0" cellPadding="4"
  width="100%" border="0">
  <TR>
    <TD class="thBorder" colSpan="7">
    <a href="#" jwcid="backLink" >Back</a>
    Events for <span jwcid="@Insert" value="ognl:formattedDate" />
    <a href="#" jwcid="nextLink">Next</a>
    </TD></TR>
  <TR>
    <TD class="td2">Sun</TD>
    <TD class="td2">Mon</TD>
    <TD class="td2">Tue</TD>
    <TD class="td2">Wed</TD>
    <TD class="td2">Thu</TD>
    <TD class="td2">Fri</TD>
    <TD class="td2">Sat</TD>
</TR>
<span jwcid="@Foreach"
  source="ognl:calendarModel.rows" value="ognl:row">
    <TR>
    <span jwcid="@Foreach" source="ognl:row" value="ognl:day">
    <TD class=td1 vAlign=top width="15%">
        <TABLE>
            <TR>
                <TD colSpan="2">
                  <span jwcid="@Conditional"
                    condition="ognl:day.notEmpty">
                    <U>
                      <span jwcid="@Insert"
                        value="ognl:day.dayOfMonth" />
                    </U>
                  </span>
                </TD>
            </TR>
<TR>
            <span jwcid="@Foreach"
              source="ognl:day.events"
              value="ognl:event">
            <TR><TD>-
            <span jwcid="@Insert"
              value="ognl:event.name" />
```

Generates the
back link,
using a
component

Generates the forward link

Displays a
formatted date

Iterates over the rows of the calendar model

Iterates over
the days

Displays an
underlined day

Iterates over
the events

```
            </TD></TR>          Displays the
              </span>          event day
            </TR>
        </TABLE>
     </TD>
     </span>
     </TR>
  </span>
  </TABLE>
  </BODY>
  </HTML>
```

As you can see in listing 8.20, in the place of the <c:forEach> and <c:out > tags that JSTL uses, normal HTML <span> tags with some extra attributes are used—most importantly, the jwcid attributes. The jwcid identifies a component (think a tag library) that generates HTML. When Tapestry parses this template, it replaces the <span> tags with the generated HTML. There are two kinds of components here: built-in (all of those with the @ symbol, such as @Foreach and @Insert), and some custom templates, such as backLink and nextLink.

Probably the most basic component, @Insert is the logically equivalent to the JSTL <c:out />. Where does it obtain the value to display? Instead of looking through the HttpServletRequest attributes, it uses Object Graph Notation Language (OGNL) to call methods on the BasePage. As an example, the ognl:formattedDate expression calls get-FormattedDate() on the BasePage object.

8.6.4 Page controller

Behind every Tapestry template is a backing page object. In this case, the template we looked at needs to get information about the Calendar-Model (so that it can iterate over it), the URL links (to navigate through the months), and the Date of the current month. That information comes from the BasePage object, which you have to implement here. Let's take a look at the CalendarPage object (listing 8.21).

Listing 8.21 CalendarPage, the page controller for Home.hml

```java
package com.manning.hq.ch08.tapestry;

import java.text.SimpleDateFormat;
import java.util.Calendar;
import java.util.List;

import org.apache.tapestry.IRequestCycle;
import org.apache.tapestry.html.BasePage;

import com.manning.hq.ch08.Event;
import com.manning.hq.ch08.CalendarDay;
import com.manning.hq.ch08.CalendarModel;
import com.manning.hq.ch08.DateUtils;
import com.manning.hq.ch08.EventManager;

public class CalendarPage extends BasePage {
    private List row;
    private CalendarDay day;
    private Event event;
    private int month;
    private int year;
    private int previousMonth;
    private int previousYear;
    private int nextMonth;
    private int nextYear;
    private CalendarModel model;

    public CalendarPage() {
        Calendar thisMonth = Calendar.getInstance();
        month = thisMonth.get(Calendar.MONTH);
        year = thisMonth.get(Calendar.YEAR);
        storeNextMonth();
        storePreviousMonth();
    }
    public List getRow() { return row; }            ◁── Defines methods for iterating over the rows, days, and events
    public void setRow(List row) { this.row = row; }
    public CalendarDay getDay() { return day; }
    public void setDay(CalendarDay day) { this.day = day; }
    public Event getEvent() { return event; }
    public void setEvent(Event event) { this.event = event; }

    public int getPreviousMonth() { return previousMonth; }
```

```java
public int getPreviousYear() { return previousYear; }
public int getNextMonth() { return nextMonth; }
public int getNextYear() { return nextYear; }
```

Allows references from template by ognl:formattedDate

```java
public String getFormattedDate(){
    SimpleDateFormat f = new SimpleDateFormat("MMMM yyyy");
    return f.format(getCalendarModel().getDate());
}
```

Allows templates to get model with ognl:calendarModel

```java
public CalendarModel getCalendarModel(){
    if(model == null){
        loadModel();
    }
    return model;
}
```

Handles the backLink and forwardLink requests

```java
public void link(IRequestCycle cycle){
    Object[] params = cycle.getServiceParameters();
    month = ((Integer) params[0]).intValue();
    year = ((Integer) params[1]).intValue();
    loadModel();
    storeNextMonth();
    storePreviousMonth();
}
```

Contains the visit, a central management object

```java
private void loadModel() {
    EventManager manager = (EventManager) getVisit();
    List eventsFor = manager.findEventsFor(month, year);
    model = new CalendarModel(month, year);
    model.setEvents(eventsFor);
}

private void storePreviousMonth() {
    Calendar previous =
        DateUtils.createCalendarMonth(month - 1,
            1, year);
    previousMonth = previous.get(Calendar.MONTH);
    previousYear = previous.get(Calendar.YEAR);
}

private void storeNextMonth() {
    Calendar next =
        DateUtils.createCalendarMonth(month + 1,
            1, this.year);
```

```
        nextMonth = next.get(Calendar.MONTH);
        nextYear = next.get(Calendar.YEAR);
    }
}
```

Looking at listing 8.21, you can see a lot of the same things that we did in the previous `Actions`. The basic responsibility of the controller is to load the events, storing them in a `CalendarModel` and making them available to the view. The controller provides methods that allow the `@Foreach` components to iterate over `getRows()`, `getDays()`, and `getEvents()`. Finally, it exposes the `getPreviousMonth()`, `getPrevious-Year()`, `getNextMonth()`, and `getNextYear()` fields so the forward and back links can be created.

The `loadModel()` method is where Hibernate shows up. One of the Tapestry central concepts is the `Visit` object, which is the central "manager"-type object that Tapestry creates for you and stores in the `HttpSession`. This allows different pages to share state without having to muck about with the session itself. The actual `Visit` object, which you can get a handle to by using `getVisit()`, can be any kind of object you want. In this case, you have a simple `EventManager` object that delegates Hibernate calls to your `EventDao`, like so:

```
public List findEventsFor(int month, int year) {
    return new EventDao().findEventsFor(month, year);
}
```

8.6.5 Page specification

You may be wondering about a couple of things: how the Home.html page knows which class to get its information from, and how the back-Link and nextLink components generate the HTML for the hyperlinks. The answer to both of these mysteries is the page specification file. The page specification is a file that shares the same name as the HTML page, which wires the Java class and HTML template together. It's roughly analogous to the struts-config.xml or xwork.xml file, except that each page gets its own file. Listing 8.22 shows the page specification for Home.html.

Listing 8.22 /WEB-INF/Home.page, the page specification for Home.html

```
<?xml version="1.0" encoding="UTF-8"?>
<!DOCTYPE page-specification PUBLIC
  "-//Apache Software Foundation//Tapestry Specification 3.0//EN"
  "http://jakarta.apache.org/tapestry/dtd/Tapestry_3_0.dtd">

<page-specification
  class=
  "com.manning.hq.ch08.tapestry.CalendarPage">        ◁⎯  Links Home.html to CalendarPage
    <component id="backLink" type="DirectLink">   ◁⎯┘ Makes backLink a hyperlink
       <binding name="listener" expression="listeners.link"/>   ◁⎯
       <binding name="parameters"                                  Calls the
    expression="{previousMonth,previousYear}"/>                    link() method
    </component>                                                    when clicked
    <component id="nextLink" type="DirectLink">
       <binding name="listener" expression="listeners.link"/>
       <binding name="parameters"
    expression="{nextMonth,nextYear}"/>
    </component>
</page-specification>
```

As you can see the, <page-specification> element defines which page class acts as Home.html's controller. Also, it defines two components: backLink and nextLink. Both of them inherit from @DirectLink, which generates an <a> link to the CalendarPage. The listener <binding> calls the link() method, passing the getPreviousYear() and getPrevious-Next() values as parameters. Looking back at the link() method, you retrieve those values from the IRequestCycle object that Tapestry provides you. Defining components in the page specification simplifies the template, which makes the page designer's job a bit easier. But the complexity has to go somewhere, so it moves to the page specification.

8.6.6 web.xml

The final piece is the web.xml. Like with the other Model 2 framework, it defines a Front Controller servlet that handles requests. In addition, Tapestry allows you to define which class acts as the Visit class (listing 8.23).

Listing 8.23 web.xml for the Tapestry web application

```xml
<web-app>
    <servlet>
        <servlet-name>calendar</servlet-name>
        <servlet-class>
          org.apache.tapestry.ApplicationServlet
        </servlet-class>
        <init-param>
            <param-name>
               org.apache.tapestry.visit-class
            </param-name>
            <param-value>
              com.manning.hq.ch08.tapestry.EventManager
            </param-value>       <--  Defines the Visit class
        </init-param>
        <load-on-startup>0</load-on-startup>
    </servlet>
    <servlet-mapping>
        <servlet-name>calendar</servlet-name>
        <url-pattern>/calendar</url-pattern>
    </servlet-mapping>
    <filter>
        <filter-name>redirect</filter-name>
        <filter-class>
          org.apache.tapestry.RedirectFilter
        </filter-class>
    </filter>
    <filter-mapping>
        <filter-name>redirect</filter-name>
        <url-pattern>/</url-pattern>
    </filter-mapping>
    <welcome-file-list>
        <welcome-file>Home.html</welcome-file>      <--  Specifies the
    </welcome-file-list>                                  welcome page
</web-app>
```

Most of what you see in listing 8.23 is a stock `web.xml` for a Tapestry project. The only variations are noted in the listing. Using a servlet `<init-param>`, you tell Tapestry what kind of class you want to use as your visit object. A `<welcome-file>` element defines which template is your welcome file.

8.7 Hibernate in the view layer

A frequent topic of debate when building web applications is what mechanism should be used to send data to the view layer. We're not referring to editable data. When editing, you'll typically convert the domain object into some easily rendered representation before presenting the form to the user. For instance, Struts uses an `ActionForm` class. We're more concerned about displaying read-only data to the user.

A common approach to displaying data in the view layer is to create a separate set of objects called data transfer objects (DTOs). DTOs are created by a transfer object assembler and sent to the view layer for display. DTOs are used because the view typically requires values from more than one domain object. A DTO is used to combine a number of requests for a given view.

If you take advantage of Hibernate's proxying and lazy collections, you can effectively bypass creating the DTOs and the logic used to create them, and simply use your domain objects in the view. The only requirement is that a Hibernate `Session` must be available in the view tier, which is possible when you use a servlet filter or Spring to manage your `Session` instances. Despite the fact that this approach is relatively easy to implement, some developers dislike doing this.

The main objection most developers have to displaying domain objects in the view tier is that it violates layer encapsulation. This objection stems from the idea that the various layers should know as little about each other as possible to avoid tightly coupling the various layers, which in turn encourages reuse.

While we agree in principle, the reality is that you need some mechanism to display object data to the user. You can either create another tree of DTOs and the logic to populate them, or you can use your pre-existing domain objects. Either way, the view has to know how to display something.

It might seem counterintuitive to claim that using domain objects to display data is preferable to using a lightweight representation of your data, but let's consider an example.

Assume you have an Event object, with a Location and a collection of Speakers. In your Hibernate mapping definition, you proxy the Location class and set the collection to be lazy. Since Location is proxied, it isn't retrieved from the database until you access it. You want to display the Event instance to the user, but you only need to display the Event and the collection of Speakers. The JSP snippet used to display the relevant fields is shown here:

```
<%@ taglib prefix="c" uri="http://java.sun.com/jstl/core" %>
Event Name: <c:out value="${event.name}"/><br/>
Event Date: <c:out value="${event.date}"/><br/>

Event Speakers: <br/>
<c:forEach var="speaker" items="${event.speakers}">
   Speaker Name: <c:out value="${speaker.firstName}"/>
                 <c:out value="${speaker.lastName}"/><br/>
</c:forEach>
```

This view is efficient because the collection of speakers is populated only when you start iterating over it. The Location attribute is never retrieved because you don't access it in the view.

This method only works if you proxy persistent classes, use lazy collections, and keep the Hibernate Session instance in the view tier. Of course, this approach may not work with your application requirements, but it's important to realize that it's available.

8.8 Summary

Java web applications always seem to have a database somewhere in the mix, which makes Hibernate an easy choice. In this chapter, you created a single simple sample application, using three different J2EE web frameworks: Struts, WebWork, and Tapestry. Looking over the code, it becomes clear that the main difference between the three is in the Presentation (sometimes called View or Web) layer. Using a good reusable data access object and Service layer ensures that the only different parts between the applications are the controller and views. Each framework has its own templating languages, tags, or components that contain slight variations, but from Hibernate's standpoint there are only a few considerations you need to worry about:

1 How long do Hibernate sessions last, and are they available to the view for lazy instantiation? In this chapter we opted for a very short duration so the actions didn't need to worry about managing Hibernate sessions. In our experience, leaving a session open for a long period of time is a recipe for trouble. Other developers on the project (beside you) need to understand too much about how long sessions are open to be productive. It's better to have the controller completely initialize all the objects for the view.

2 How do controllers get a handle on the `SessionFactory`? In this chapter the `EventDao` uses a static field to store the `SessionFactory`, but you can also store it in the `ServletContext`.

3 How much logic goes into the controller? It's our general preference to have very "thin" actions, so we opted to move all the Hibernate query logic into the DAO, leaving only coordination and presentation logic for the controller.

4 How reusable are controllers? This goes hand in hand with point 3. Generally, we don't favor reusing controllers, especially in a framework like WebWork or Struts. Action chaining (reusing logic by having an `Action` call another `Action`) is essentially programming in XML (your config file), which we find cumbersome and hard to

test. By moving logic into a Service layer, or Data Access layer, you can program in Java, not XML.

5 When updating objects, do you use a query and update every request, use detached objects in an HttpSession, or use long application sessions? Our general preference for the sake of simplicity is to use a query and update in a request. But this is still an open question for the community, and one that *Hibernate in Action* (Manning, 2004) tackles in depth.

While we certainly could show you how to tightly couple your web application to Hibernate and put Hibernate logic directly into a Web-Work or Struts Action, we generally try to avoid that. If you are like us, you work on lots of projects, with lots of different web frameworks, so knowing a web framework to get the job done is a bit more useful.

9

Hibernating with XDoclet

This chapter covers

- *Understanding how XDoclet reduces duplication by generating mapping files for you*
- *Making classes persistent by marking them with XDoclet tags*
- *Defining relationships, such as components and collections, using XDoclet*

In the examples we have demonstrated so far in this book, making a class Hibernate-persistable requires at least two files for every class: the .java file and an additional mapping file (.hbm.xml), which maps the class properties to the associated columns in the database. It is, at best, a necessary evil, since it requires a bit of duplication between the class and mapping file. The name of the class is declared twice, as is every property. It would be nice if you could put at least some of the mapping information right into the Java file itself. Unfortunately, Java 1.4 doesn't provide any standardized way to do that.

Alternatively, you could use the .java file to generate the mapping file. Considering that in our examples you have already been using the mapping file to automatically generate the SQL for the database, this seems to be a pretty reasonable approach. You could write your Java class, then automatically generate both .hbm.xml files and your database from it. You would only need to maintain a single file, your Java class, and make any subsequent changes only once.

By itself, Hibernate doesn't provide any mechanism to generate the mapping files. Instead, in this chapter we are going to use another open source tool, XDoclet. As a generic code-generation tool, XDoclet can be used to generate just about any type of file, including Hibernate mapping files.

XDoclet uses a variation of the standard JavaDoc tool to read Java source files and write out new files. When you insert special JavaDoc tags into the .java source files, XDoclet can read those tags and generate the mapping file using that information. As a bonus, by adding more comments to your Java file, you help document the Java classes as well. This gives follow-on developers additional information about the persistent relationships of your object model.

Chapter goals

This chapter is all about installing, configuring, and using XDoclet to generate your mapping files. You will learn to

- Download and install XDoclet.
- Configure it using Ant so that it reads your persistent classes and generates the mapping files for you.
- Mark up basic persistent Java files, thus allowing XDoclet to read them.
- Create mappings for several complex Hibernate relationships, such as collections and components, using XDoclet.

Assumptions

Building on previous chapters, you won't be learning any new Hibernate mappings, but you will learn how to write them differently. So we assume that you understand how to do the following:

- Write basic persistent class mappings.
- Create mappings for common associations.
- Express collections and components in a mapping file.

9.1   Essential XDoclet

XDoclet is an open source project with an Apache-style license, hosted at sourceforge.net. By using it in conjunction with Hibernate, you can avoid having to manually write mapping files. For example, having written your Event.java, you would normally then have to write an Event.hbm.xml file to define which Event fields are persistent and how they map to database columns. Instead, if you add some special comments to the Event.java file, XDoclet will write your Event.hbm.xml file for you.

XDoclet is based on the JavaDoc tool, which is how all Java API documentation is generated. JavaDoc inspects the Java source files, and then generates HTML documents that list the methods and fields of the class, along with developer comments about them. It allows developers to keep documentation close to the code. XDoclet is used during the build step, so it goes hand in hand with Ant. Adding XDoclet to the build process allows you to compile your Java files and generate the mapping files all in a single step.

This section will cover the basics of how JavaDoc works and how you can add XDoclet tags to your persistent classes. It will also explain how to install XDoclet and integrate it into your Ant build process.

9.1.1   JavaDoc basics

As mentioned earlier, XDoclet works by parsing Java source files, using a modified version of JavaDoc. In case you aren't familiar with JavaDoc, it is a tool that comes with the basic JDK. It reads source files, looking for specially formatted comments on classes and methods. It then generates HTML documents that help developers understand the API. Even if a developer doesn't include comments, JavaDoc will still give a detailed overview of the available public methods and fields. Here's a sample JavaDoc:

```
package com.manning.hq.ch09;

/** Special ** multiline comment denotes this as a JavaDoc comment
 * A persistent Hibernate object.
 *
 * @author Patrick Peak This JavaDoc tag marks the author
 * @author Nick Heudecker
 */
public class Event implements Serializable {
}
```

Notice that this code contains a JavaDoc comment immediately before the class declaration. In addition, it uses two *s instead of the typical single *. This marks the comment as "special" for JavaDocs. A simple comment follows that explains a bit about the class. Next are two @author tags, which provide additional information to JavaDoc. In this case, JavaDoc knows that there are two authors who worked on this class and can generate the API documentation accordingly. JavaDoc knows how to read a basic set of tags, including the @author tag, as well as other class tags, such as @deprecated, @see, and @version. Method- and field-specific tags are also available, such as @param, @throws, and @return.

9.1.2 XDoclet: Building your own tags

XDoclet works by defining its own set of custom tags. More precisely, each XDoclet module (of which there are quite a few) defines its own set of tags. There are XDoclet modules for handling EJBs, Struts, WebWork, JDO, and most importantly for our purposes, Hibernate. Instead of generating HTML files for documentation purposes, XDoclet can generate any sort of files, using a JSP-like template syntax. The generated files can be HTML, XML, Java, C#, or whatever the template author wants. The following uses the prebuilt Hibernate templates to generate the mapping XML files for you:

```
/**
 * @hibernate.class table="events"
 */
public class Event implements Serializable {
    /**
     * This tag marks the primary key field
     * and column in database.
     * @hibernate.id generator-class="native" column="uid"
     */
    public Long getId() { return id; }
}
```

Here you see a Hibernate tag called @hibernate.class. This marks this class as a Hibernate persistent class. Normally you would have to manually write an Event.hbm.xml file. Instead, when XDoclet processes this file, it will generate a basic Event.hbm.xml file for you. One of the new things you see here is the table attribute. Typically, JavaDoc just parses the text immediately after the tag. XDoclet needs more specific information to work with, so tags can include attributes, such as the table attribute you see here. This allows you to tell XDoclet what table Event maps to. In fact, with just the previous lines of code XDoclet will generate a file that looks like the one shown in listing 9.1.

Listing 9.1 Generated Event.hbm.xml

```
<?xml version="1.0"?>
<!DOCTYPE hibernate-mapping PUBLIC
    "-//Hibernate/Hibernate Mapping DTD 3.0//EN"
    "http://hibernate.sourceforge.net/hibernate-mapping-3.0.dtd">
<hibernate-mapping>
    <class
        name="com.manning.hq.ch09.Event"    ⟵  Generates the
                                                class name
        table="events"    ⟵
        dynamic-update="false"    Writes out the event
        dynamic-insert="false"    table attribute
    >
        <id
            name="id"    ⟵  Extracts the
                            id property
```

```
            column="uid"                    | Determines
            type="java.lang.Long"    ◁──┘   | correct field type
        >
            <generator class="native">
            </generator>
        </id>
        <!--
            To add non-XDoclet property mappings,
            create a file named hibernate-properties-Event.xml
            containing the additional properties and place it
            in your merge dir.
        -->
    </class>
</hibernate-mapping>
```

With two brief lines of XDoclet comments, you have generated an 18-line file (excluding whitespace and comments). In addition, most of the necessary class and field type information has been gathered from the source file itself, without you having to specify it. The fully qualified name of the class (com.manning.hq.ch09.Event) is included, as well as the Long field id.

9.1.3 Installing XDoclet

Having covered some of the basic details of how XDoclet works, let's dig down a little deeper and work on some examples. You first have to get a copy of XDoclet, so head to its home page at http://xdoclet. sourceforge.net/xdoclet/index.html.

Choose the download/installation link from the left menu, and then select the SourceForge download page. At the time of this writing, the latest stable version is 1.2.3; support for Hibernate 3 has been added. Select the bin version, which should be the most complete package; it will be named something like xdoclet-bin-1.2.3.zip.

After getting a distribution, extract it to your applications directory. When you've finished, take a look; the directory should be named something like /applications/xdoclet-1.2.3. You should see at least three directories: docs, lib, and samples. The docs directory contains the documentation for the project, which is mostly a duplicate of the website, including the JavaDocs. The samples directory contains some code samples of XDoclet in action. And finally, the lib directory contains all the XDoclet JAR files and XDoclet's dependencies. If you want a complete list of all the XDoclet tags, check out the tag reference by opening up docs/index.html and choosing the tag reference link for Hibernate from the left menu.

That's all there is to the install. In the next section, you'll integrate XDoclet into your Ant build file.

9.1.4 Configuring Ant

So far, we have glossed over the details of how XDoclet actually processes the files. XDoclet works strictly at build time. In fact, the only way to use XDoclet is as a part of an Ant build process. You'll need to create targets and tasks in your build.xml file to instruct it to process the Java files and then generate the hbm.xml files. Go ahead and make a copy of the build.xml file we have been working with in the previous few chapters, this time naming it build09.xml. Modify it to look like so:

```xml
<project name="build09.xml" default="build">

    <property name="src.java.dir" value="src/java"/>
    <property name="build.classes.dir" value="build/classes"/>
    <!-- Other properties excluded -->
    <import file="hibernate-build.xml"/>
    <property name="xdoclet.version" value="1.2.3"/>
    <property name="xdoclet.lib.dir"
        value="${applications.dir}/xdoclet-${xdoclet.version}"/>
    <path id="xdoclet.lib.path">
        <fileset dir="${xdoclet.lib.dir}\lib">
            <include name="**/*.jar"/>
        </fileset>
    </path>
    <path id="project.classpath">
        <pathelement location="${build.classes.dir}"/>
    </path>
    <path id="runtime.classpath">
        <path refid="project.classpath"/>
```

Defines the location where XDoclet is installed

Creates a path element for XDoclet

```
            <path refid="hibernate.lib.path"/>        | Adds XDoclet to
            <path refid="xdoclet.lib.path"/>    <----- | the classpath
            <pathelement location="${jdbc.driver.jar}"/>
            <pathelement location="${src.java.dir}"/>
        </path>
        <!-- Other attributes excluded -->
        <target name="generate-hbm" depends="compile">
            <taskdef                          <--------| Defines the Hibernate
                name="hibernatedoclet"                 | Doclet task
            classname="xdoclet.modules.hibernate.HibernateDocletTask"
                classpathref="runtime.classpath"
                />
            <hibernatedoclet                           | Specifies the output
                destdir="${build.classes.dir}"  <-----| directory for the
                verbose="true">                        | .hbm.xml files
                <fileset dir="${src.java.dir}">   <---- | Contains location of
                    <include name="**/*.java"/>         | the Java files, parsing
                </fileset>                              | all of them
                <hibernate version="3.0"/>
            </hibernatedoclet>
        </target>
    </project>
```

(We left out a few of the attributes and tasks from the overall build file
to highlight the new additions.) Overall, you do quite a few things with
this code. You add XDoclet to the classpath by defining the location
where you installed it. By making the xdoclet.version a property, you
make it easy to upgrade to a new version. You define a path element,
xdoclet.lib.path, which includes all the XDoclet JARs and dependencies. Finally, you define a new Ant task, called hibernatedoclet,
which will be used to generate the .hbm files. Running this task from
the command line yields the following:

```
$ant -f build09.xml generate-hbm
Buildfile: build09.xml

init:

compile:

generate-hbm:
```

```
[hibernatedoclet](XDocletMain.start 47  ) Running <hibernate/>
[hibernatedoclet] Generating mapping file
                 for com.manning.hq.ch09.Event.
[hibernatedoclet]    com.manning.hq.ch09.Event

BUILD SUCCESSFUL
Total time: 4 seconds
```

As you notice, the task processed a single Java class, your Event class, and generates its mapping file. If you look in the build/classes directory, you should find an Event.hbm.xml file sitting along with the compiled Event.class. You can add Event to your SessionFactory now and persist classes just as if you wrote the Event.hbm.xml file by hand. And as you can see by looking at Event.java, the Hibernate tags you added make the purpose and intent of the class a bit clearer. So you have reduced the number of files that future developers (which may include you) need to read and comprehend, as well as documenting the files they do read.

9.2 Making single objects persistent

So far we have covered a basic example of how XDoclet works. Let's take a step back and look at what mapping elements Hibernate requires to make a class persistent. Generally, each Hibernate element has a corresponding XDoclet tag that generates it. This section covers four of the basic tags you need to make a single class persistent: @class, @id, @property, and @column.

Each of these tags has its own set of allowable properties, which you'll likely need to configure; some of them have very reasonable defaults. What follows is not an exhaustive list but just a listing of properties that you may need to use. For complete tag details, check the documentation that comes with XDoclet.[1]

---

[1] The Hibernate tag documentation is in that docs directory we pointed out in section 9.1.

9.2.1 The @hibernate.class tag

The @hibernate.class tag has quite a few properties (many of which you will use when we start discussing polymorphism and subclasses), but table 9.1 shows the one that's commonly used.

Table 9.1   A common @hibernate.class attribute

Attribute	Description	Default
table	Contains the name of the table where instances of this class will be persisted to.	The unqualified name of the class.

Tags are valid only when placed in certain spots. In this case, you put this tag only in the class-level JavaDoc comments. It would be meaningless to put it on a method, for example. Note that while the table attribute isn't mandatory, we also recommend specifying it for the sake of clarity (and because database and Java naming conventions differ a bit).

Also, for the class-based tags, be sure the JavaDoc comments are right before the class declaration. If you put a class-based tag in the wrong place, XDoclet will silently do nothing and leave you frustrated and confused. For example, don't do this:

```
/**
 * Don't do this! Class tags can't appear before the
 * package statement.
 * @hibernate.class
 */
package com.manning.hq.ch09;

public class Event implements Serializable { }
```

Many classes have a big block of comments appear at the beginning of the file, which is fine. But if you want XDoclet to parse them, be sure to put the JavaDoc right up next to the class declaration like so:

```
/*
 *    Some other comments about the Event class go here.
 */
package com.manning.hq.ch09;
/**
 * This is the right place. XDoclet looks for
 * class-level tags here.
 * @hibernate.class
 */
public class Event implements Serializable { }
```

9.2.2 The @hibernate.id tag

Table 9.2 list the common properties of the @hibernate.id tag.

Table 9.2 Common @hibernate.id attributes

Attribute	Description	Default
generator-class	Contains the key genera-tor that Hibernate will use to insert new instances.	None. It's mandatory so you have to pick one. When in doubt, using native will work for most databases.
type	Specifies the Hibernate type for this field.	The return type of the field; as primary keys tend to be Longs or Strings, it usually isn't necessary to specify this.
column	Contains the name of the column.	The property name.
unsaved-value	Contains a value that will distinguish transient instances from persis-tent ones.	Null. Generally, if you use a String or Long as the primary key, you don't need to specify this.
length	Specifies the size of the database column.	The default size for the field type. For a Long, it's a given, but for a String key, you might need to specify it.

That's actually all of the properties you can specify for the id field. Generally, unless you are doing something fairly complex, you just need the generator-class and possibly the column field.[2] The @hibernate.id tag is a property-level tag, so it only goes along with a property, not with a class.

You need to keep in mind a few tricky things about property-based tags. For example, you have to mark the getter method, not the field itself or the setter methods. The following is wrong:

```
/**
 * Wrong! Don't put on the field.
 * @hibernate.id generator-class="native" column="uid"
 */
private Long id;

/**
 * Wrong! Don't put on the setter method either.
 * @hibernate.id generator-class="native" column="uid"
 */
public void setId(Long id) {
    this.id = id;
}
```

This is the correct place to put it: on the getId() method.

```
/**
 * The right place for the tag, on getter method.
 * @hibernate.id generator-class="native" column="uid"
 */
public Long getId() {
    return id;
}
```

---

[2] Most property-based tags (including both property and id) will have a column attribute, which is usually optional. We think it's good practice to specify it, though, since it makes columns obvious in the class documentation.

Another aspect that might be confusing is unsaved-value.

unsaved-value

The issue we'll discuss next isn't related just to XDoclet, but is a more general Hibernate one. We discussed this issue earlier in chapter 3, but a quick review might be in order. When Hibernate goes to save an object, it looks at the value of the identifier field to determine whether the object is new (transient) and needs to be inserted or whether it is persistent. If a transient object is passed to saveOrUpdate(), a new row is created. If the identifier is anything else, an update for the matching row is performed.

For most persistent classes, if the identifier is an object, such as a Long or a String, the default unsaved-value of null is fine. This is the case with your Event, which has an id field that's a Long, so you don't need to specify a value for unsaved-value. So the following would create a new Event row in the database:

```
Event event = new Event();
session.saveOrUpdate(event);
```

So when you create a new Event, its id is null to start and thus will be inserted. If you are using a primitive for a key (like long or int), you should set the unsaved-value attribute to 0. So if you changed your Event.id field to be a long, you'd have to specify the unsaved-value field like this:

```
/**
 * Using a primitive long instead of a Long to
 * demonstrate unsaved-value.
 * @hibernate.id generator-class="native"
 *   column="uid" unsaved-value="0"
 */
public long getId() {
    return id;
}
```

9.2.3 The @hibernate.property tag

Now let's look at a new tag, @hibernate.property. You will use this tag quite a bit. It is a direct replacement for the Hibernate <property> element and has most of the same attributes you see there. Like the @hibernate.id tag, it has to go on the getter, not on the field. Table 9.3 contains the most commonly used tag attributes.

Table 9.3 Common @hibernate.property **attributes**

Attribute	Description	Default
column	Contains the name of the column this property maps to.	The name of the field.
length	Specifies the column size.	The default length for a field (i.e., 11 for Longs, 255 for Strings).
not-null	Specifies that a not-null constraint should be enforced.	false.
unique	Specifies that a unique constraint should be enforced.	false.
type	Specifies the Hibernate type.	If you don't specify the type attribute, XDoclet makes an educated guess based on the return type of the field.

Its attributes are not much different from those of @hibernate.id. The important ones @hibernate.property adds are the not-null and unique column constraints, which are also present by default for an id/primary key column. With that in mind, you can expand on the Event example and put some of the properties you left out earlier back in using XDoclet (see listing 9.2).

Listing 9.2 Event with @hibernate.property tags

```
package com.manning.hq.ch09;

import java.io.Serializable;
import java.util.Date;
```

```java
public class Event implements Serializable {
    private Long id;
    private int duration;
    private String name;
    private Date startDate;

    /**
     * @hibernate.id generator-class="native" column="uid"
     */
    public Long getId() { return id; }
    public void setId(Long id) { this.id = id; }

    /**
     * @hibernate.property column="name"
     */
    public String getName() { return name; }
    public void setName(String name) { this.name = name;    }

    /**
     * @hibernate.property column="start_date"
     */
    public Date getStartDate() { return startDate; }
    public void setStartDate(Date startDate) {
        this.startDate = startDate;
    }

    /**
     * @hibernate.property column="duration"
     */
    public int getDuration() { return duration; }
    public void setDuration(int duration) {
        this.duration = duration;
    }
}
```

We have added three properties, of differing types: a String, a Date, and an int property. XDoclet will parse this file and correctly create the mapping document we have seen in previous chapters. Rerunning the generate-hbm target in Ant should regenerate the Event.hbm.xml file with the following additions:

```
<property
    name="name"
    type="java.lang.String"
    update="true"
    insert="true"
    access="property"
    column="name"
/>

<property
    name="startDate"
    type="java.util.Date"
    update="true"
    insert="true"
    access="property"
    column="start_date"
/>

<property
    name="duration"
    type="int"
    update="true"
    insert="true"
    access="property"
    column="duration"
/>
```

Working in an iterative fashion, you can see how easy it is to add properties to an existing persistent object in this way. Add the new field to the class, mark it with XDoclet tags, generate the mapping files, and then run the SchemaUpdate or SchemaExport task to add the new columns to the database.

9.2.4 The @hibernate.column tag

Making a field a simple Hibernate property in most cases only requires the services of the @hibernate.property tag. However, at times more information is needed, and this is where the @hibernate.column tag comes in handy. Its purpose is to allow you to provide additional information about the database column mapping. It is also the first example we have considered where you can use two Hibernate tags on a single field. We will see more examples of this later, in section 9.4, when we cover collections. Table 9.4 contains the most common attributes in the @hibernate.column tag.

Table 9.4 Common @hibernate.column attributes

Attribute	Description	Default
name	Contains the name of column this property maps to.	It's mandatory, so no default.
length	Specifies the column size.	The default length for a field (i.e., 11 for Longs, 255 for Strings) or the size implied by sql-type.
not-null	Specifies that a not-null constraint should be enforced.	false.
unique	Specifies that a unique constraint should be enforced.	false.
index	Contains the name of a table index for this column.	No named index created.
unique-key	Creates a uniquely named constraint with this name.	No constraint created.
sql-type	Specifies a database-specific column type, like TEXT or LONGBLOB.	The type implied by the length.

Looking at tables 9.3 and 9.4, you can see some duplication of attributes between the @hibernate.property and @hibernate.column tags, especially considering that they will be used together for a single field. It's because the column tag is intended to be an overriding, more specific version of the property tag. Information from the column tag is used to create a nested <column> element inside the property tag.

The question you might be asking yourself now is, "Why would I want to use this; @hibernate.property seems to have all I need?" Take, for example, the case of the humble java.lang.String. In Java, a String can be as big or as small as needed. A developer doesn't have to choose between a String256, a StringBig, or a StringTiny—there's a one-size-fits-all String. The world of the database isn't so simple. You have to declare columns to be of a specific size ahead of time. If you create a VARCHAR(255) column and then attempt to stuff a 1,055-character college essay into it, hopefully you still have the original since the database is probably going to truncate everything after its size limit has been reached.[3]

In our example, you want to specify the Event's name to be really long. In MySQL terms, you want it to be a TEXT column type. You could do one of two things: declare the length of the property to be 65535 (which happens to be the exact size of the column), or use a @hibernate.column with a sql-type="TEXT". The first approach is workable and likely to be more database portable. The second is a lot easier to remember and read.[4] Let's give the second strategy a try. Go ahead and modify the getName() method on the Event class:

```
/**
 * @hibernate.property
 * @hibernate.column name="name" sql-type="TEXT"
 * @return
 */
public String getName() { return name; }
```

Here you've removed the column attribute from the property tag and specified it in the column tag. Now when you regenerate the hbm.xml files, you should see the following altered version of the name property:

---

[3] The database's behavior when you try to fit too much data into a column that is too small to hold it all is specific to that database. MySQL truncates; other databases are free to do different things.

[4] If database portability becomes a concern here, you can also use Ant property substitution, detailed in section 9.5. It allows you to regenerate the hbm.xml files for different databases fairly easily.

```
<property
    name="name"
    type="java.lang.String"
    update="true"
    insert="true"
    access="property"
>
    <column
        name="name"
        sql-type="TEXT"
    />
</property>
```

That's all there is to it. While this might seem to be an unusual case, the approach is extremely handy when you are using SchemaExport to generate the database, since the newly created columns will be the right size. If you run this against a MySQL database, it will create the name column as type TEXT rather than the often-too-short default VARCHAR size of 255.

9.3 Basic relationships

Having covered the basics of generating a single persistent class mapping file, with its properties, let's next examine how basic relationships can be generated. The two basic relationships we have seen before, many-to-one and components, can be generated by XDoclet using the two new tags we'll cover next: @hibernate.many-to-one and @hibernate.component.

9.3.1 The @hibernate.many-to-one tag

The many-to-one relationship works essentially like the property tag, except that it stores a foreign key to another table, as opposed to a single column property value. As such, it shares many of the same attributes as the @hibernate.property tag. Table 9.5 contains some of the common ones.

Table 9.5 Common @hibernate.many-to-one attributes

Attribute	Description	Default
column	Contains the name of column in the database.	The name of the field.
class	Contains the associated persistent class.	The class of the field. Usually XDoclet can guess this so it's not necessary to specify.
cascade	Specifies how cascading operations should be handled from parent to child.	None. Acceptable values include all, none, save-update, or delete.
unique	Specifies that a unique constraint should be enforced.	false.
not-null	Specifies that a not-null constraint should be enforced.	false.

In most cases, only cascade and column need to be specified. As an example, let's add the many-to-one relationship between Event and Location using the @hibernate.many-to-one tag. First, add the following to the Event class:

```
public class Event implements Serializable {
    private Location location;
    /**
     * @hibernate.many-to-one column="location_id"
     * cascade="save-update"
     */
    public Location getLocation() { return location; }
    public void setLocation(Location location) {
        this.location = location;
    }
}
```

Here you see @hibernate.many-to-one in action. You've mapped the location field to a location_id column in the events table. XDoclet will extract the correct class, in this case com.manning.hq.Location, by looking at the return type of the getLocation() method. The next step is to make sure that Location itself has a mapping file, which you can generate via XDoclet as well:

```
package com.manning.hq.ch09;

import java.io.Serializable;
/**
 * @hibernate.class table="locations"
 */
public class Location implements Serializable{
    private Long id;

    /**
     * @hibernate.id generator-class="native" column="uid"
     */
    public Long getId() { return id; }
    public void setId(Long id) { this.id = id; }

}
```

There's nothing really new here; you've just defined the Location object with an id field. Now when you run the generate-hbm task via Ant, XDoclet adds the following to the Event.hbm.xml file:

```
<many-to-one
    name="location"
    class="com.manning.hq.ch09.Location"
    cascade="save-update"
    outer-join="auto"
    update="true"
    insert="true"
    access="property"
    column="location_id"
/>
```

A complete many-to-one element has been added to the Event.hbm.xml file. In addition, you may notice the previous code has a few attributes that you might not be familiar with. Check the Hibernate manual and XDoclet manuals for more information.

9.3.2 The @hibernate.component tag

The next basic relationship we want to cover involves components. As you might remember, components are not full-blown entities, like Event or Location, but are just simple value objects whose values are stored in the same table as their parent objects. XDoclet can be used to mark both the component object itself (where the field-to-column mapping must be done) and the component field on the entity object. We'll use the example from chapter 4, where our Location object had an Address component. When XDoclet parses the Java files, it will combine the information from the Address class and Location class into a single Location.hbm.xml. Remember that since Address is a component, it doesn't need its own Address.hbm.xml file.

Using a single component

Generating the mapping files for a component isn't much different than what you've seen. You add @hibernate.property tags to the fields of the component object, but you don't need to declare a @hibernate.class tag on the component. The parent class then uses the @hibernate.component tag to pull the information from the component object. It's a simple tag, with only a few attributes, as table 9.6 shows.

Table 9.6 @hibernate.component **attributes**

Attribute	Description	Default
class	Contains the fully-qualified class name of the component.	The return type of the getter method (XDoclet can usually guess).
prefix	Contains a column prefix that allows multiple components of the same type on a single entity.	No prefix, which is fine when only one component exists per class.

For the simplest cases, neither attribute needs to be specified. XDoclet can usually guess the name of the class, so you don't have to include class. The prefix attribute is only used when you need multiple components of the same type. We look at this prefix in the short section that follows.

Let's put the @hibernate.component tag into motion by marking up our component, the Address object (see listing 9.3).

Listing 9.3 An Address component, XDoclet-style

```
package com.manning.hq.ch09;
import java.io.Serializable;

/** An Address component, it does not have its own identity  */
public class Address implements Serializable {
    private String streetAddress;
    private String city;
    // Other properties omitted

    /**
     * @hibernate.property column="street_address"
     */
    public String getStreetAddress() { return streetAddress; }
    public void setStreetAddress(String streetAddress) {
        this.streetAddress = streetAddress;
    }

    /**
     * @hibernate.property column="city"
     */
    public String getCity() { return city; }
    public void setCity(String city) { this.city = city; }

    // Other getter/setter methods omitted
}
```

As you can see, we have marked the properties as persistent, but there is no @hibernate.class tag that would mark it as a persistent entity. Next, add the following to the Location class you created earlier in this chapter:

```
public class Location implements Serializable{
    // Other properties omitted
    private Address address = new Address();

    // Other getter/setters methods omitted

    /**
     * @hibernate.component
     */
    public Address getAddress() { return address; }
    public void setAddress(Address address) {
        this.address = address;
    }
}
```

The Address component is declared, almost as if it were a many-to-one relationship. Rerun the Ant generate-hbm target and check out the Location.hbm.xml file. Look for the Address component and you should see the following fragment:

```
<component
    name="address"
    class="com.manning.hq.ch09.Address"
>
<property
    name="streetAddress"
    type="java.lang.String"
    update="true"
    insert="true"
    access="property"
    column="street_address"
/>

<property
    name="city"
    type="java.lang.String"
    update="true"
    insert="true"
    access="property"
    column="city"
```

```
/>
<!-- Other properties omitted -->
</component>
```

This fragment shows that XDoclet has combined the property information from `Address` and the component declaration from `Location` into a single Location.hbm.xml mapping file. For an investment of three lines of documentation, we get an approximately 18-line return (excluding whitespace), so how's that for ROI? And consider the time savings if three or four classes used this component. Each one would only need to declare the `@hibernate.component` tag and would have all the same property information generated.

Multiples components on a single class

One of the things you may have noticed from the previous example is that the column information is stored in the `Address` object rather than the `Location` object. What if your `Location` needed two address fields, perhaps a `mailingAddress` and a `billingAddress`? You clearly can't have two city columns in a table, so do you have to resort to the hassle of handwriting the mapping file? Nope. Fortunately, XDoclet provides the `prefix` attribute, which allows you to prefix the column names easily, allowing mailing and billing addresses to coexist peacefully alongside each other on a single `Location`. Modify the `Location` class to add the following changes:

```
public class Location implements Serializable{
    // Other properties omitted
    // Renamed from address to mailingAddress
    private Address mailingAddress = new Address();
    // Added second component, the billingAddress property
    private Address billingAddress = new Address();
    // Other getter/setter methods omitted.
    /**
     * @hibernate.component prefix="mailing_"
     */
    public Address getMailingAddress() { return mailingAddress; }
    public void setMailingAddress(Address mailingAddress) {
```

```
    this.mailingAddress = mailingAddress;}

      /**
       * @hibernate.component prefix="billing_"
       */
      public Address getBillingAddress() { return billingAddress; }
      public void setBillingAddress(Address billingAddress) {
    this.billingAddress = billingAddress; }
    }
```

In this code, you rename one of the properties (address becomes mailingAddress) and add a second property, billingAddress, and then declare prefixes on both of these. Rerunning the Ant generate-hbm target adjusts the Location.hbm.xml with the fragment below. Note that the whitespace has been rearranged a bit.

```
    <component name="mailingAddress"
       class="com.manning.hq.ch09.Address" >
       <property
          name="streetAddress"
          type="java.lang.String"
          update="true"
          insert="true"
          access="property">
             <column name="mailing_street_address"/>
      </property>
    <!-- Other properties omitted. -->
    </component>

    <component name="billingAddress"
       class="com.manning.hq.ch09.Address">
    <property
       name="streetAddress"
       type="java.lang.String"
       update="true"
       insert="true"
       access="property">
    <column name="billing_street_address"/>
    </property>
    <!-Other properties omitted -->
    </component>
```

There is only one trick to getting this to work, which even caught this author off guard at first. (This trick has only been well documented in the latest 1.2.3 version of XDoclet.) You have to modify the `Address` class to use `@hibernate.column` tags, in addition to the `@hibernate.property` tags. Doing this allows XDoclet to prepend the prefix to each column. So looking at the `Address` class, take this:

```
/**
 * @hibernate.property column="street_address"
 */
public String getStreetAddress() { return streetAddress; }
```

and change it into this:

```
/**
 * @hibernate.property
 * @hibernate.column name="street_address"
 */
public String getStreetAddress() { return streetAddress; }
```

These two mappings are functionally the same, but only the second one allows multiple identical components for XDoclet to work.

9.4 Building collections

After discussing XDoclet's ability to generate persistent entities and basic relationships, the only major remaining piece of the puzzle to discuss is collections. The bulk of the XDoclet tags are devoted to handling collections. They are the most complicated of the relationships, and numerous variations exist. As varied as they are, the basic uses between a one-to-many set, a many-to-many list, and a map of components are all fairly similar. So here we are going to cover a simple case and leave the specifics of each association to the appendix.

9.4.1 One-to-many: a kicking set of Speakers

Our next example is a remake of the original Event and Speaker example from chapter 5. Recall that an Event has a one-to-many relationship with Speakers, stored as a Set property on Event. To build a collection with XDoclet, you can't just use a single tag, as we did with the @hibernate.id and @hibernate.many-to-one tags. Instead, you have to use multiple cooperating tags, such as the @hibernate.property and @hibernate.column tags. One of the things that makes XDoclet generation difficult is knowing which tags to use together, something that the XDoclet tag reference documentation doesn't currently make clear. Typically you will need at least three tags, one for each nested element and one for the collection element. The net result is something that is easier to demonstrate than it is to explain, so let's demonstrate first. Modify the Event class as shown in listing 9.4 to give it a set of Speakers and the corresponding XDoclet tags.

Listing 9.4 Event with a set of Speakers

```
import java.util.LinkedHashSet;
import java.util.Set;

/**
 * @hibernate.class table="events"
 */
public class Event implements Serializable {
    // Other properties omitted.
    private Set speakers = new LinkedHashSet();

    // Other getter/setters omitted.

    /**                                              Declares the              Declares the
     * @hibernate.set cascade="save-update"          collection type           foreign key
     * @hibernate.collection-key column="event_id"                              from Speaker
     * @hibernate.collection-one-to-many                                        to Event
class="com.manning.hq.ch09.Speaker"
     */                                      Declares the collection a one-
    public Set getSpeakers() { return speakers; }   to-many along with the class
    public void setSpeakers(Set speakers) {
        this.speakers = speakers; }
}
```

Needing three tags to generate the mapping for just one property may seem a bit overwhelming. This code tells XDoclet that the collection is a Set, which column on the Speaker object is the foreign key back to Event, and that it's a one-to-many (as opposed to a many-to-many) relationship between Events and Speakers. XDoclet cannot inspect the code to determine what class of object the speaker's collection holds, so you must explicitly tell it that it holds a set of com.manning.hq.ch09.Speaker instances. If you rerun the Ant generate-hbm task, the task will add the following fragment to the Event.hbm.xml file:

```
<set name="speakers"
    lazy="false"
    inverse="false"
    cascade="save-update"
    sort="unsorted" >
      <key column="event_id" ></key>
<one-to-many ="com.manning.hq.ch09.Speaker" />
</set>
```

Here the method to XDoclet's madness is made clear. The Rule of XDoclet collections is: To generate collections, every element requires a single XDoclet tag. If you know what the end resulting mapping fragment looks like, you should be able to reasonably determine which tags you need to generate it. For our previous example you needed three elements, as shown in table 9.7, which offers a line-by-line comparison.

Table 9.7 Matching Hibernate mapping elements to XDoclet tags

Mapping Element	XDoclet Tag
<set />	@hibernate.set
A nested <key />	@hibernate.collection-key
A nested <one-to-many />	@hibernate.collection-one-to-many

Given the comparison in table 9.7, what tag do you think you would need if you wanted to change the Speaker to Event one-to-many relationship into a many-to-many relationship? Assume that the end result is an element like this:

```
<set name="speakers" table="as_event_to_speaker">
    <key column="event_id" ></key>
    <many-to-many class="com.manning.hq.ch09.Speaker"
            column="speaker_id" />
</set>
```

If you guessed @hibernate.collection-many-to-many, you'd be absolutely correct. And the prize is that you don't need to scour the XDoclet tag reference using trial and error to guess which one you need to use.[5]

9.4.2 The @hibernate.set tag

Having seen the @hibernate.set tag in action, let's step back and take a look at its common attributes. Since a set supports both many-to-many and one-to-many, some of the attributes are used for each of those cases, as table 9.8 shows.

Table 9.8 Common @hibernate.set attributes

Attribute	Description	Default
cascade	Specifies how cascading operations should be handled from parent to child.	None. Acceptable values include all, none, save-update, all-delete-orphan, and delete.
table	For the many-to-many association only, contains the association table name for joins.	For a many-to-many, it uses the name of the field.

---

[5] Unfortunately, the trial-and-error guessing game of which tag matches which element isn't a particular fun one for us anyway. This is one of the reasons why we created the appendix, which is called "The complete Hibernate mapping catalog."

Table 9.8 Common `@hibernate.set` **attributes (continued)**

Attribute	Description	Default
lazy	Specifies whether the collection should be lazily initialized.	false.
sort	Specifies whether the collection should be sorted in memory. Allows values are unsorted, natural, or the fully qualified class name of a java.util.Comparator.	Collection is not sorted.
order-by	Specifies whether the query to fetch the collection should add a SQL ORDER BY clause. Allowable syntax is column_name asc | desc.	No ORDER BY added. Note that it's a *column* name, not a *property* name.
inverse	Specifies whether the collection is inverse (determines which end of the collection is the parent).	false.

The simplest cases of one-to-many relationships will not likely need any attributes. You can add sorting, ordering, or laziness as your domain model dictates. The `@hibernate.set` tag is not the only collection type allowed; alternatively, `@hibernate.array`, `@hibernate.primitive-array`, `@hibernate.bag`, `@hibernate.list`, and `@hibernate.map` are possible top-level tags as well. In addition, the `@hibernate.set` tag needs the support of two more tags: `@hibernate.collection-key` and `@hibernate.collection-one-to-many` (or `@hibernate.collection-many-to-many`).

9.4.3 The `@hibernate.collection-key`

All of the collections require the use of the <key> element. Otherwise, there is no foreign key to trace back from the individual object to the parent object. Therefore, a `@hibernate.collection-key` tag is necessary as well. It has only one attribute, as you can see in table 9.9.

Table 9.9 `@hibernate.collection-key` **attribute**

Attribute	Description	Default
column	Contains the name of the foreign key column on the object in the collection.	No default; it's mandatory.

One thing might be confusing about this: when dealing with a many-to-many relationship, which foreign key column is which? The `<key>` element/`@hibernate.collection-key` tag/key column is always on object in the collection. The way we like to remember it is that the `<key>` is named after the parent object. So on our example `Event` class, the `<key>` looks like this:

```
<!--This is right. Name the key column after the parent object -->
<key column="event_id"/>
```

and not like this:

```
<!-- Wrong! Don't name keys after the collection -->
<key column="speaker_id"/>
```

9.4.4 The @hibernate.collection-one-to-many tag

The `@hibernate.collection-one-to-many` and the `@hibernate.collection-many-to-many` tags are mutually exclusive because a single collection can only be one or the other. This section details the syntax associated with one-to-many. The many-to-many tag is functionally similar; you can find details about it in the appendix. This simple tag has one attribute, as table 9.10 shows.

Be sure to spell the name of the class correctly; XDoclet won't warn you of a `ClassNotFoundException` during the generation process. A spelling error appears only at runtime (or unit-test time, whichever comes first).

Table 9.10 `@hibernate.collection-one-to-many` **attribute**

Attribute	Description	Default
class	Contains the fully qualified name of the class in the collection.	No default. Though not officially mandatory, since XDoclet can't guess and leaves it blank, you need to specify the class name.

9.5 Going where no XDoclet has gone before

As you may have guessed, most Hibernate relationships can be generated with XDoclet—but certainly not all. As a dynamic open source project, Hibernate is a moving target. New features are added frequently. XDoclet is a separate project from Hibernate, maintained by a separate group of developers, so the features it supports will inevitably lag behind by a bit.

This section covers the way in which you can work around or handle Hibernate mappings that XDoclet won't completely handle. Any code-generation tool has a few scenarios that it isn't fully prepared to cover; obviously, the developers can't code for every possible situation. A good tool like XDoclet provides a number of workaround routes that you can use. Here are a couple of strategies to use with XDoclet if somehow it won't generate what you need:

- Merge points
- Ant property substitution

Which approach you should use depends mainly on the situation and how close the generated files are to what you want them to be. Let's look at each strategy in turn.

9.5.1 Merge points

Perhaps a new version of Hibernate is released that defines a new property mapping that XDoclet doesn't support yet. You don't want to handwrite the entire .hbm.xml file—just the single property. The most common solution for this problem is to use XDoclet's built-in merge feature. Since you shouldn't hand-edit actively generated code,[6] XDoclet lets you inject handwritten code into the final actively generated file. XDoclet refers to these as merge points. The Hibernate module supports injecting handwritten XML configuration into each hbm.xml file. If you look at the generated Event.hbm.xml file, you should see a helpful comment that looks like this:

```
<!-- To add non XDoclet property mappings, create a file named
hibernate-properties-Event.xml containing the additional
properties and place it in your merge dir. -->
```

This tells you that if you write a file called hibernate-properties-Event.xml and put it in the magical merge directory, XDoclet will insert it in the finished Event.hbm.xml file. Suppose, for example, you didn't have access to the Address object. You cannot insert XDoclet tags to nicely generate the component mapping. Instead, you have to include a handwritten component mapping and merge it into the Location.hbm.xml file.

Create a directory named /work/calendar/src/xdt. This will be your merge directory, where your handwritten merge files will go. Then create a file called hibernate-properties-Location.xml in the merge directory. One tricky thing is that the directory structure where the merge file is needs to match the package structure of the class. In this case, create a directory structure that looks like /work/calendar/src/xdt/com/manning/hq/ch09. The hibernate-properties-Location.xml file goes in that directory. Here's what the file should contain:

---

[6] Actively generated code can be automatically regenerated at any time and therefore should not be hand-edited since changes will be lost. This is opposed to passively generated code, which is generated once, and then modified, edited, and checked into source control like any source file would be. All the examples from this chapter have featured active generation.

```xml
<component name="address" class="com.manning.hq.ch09.Address" >
    <property name="streetAddress"
        type="java.lang.String"
        column="street_address"      />
    <!-- Other properties omitted -->
</component>
```

Next, you need to modify the `hibernatedoclet` task in Ant so that it knows where the merge directory is. Make the following modification to the build9.xml file:

```xml
<hibernatedoclet
    destdir="${build.classes.dir}"
    verbose="true"
    mergeDir="src/xdt">
```

This tells XDoclet to use the relative directory of src/xdt as the merge directory. Finally, since you do actually have control over the `Address` source file, you want to modify `Location`'s `address` property. Otherwise, you would have two properties generated, one by XDoclet and one from the merge file. Modify the `getAddress()` method and remove the `@hibernate.component` tag as shown here:

```java
/**
 * Mapping handled by hibernate-properties-Location.xml
 */
public Address getAddress() { return address; }
```

At this point, rerun the `generate-hbm` task. Inspect the Location.hbm.xml file and you should see that the component fragment has been inserted, and the merge comment will be gone.

9.5.2 Property substitution

The primary way Ant can be customized for different deployment environments is by the use of properties. XDoclet builds on this by allowing the use of Ant properties inside an XDoclet tag. Suppose you want to customize the key-generation algorithm for different database deployments. In one case, you want to use hilo, and in another, identity. You'll need two targets in your Ant build.xml, one for each environment that sets the property accordingly:

```
<target name="generate-identity">
    <property name="hibernate.id.value" value="identity"/>
    <antcall target="generate-hbm"/>
</target>
<target name="generate-hilo">
    <property name="hibernate.id.value" value="hilo"/>
    <antcall target="generate-hbm"/>
</target>
```

Calling one target or the other will set the Ant property for that environment; it then regenerates the mapping files. Next you need to modify the Event class to make the @hibernate.id tag dynamic:

```
/**
 * @hibernate.id generator-class="${hibernate.id.value}"
 *   column="uid"
 */
public Long getId() { return id; }
```

Here you have basically inserted an Ant property directly into the XDoclet tag. You can do this for any XDoclet property as well, so there are a huge number of possibilities. It lets you move the details out of the Java classes (where some developers may not want to put things such as table or column names) and into Ant, which can be tweaked for different environments.

Run the generate-hilo target. If all has gone well, when you inspect the Event.hbm.xml file you should see something like this fragment:

```
<id name="id" column="uid" ="java.lang.Long"
    <generator class="hilo"><generator>
</id>
```

The correct Ant property has been inserted during generation, providing a new level of customization for your XDoclet generated files. Alternatively, if you see this you know the Ant property hasn't been set correctly:

```
<id name="id" column="uid" ="java.lang.Long"
   <generator class="${hibernate.id.value}"><generator>
</id>
```

The ${} is a debugging hint: it means the Ant property wasn't set before you ran the hibernatedoclet task, so it just inserted the literal string value. Double-check the order that Ant tasks are being run.

9.6 Generating the hibernate.cfg.xml file

Even removing most of code duplication, you still had to handwrite one file: hibernate.cfg.xml. As you added persistent classes you had to manually add the path of the mapping files to it. Well, no longer. With XDoclet 1.2.3, you can now generate the hibernate.cfg.xml file as part of the build process. It will include all the classes that you have marked with the @hibernate.class tag, as well as the database connection information. You do this by adding a new subtask to the hibernate-doclet task. Add the code in listing 9.5 to the build09.xml.

Listing 9.5 Excerpt from build.xml with hibernatecfg subtask

```
<property file="../hibernate.properties"/>       ◁⎯┐ Loads database
<hibernatedoclet                                       properties as
    destdir="${build.classes.dir}"                     Ant properties
    verbose="true">
    <fileset dir="${src.java.dir}">
        <include name="**/*.java"/>
    </fileset>
    <hibernate version="3.0"/>
    <hibernatecfg
            dialect="${hibernate.dialect}"
            jdbcUrl="${hibernate.connection.url}"
```

```
          driver="${hibernate.connection.driver_class}"
          userName="${hibernate.connection.username}"
          password="${hibernate.connection.password}"
          showSql="false"
          version="3.0"
     />  ◁
  </hibernatedoclet>        | **Uses Ant properties to**
                            | **generate the cfg.xml file**
```

Notice that you add the `hibernatecfg` subtask after the `hibernate` subtask (which as you might remember generates the .hbm.xml files). This will generate the hibernate.cfg.xml file in the `${build.classes.dir}`. Note that since the `hibernatecfg` subtask actually requires the `dialect` attribute, just go ahead and specify all the database connection properties. This means you don't need to add the hibernate.properties file to the classpath but rather load it as Ant properties. Then use them to specify the needed properties to the `hibernatecfg` subtask. Finally, the `version` attribute refers to the target version of Hibernate and can accept either `3.0` or `2.0`.

9.7 Summary

We've covered a lot of ground in this chapter, but there's much that we haven't covered. For more information on other collection types, I recommend you check out the XDoclet Hibernate Tag Reference and the Hibernate Reference documentation. Both are packaged with their respective applications. We often bounce between them to find the details of what our mapping files should look like, and then match up the needed XDoclet tags to reverse-engineer our desired mapping files.

As you've learned in this chapter, while Hibernate requires mapping files, you don't need to be burdened with writing them. The single definitive source for the association and relationships can and should be the Java source code. Information should not be duplicated between files, and class information should stay in that class.

XDoclet is a code-generation tool that allows you to generate mapping files from the single definitive source: the source code. It cuts the hand-written work, reduces the errors that evils of duplication cause, and facilitates rapid evolution of a project.

In this chapter, we explained how to install XDoclet, a tool that is used during the build phase of a project. We explored how single object associations can be expressed and generated with XDoclet, including components. All of the essential Hibernate mapping elements can be generated, such as <class>, <id>, and <property>. XDoclet can create collection association elements like <map>, <list> and <set>. Most of the associations that Hibernate allows can be expressed using XDoclet, and, where that's not possible, XDoclet provides extension points such as merge points and property substitution.

Overall, XDoclet is a popular open source code-generation tool that belongs in any Java developer's toolkit. It's a great timesaving tool that can be used with Hibernate as well as a number of other projects.

10

Unit testing with JUnit and DBUnit

This chapter covers

- Learning to write tests with JUnit
- Using JUnit to test Hibernate
- Applying DBUnit to reset database state

When the coding is done, how do you know your program is working as you intended? Generally, the answer is testing. Writing code is only half the battle; you need to verify that the code is doing what you think it should. There are many types of testing, often done by members of your staff. You may have acceptance testing done by the Quality Assurance department on behalf of the customer, or integration testing defined by your architect or development lead to make sure all the parts of the system are working together. But the bedrock beneath all the higher-level tests is the unit test. Developers unit-test their code by making sure the small bits of code (usually methods or classes) work in isolation.

Unit tests can be carried out either manually or automatically. Manual testing is merely acceptable, allowing a developer to spot-check that one or two methods are working correctly. In Java it usually results in a lot of `System.out.println()` statements or clicking around on a GUI. This approach has the benefit of requiring little investment, but is labor intensive and doesn't catch bugs in parts of the system that aren't being actively tested. Automatic testing, on the other hand, takes a bit of work up front, but once you write your tests, you have a suite that can be frequently and automatically run, assuring that bugs stay fixed.

This chapter is all about writing the automatic tests for your Hibernate projects. We introduce an open source framework, JUnit, which is the de facto standard for writing unit tests in Java. Unit testing is easy for simple cases, but testing persistence layers, like Hibernate, is more complex. This chapter aims to make that easier.

Chapter goals

By the end of the chapter, you should be able to do the following:

- Understand why unit testing is important.
- Know to how to get and install JUnit.
- Create a basic test with JUnit.
- Set up your environment and write tests for your Hibernate layer.
- Use DBUnit to set up and tear down a database for testing.

Assumptions

Since this chapter covers how to test Hibernate, we expect you to understand the basics of Hibernate. In addition, while we'll cover some basic tenets of how to write unit tests, you should have some understanding of how to do testing, either manually or automatically. We'll build on this basic knowledge to explain how Hibernate should be tested.

10.1 Introduction to unit testing

The core philosophy behind automated unit testing is that you should test everything that could possibly break. As you build your program, you write unit tests in the same code in which you're writing the program. Method by method, class by class, verify that everything works as it should, and when you're done, you have a suite of tests for the life of your program that can be used to make sure it stays working.

10.1.1 Automate those tests

Unlike with visual inspections, you don't manually evaluate what each method is doing every time you test it. Instead, you write code that exercises and verifies that your methods do exactly what you think they should. Using a framework like JUnit facilitates this by providing a support structure to collect and run all the tests together.

To write some tests, you need to have a class to test. In this chapter, let's start with the basic Event we have seen in previous chapters. We'll add a method to it, isScheduledBefore(), which determines whether the event is scheduled to start before a given date. This is the type of method you might often see on a domain object, because it encapsulates logic about the domain object where it belongs, inside Event. The method looks like this:

```
/**
 * Determines if this event is scheduled before the given date.
 * @param date - The date to compare against.
 * @return true - if the event.startDate is prior to the given
   date.
 */
public boolean isScheduledBefore(Date date) {
    return this.startDate.getTime() < date.getTime();
}
```

This is a fairly simple method, but there could easily be a bug in it, for example, if you used a > instead of a <. It's worth writing a unit test to verify that the method works as expected, and stays working if you later need to modify it. So let's write a sample unit test.

10.1.2 Assertions

Using JUnit, you start by extending the basic junit.framework.TestCase class. Typically, for every class you test, you create at least one TestCase. Here, for the Event class, create a TestEvent. It helps to follow a consistent naming convention, so for a Class X, you create a TestX or XTest.

JUnit works on the basis of assertions. Each test runs a method, given a set of inputs, and verifies that the methods return the expected values. If an assertion fails, it throws an exception, which JUnit collects for you, and generates a report. Listing 10.1 shows the TestEvent.java file you should create now.

Listing 10.1 TestEvent.java, the JUnit test for Event

```
package com.manning.hq.ch10;

import junit.framework.TestCase;

import java.util.Calendar;
import java.util.Date;

public class TestEvent extends TestCase {
    public void testIsScheduledBefore() {
        Calendar c = Calendar.getInstance();
        c.set(2004, 5, 1);
        Date beforeDate = c.getTime();

        c.set(2004, 6, 1);
        Date actual = c.getTime();

        c.set(2004, 7, 1);
        Date afterDate = c.getTime();

        Event event = new Event();
        event.setStartDate(actual);

        assertTrue("Should be before",
    event.isScheduledBefore(afterDate));
        assertFalse("Should be after",
    event.isScheduledBefore(beforeDate));
    }
}
```

❶ Sets up sample dates

❷ Populates the data on our event

❸ Asserts that the method returns true

❹ Asserts that the method returns false

As you can see, this class has a single method, testIsScheduled-Before(), which follows yet another naming convention. Any method that starts with testXXX will be automatically collected into a suite and run by the JUnit framework. You'll see how this works in section 10.2, but for now, just know that all your test methods should be named in this way. Here's a breakdown of what the method is doing:

❶ The test needs sample data to use. So create three Date objects: your actual start date, and then a date before and after.

❷ Create an event, and populate it with the sample data.

❸ The assertTrue() method takes two arguments: a description and a Boolean condition. Here the Boolean condition is the isScheduledBefore() method. You expect that if you pass it afterDate, it will return true.

❹ Here you expect isScheduledBefore() to return false, since you're passing in a date that is prior to your event. The assertFalse() method verifies this.

10.1.3 Expect failures

So you have coded exactly how your method should work. When you run your test method, as you'll learn how to do in section 10.2, you should get the message "All Tests Passed." Suppose, instead, you'd made an error in your isScheduleBefore() method; what would the failure message look like? Something like this:

```
    [junit] Testcase:
testIsScheduledBefore(com.manning.hq.ch10.TestEvent):
FAILED
    [junit] Should be before
    [junit] junit.framework.AssertionFailedError: Should be before
    [junit]      at
com.manning.hq.ch10.TestEvent.testIsScheduledBefore
(TestEvent.java:27)... (Stack Trace continued)
```

The message indicates a few things. First, you can see the name of the test class and method that failed. Second, often you may have more than one assert in a test method, so the assert description you put in your assert method ("Should be before") is also displayed. Finally, a portion of the stack trace, with the exact line of code that threw the exception (27) is displayed, so that you can easily debug the method. Note that for the exact line number to appear, you must compile with debug mode on, which we'll look at in the next section. Both assertion labels and exact line numbers in the exception will help to rapidly determine that your method is broken, as well as where it is broken, so that it can be fixed just as quickly.

Having written a basic unit test, let's look at how to install a JUnit, set it up in your build file, and run your unit test. Also, we'll discuss a few tips on how to organize the unit tests for best results.

10.2 JUnit

Having seen what a simple unit test looks like, let's cover how to install JUnit and incorporate it into our build process. This may be familiar to some readers already, so if you already know how to get and install JUnit, feel free to skip ahead to section 10.3.

The first thing you need to do is download the JUnit library. You can find it at www.junit.org, along with sample documentation. At the time of writing, the current version was 3.8.1. Download the zip file and install it alongside your other applications (on Windows, extract to C:\applications\junit3.8.1). If you look into the expanded directory, the really important file is the junit.jar file; the other files consist of user guides, sample code, and JavaDocs.

10.2.1 Test-infecting your build file

One of the terms used to describe developers who enjoy (yes, it is possible) writing unit tests is "test infected"—they catch the "bug" and find writing tests to be extremely productive and satisfying. So on your path to positive testing karma, the next step is to introduce it into your Ant build file.

Ant provides several tasks specifically for working with JUnit: `junit` and `junitreport`. Both are optional tasks, and both depend on having the junit.jar file in the classpath. Ant actually makes this easy on you and already includes a copy of the junit.jar file.

The JUnit task

The `junit` task runs one or more JUnit tests and compiles the results. When you run tests, you obviously want to see the results. By default it just reports the overall successes and failures, so you generally want more information. For more detailed results, the task allows a number of possible outputs, called formatters, including straight to the console, or a formatted plain-text or XML file. If you generate an XML file, you can use the next task, `junitreport`, to nicely format the results in an HTML page. Here's a sample of what a JUnit task would look like in your build file:

```
<junit printsummary="true" >
    <classpath refid="runtime.classpath"/>
        <batchtest todir="${reports.dir}">
            <fileset dir="${build.classes.dir}"
                includes="**/Test*.class"/>
        </batchtest>
        <formatter type="brief" usefile="false"/>
        <formatter type="xml" usefile="true" />
</junit>
```

Here's what this task is doing. First, by specifying `printsummary="true"`, it summarizes all the test methods with a single class and prints a line to the console that looks like this:

```
[junit] Running com.manning.hq.ch10.TestEvent
[junit] Tests run: 1, Failures: 1, Errors: 0,
    Time elapsed: 0 sec
```

Next, you need to specify the classpath that contains your test case (TestEvent.class), any class being tested (Event.class), junit.jar, and the third-party JAR files (like Hibernate).

Next you run a batch test, which is extremely useful. Recall our point about consistently naming the TestCases? Here's where it pays off. The <batchtest> element finds and runs any TestCase that matches the **/Test*.class pattern. So any class in any directory that starts with Test will be run. In addition, any generated files will be written out to the ${reports.dir} directory.

At this point, the brief formatter prints details for the tests that fail to the console, such as the stack trace and description you saw in section 10.1.3.

The XML formatter then generates an XML file, in the ${reports.dir} directory, with detailed statistics on each test case. One report file will be generated for each TestCase class; by default it's based on the class name, and would be called TEST-com.manning.hq.ch10.TestEvent.xml.

With the junit task set up, you can create new TestCases anywhere in your project, and it will automatically pick them up and run them. Let's now look at how you can nicely format the test results in a publishable HTML file.

The junitreport task

Once you have your results, you might want to publish the results, perhaps on your corporate intranet. To do this, add the junitreport task to your build file. This task has an external dependency on the Xalan Extensible Stylesheet Language Transformation (XSLT) processor (2.x or later). It collects all test results and runs an XSLT style sheet on them to generate the HTML files. Let's take a look at a sample task that will convert the raw XML generated from the previous section into a nicely formatted HTML page, complete with navigable frames.

```
<junitreport todir="${reports.dir}">
    <fileset dir="${reports.dir}">
```

```
            <include name="TEST-*.xml"/>
        </fileset>
        <report format="frames" todir="${reports.dir}/html"/>
    </junitreport>
```

The whole process consists of two steps; first, the task compiles all the individual test case reports into a single XML document, by default called TESTS-TestSuites.xml. It then converts that to HTML. Here's a detailed breakdown of the task:

In the first line, the task specifies where the aggregate report (TESTS-TestSuites.xml) will be written out. Next, the fileset specifies the location where all the individual class report XML files are. (For this example, this is the same directory where you generate the aggregate report.)

Finally, the <report> element specifies the directory to write out the HTML files and to use frames for navigation.

When you are done, you should have a reports/html directory, which contains the nicely formatted text. To see the reports, open the index.html file in your web browser. Figure 10.1 shows a sample of what the output looks like.

Both the junit and junitreport tasks work together to make adding and running tests an easy part of your build process. Next, let's take a look at a more complete build file that puts everything together.

10.2.2 Polishing off the build file

Although you've seen the syntax for the individual JUnit tasks, you haven't seen how they fit into the overall build file. You have a few remaining things to do, including creating the reports directory and adding a new target to the build file.

What you shouldn't need to do is add the junit.jar file. For the simple cases, you don't have to do anything to get JUnit into the classpath. A copy of it comes bundled with Ant, so no additional action is needed. This is more of an issue with older versions of Ant; thankfully this

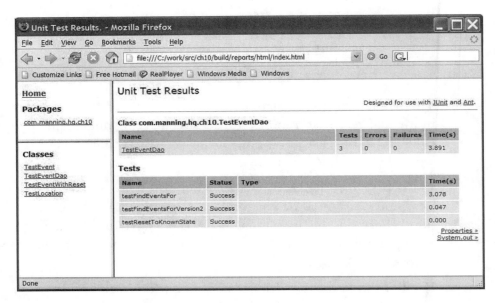

Figure 10.1 HTML output for the `junitreport` task

problem has disappeared due to more convenient packaging in the more current versions.

Building the reports directory

Because your reports are derived products from your source code, much like .class files, they are not checked in version control and are regenerated each time you build the project. So you want to rebuild the reports directory each time you run the complete build. You also want to create the properties that you can reuse throughout the build file. Here's what that looks like:

```
<property name="build.classes.dir" value="build/classes"/>
<property name="reports.dir" value="build/reports"/>
<!--Other properties and targets omitted -->
<target name="clean">
    <delete dir="${build.classes.dir}"/>
    <delete dir="${reports.dir}"/>
</target>
<target name="init">
```

```
        <mkdir dir="${build.classes.dir}"/>
        <mkdir dir="${reports.dir}"/>
    </target>
```

As you can see, this code features a new property, `${reports.dir}`, which should go near the top of the file, next to the `${build.classes.dir}` property. You've also modified the clean and init tasks so that they delete and create the directory each time.

Adding a testing task

Finally, you want to create a new task, which will run your unit tests and will be called when your normal build target is called. Listing 10.2 shows the new target, as well as the modified build target.

Listing 10.2 A new target, test, that runs the unit tests and generate reports, along with the modified build target

```
    <target name="test">
       <junit printsummary="true">
           <classpath refid="runtime.classpath"/>
           <batchtest todir="${reports.dir}" >
               <fileset dir="${build.classes.dir}"
                   includes="**/Test*.class"/>
           </batchtest>
           <formatter type="brief" usefile="false"/>
           <formatter type="xml" usefile="true"/>
       </junit>
       <junitreport todir="${reports.dir}">
           <fileset dir="${reports.dir}">
               <include name="TEST-*.xml"/>
           </fileset>
           <report format="frames" todir="${reports.dir}/html"/>
       </junitreport>
    </target>
    <target name="build"
        depends="clean,generate-hbm,test"
        description="Compiles all the classes in the chapter,
            generates the .hbm.xml and runs the unit tests.">
    </target>
```

As you can see, the new target just runs both JUnit tasks in the proper order. You've also modified the build target to make sure it runs the unit tests as a standard part of the build. You've now integrated the JUnit framework into your build process. It should be very straightforward to extend your test coverage by adding new test cases. So having covered a simple unit test, let's kick it up a notch by learning how to test Hibernate code.

10.3 Testing the persistence layer

Let's be honest: using JUnit to test a simple class in isolation is pretty darn trivial. It gets quite a bit more complex when you try to test code that is "connected" to other systems, such as a database. Some people recommend using Mock objects to stub out things like databases. This works fine, if you're trying to test something like a Struts Action, and you mock your DAOs to return sample data rather than go to the database. But how do you know that your DAOs work correctly? Did you write your HQL correctly?

This section covers the basics of testing your persistence layer, what to test, and when testing is valuable. We'll discuss the fundamentals of what testing a database is all about, as well as what about Hibernate we are testing.

10.3.1 What do we want to test?

The first thing you should decide is what you're going to test. An Agile methodology, like Extreme Programming (www.extremeprogramming.org), recommends that you test everything that could possibly break. For your persistence layer, Hibernate, there are a number of things you expect to work. You have to verify them somehow, and unit tests are a great way to do this. Here is an overview of some of the common things you should verify.

Expect classes to be persistent

The most basic error is that you try to save a class that hasn't been declared persistent, i.e., you failed to add its mapping file to the hibernate.cfg.xml file or to your Spring applicationContext.xml file. Or you didn't create a mapping file at all. Unit testing can verify that classes can be saved or loaded.

Expect mapped fields to persist

A second point of failure involves the details of our mapping files. You want to make sure you've defined your persistence mappings correctly. The error could be a misspelled field name or more likely a completely missing field. The latter would mean a field is actually just transient and never gets written out to the database. This category of bugs includes mistakes in field/columns modifiers, such as expecting a field to be unique or holding more than 255 characters.

Expect persistent entities to cascade

In addition to the simple fields, bugs can exist in the more complex relationships, such as many-to-one or collections. Here you want to verify both that the entities save to the database correctly and that the cascades you declared work correctly. For example, if you create a new Event with a corresponding many-to-one Location, you want to verify that the cascade="save-update" is actually saving both new objects with a single save() call.

Expect queries to return the right objects

In a Hibernate application, you'll typically write a lot of HQL queries. You expect these queries to return the right set of objects based on the criteria you specified. If you take our recommendation and collect all your HQL into a data access layer, this essentially amounts to testing the DAO layer. A unit test can verify that a query works at all (i.e., an HQL syntax check), that it returns the objects it should, and that it doesn't return objects it shouldn't.

10.3.2 Testing basic persistence

Having now covered some of the basic scenarios you'd want to write unit tests for, let's go ahead and actually write a few tests. In this section, you'll write a simple test that verifies that Events persist correctly, along with a few of their fields.

Organizing your tests

You'll modify the TestEvent you created in section 10.1.2, but before you do, let's back up and talk about organizing your test files. The question to answer is: where do you actually create the TestEvent file?

Typically, you want a test class to be in the same package as the class being tested. This allows you to call and test package-scoped methods, which can be useful. But you also don't want to make it too difficult to separate the unit tests from the production code. The solution is to create a mirror directory structure, which allows keeping the source separate but in the same package.

So create a /test directory in parallel to the /java directory. This directory will hold all the JUnit tests. Within that directory, create a com/manning/hq/ch10 directory, and add the TestEvent.java file there. When you're done, you should have something similar to the following directory structure:

```
/src/java/com/manning/hq/ch10/Event.java
/src/test/com/manning/hq/ch10/TestEvent.java
```

Since the TestEvent.java file isn't in our Ant-defined directory, ${src.java.dir}, it won't be compiled along with the production source code. So you need to add the following to your Ant build file to compile the test code:

```
<property name="test.java.dir" value="src/test"/>

<target name="compile" depends="init">
    <javac srcdir="${src.java.dir}"
        destdir="${build.classes.dir}" debug="true">
        <classpath refid="hibernate.lib.path"/>
    </javac>
    <javac srcdir="${test.java.dir}"
        destdir="${build.classes.dir}" debug="true">
        <classpath refid="hibernate.lib.path"/>
```

```
        </javac>
    </target>
```

The new portions appear in bold. You define a new property for the directory of the tests and then add a second compile task to compile the source code to the same location as the production code. At this point, you have everything you need to add the modifications to write your persistence test next.

Event, persist thyself!

In this section, you'll persist an event and make sure it works for saves and loads correctly. Listing 10.3 contains the test method.

Listing 10.3 TestEvent.java, with a `testPersists()` method which verifies that an Event saves and loads correctly

```
package com.manning.hq.ch10;
import org.hibernate.Session;
import com.manning.hq.ch10.HibernateFactory;
                                                          Opens two    ❶
                                                           different
public void testPersists() throws Exception {             sessions
    HibernateFactory.buildSessionFactory();
    Session session = HibernateFactory.openSession();
    Session session2 = HibernateFactory.openSession();

    Event event = new Event();                      ❷  Creates your
    event.setName("Hello, I'm an Event!");             transient event
    try {                                              and populates it
        session.save(event);          ❸  Saves the event and
        session.flush();                 flushes changes to
                                         the database

        Event actualEvent = (Event)            Loads the event from  ❹
            session2.load(Event.class, event.getId());   a different session
        assertNotNull("Should return an object", actualEvent);
        assertEquals("Ids should match",
            event.getId(), actualEvent.getId());     Verifies the   ❺
        assertEquals("Check names",                    object is
            event.getName(), actualEvent.getName());   loaded
    } finally {                                         correctly
        session.delete(event);     ❻  Restores the database and
        session.flush();              cleans up the sessions
```

```
        HibernateFactory.close(session);
        HibernateFactory.close(session2);
    }
}
```

Overall, the testPersists() method creates an Event, saves it, loads it, and finally cleans up and deletes it. So if it works, it verifies a number of the conditions we mentioned in section 10.3.1. Here's a detailed breakdown:

❶ You initialize the SessionFactory and create two different sessions. Why two? Remember that sessions keep an in-memory cache of all the objects that they save or load for performance reasons. So if you saved an event and then loaded it through the same session, it wouldn't really tell you that the new row was created in the database. Using a second session is one way to verify it's a complete trip to the database.

❷ Here you create your event and give it some sample data.

❸ Next, you save the event and flush the changes to the database.

❹ Here you load the event through the second session, using the primary key that was assigned to the event object by Hibernate.

❺ Do a few tests to make sure the object was returned (not null), and that it matches the id and name field. You can easily verify that other fields are persisting as well by adding them to the method, just like the name field.

❻ After your test is done, you need to clean up after yourself. You want to reset the database to its original state before the test so that you don't alter the behavior of other unit tests. So you delete the event that you created and close the sessions.

That's a sample unit test in a nutshell. It certainly could use a bit of refactoring, but it gets the job done. Some potential points of refactoring include moving the setup of data and cleanup into JUnit's setUp() and tearDown() methods, which you'll see in section 10.3.4.

10.3.3 Testing queries

Much like testing basic persistence, you can also do tests to verify that your queries work correctly. The general rule to follow involves putting a few objects into the database, some of which should be returned and others that will not. This allows you to avoid both false positives and negatives, where a query returns either too much or too little data.

Assume for a moment that you want to test the `findEventsFor()` method from the `EventDao` class in chapter 8, which looked like this:

```
public List findEventsFor(int month, int year);
```

It returns all `Events` based on a `Date` for a given month and year. Under the covers, it uses an HQL query that looks something like this:

```
from Event event where event.startDate >=
    :firstDay and event.startDate < :lastDay
```

You want to verify that the HQL is written correctly and that your method works as expected, so you need to write a unit test for it. Go ahead and create a `TestEventDao` (listing 10.4) in the same directory as the `TestEvent` class.

Listing 10.4 TestEventDao.java, with a `testEventsFor()` method

```
package com.manning.hq.ch10;

import java.util.List;
import org.hibernate.Session;
import com.manning.hq.ch10.HibernateFactory;
import com.manning.hq.ch10.EventDao;
import com.manning.hq.ch10.DateUtils;
import junit.framework.TestCase;

public void testFindEventsFor() throws Exception{
    Event eventBefore = new Event();      ◁── Creates three events
    Event eventIn = new Event();
    Event eventAfter = new Event();                   Sets dates for
                                                   months being testing
    eventBefore.setStartDate(DateUtils.newDate(6, 1, 2005));  ◁─
    eventIn.setStartDate(DateUtils.newDate(7, 1, 2005));
```

```
eventAfter.setStartDate(DateUtils.newDate(8, 1, 2005));

EventDao eventDao = new EventDao();
Session session = HibernateFactory.openSession();
try {
    session.save(eventBefore);   ←—— Persists the test events

    session.save(eventAfter);
    session.save(eventIn);
    session.flush();                              Runs the query

    List eventsFor = eventDao.findEventsFor(7, 2005);   ←—
    assertEquals("Should return 1", 1, eventsFor.size());   ←—
    Event actualEvent = (Event) eventsFor.get(0);
    assertEquals("Should be eventIn, not the other events.",
        eventIn.getId(), actualEvent.getId());    Verifies the
} finally {                                       results of
    session.delete(eventBefore);   ←—— Cleans up  the query
    session.delete(eventIn);
    session.delete(eventAfter);
    session.flush();
    HibernateFactory.close(session);
    }
}
```

Let's review the code more in depth. First, by creating three events, you can test that the query returns events in the given month, but not those from the two surrounding months. Note that you save the months using the session, rather than the EventDao, since you're testing the find-EventsFor(), not the create() or delete() method. After running the query, check the size of the results list. Verify that only one event is returned, and that the event you expected was the one returned.

Note that there is a pretty big assumption underlying this test: as it's written, you might get false negatives. In other words, this method can actually fail, even though the findEventsFor() method works correctly. If there are excess objects (events) in the database (maybe from other tests), they could be returned by the query, causing failures. We discuss ways to avoid this in the next section.

10.3.4 General database testing tips

In the previous sections, we looked at examples of writing unit tests for your Hibernate code. The tests so far illustrate a few of the important items you should test and how to test them. This section adds more tips, which should streamline your database testing.

Use multiple databases

To test a database, you must have a database to test against. We've assumed you're using a local developer database. On a project, each developer should have his or her own local database, which the developer uses to run the tests against. This approach has multiple benefits.

For one, database testing is naturally slow even when you run tests against a local copy of the database; you don't add network latency into the equation by testing against a remote database, which would make it slower still. Second, and more important, it's safer because you're isolated from other database operations. This means you can do whatever is necessary to the database without worrying about affecting production data or other developers.

As an additional step, you may even want to have a second local database, specifically for automated testing. This allows for a populated local database to perform manual tests without having to worry about them affecting the automated tests.

With the examples thus far, you've used the `events_calendar` database for your web application and other tests. A second automated test database might be called `events_calendar_testing`. The only mild complication is how you configure the hibernate.cfg.xml file to point to the different databases, one for deploying your application and the other for unit testing. What you definitely don't want to do is write two different hibernate.cfg.xml files; duplication is bad news.

Several courses of action are at your disposal. In chapter 3, we looked at using both a hibernate.cfg.xml and a hibernate.properties file. You can have multiple hibernate.properties, for multiple databases.

A second method available is Ant filtering, as used with XDoclet property substitution in chapter 9. When you insert special @ symbols around properties in the file, Ant can replace them at build time. Here's what the prefiltered hibernate.cfg.xml file would look like:

```
<hibernate-configuration>
  <session-factory>
    <property name="connection.username">@db.username@</property>
    <property name="connection.password">@db.password@</property>
    <property name="connection.url">@db.url@</property>
    <property
      name="connection.driver_class">@db.driver@</property>
    <property name="dialect">@db.dialect@</property>
    <mapping resource="com/manning/hq/ch10/Event.hbm.xml"/>
    <mapping resource="com/manning/hq/ch10/Speaker.hbm.xml"/>
    <mapping resource="com/manning/hq/ch10/Location.hbm.xml"/>
  </session-factory>
</hibernate-configuration>
```

This code allows a single file to be deployed against any number of databases, and can even be used to deploy an application to development, testing, and production servers. The next step is to filter the file using Ant filter targets and separate properties file for each database. Here's what the unit-test.properties file might look like:

```
db.username=root
db.password=
db.url=jdbc:mysql://localhost/events_testing
db.driver=com.mysql.jdbc.Driver
db.dialect=org.hibernate.dialect.MySQLDialect
```

The final step is to write the Ant filter (listing 10.5) that copies and replaces the database values.

Listing 10.5   Portion of build10.xml, demonstrating how to load the properties file and the filter hibernate.cfg.xml

```
<target name="set-unit-testing">
    <property file="unit-test.properties" />          ◁──┐ Loads properties
</target>                                                  │ from a properties file
<target name="filter-cfg">
    <filterset id="db.filtering" >                    Replaces @db.username@
        <filter token="db.username" value="${db.username}" />  ◁──┐ with property value
        <filter token="db.password" value="${db.password}" />
        <filter token="db.url" value="${db.url}" />
        <filter token="db.driver" value="${db.driver}" />
        <filter token="db.dialect" value="${db.dialect}" />
    </filterset>
    <copy todir="${build.classes.dir}">
        <fileset file="src/config/hibernate.cfg.xml" />
        <filterset refid="db.filtering" />
    </copy>
</target>
<target name="generate-unit-testing"                      ┐ Loads properties file
    depends="set-unit-testing,filter-cfg"/>   ◁──┘ and runs filter
```

Listing 10.5 shows how the same filtering logic can be used to filter and deploy the same hibernate.cfg.xml file for multiple environments. Using this technique allows you to run your tests against any database that you need to.

Write nonbrittle tests

Another way to make sure your tests are quite robust is to not assume too much knowledge about what rows might be in database already. It would be counterproductive for a query test to fail just because there was an extra event in the database. Take, for example, this test from section 10.3.3:

```
List eventsFor = eventDao.findEventsFor(7, 2005);
assertEquals("Should return 1", 1, eventsFor.size());
Event actualEvent = (Event) eventsFor.get(0);
```

```
assertEquals("Should be Event In, not the other events.",
    eventIn.getId(), actualEvent.getId());
```

Here you expected exactly one row to be returned. That's great if you can be 100 percent certain that only one row should come back. But it's a bit brittle. Below is a more robust version, but still you get only the event you expect and not the ones you didn't:

```
assertTrue("Should return 1", eventsFor.size() >= 1);
assertTrue("Should contain", contains(eventsFor, eventIn));
assertFalse("Shouldn't contain before", contains(eventsFor,
eventBefore));
assertFalse("Shouldn't contain after", contains(eventsFor,
eventAfter));
```

This, of course, requires you to add a method to TestEvent.java to verify that the list contains your event:

```
import java.util.Iterator;
import java.util.List;

private boolean contains(List list, Event contained) {
    for (Iterator it = list.iterator(); it.hasNext();) {
        Event event = (Event) it.next();
        if(event.getId().equals(contained.getId())){
            return true;
        }
    }
    return false;
}
```

The new assertions are less likely to fail when there is other extraneous data in the returned list. You just need to add a new method to iterate over the result set, since you can't know where the extra objects might be.

If you know exactly what is in the database, this technique might not be necessary. But in case you don't, avoid brittle tests.

Reset the database to a known state

As mentioned earlier, one of the most important principles of testing is that the results for each test shouldn't affect any other tests. With database testing, this requires extra caution; because the database is shared between all the tests, what you leave in the database in one test can easily affect the next one.

The best way to avoid this problem is to reset the database to a known state between test runs. You've done a fairly simple form of this in your unit tests so far, by using a `finally` block to delete each object that you insert, like so:

```
Session session = HibernateFactory.openSession();
try {
    session.save(eventBefore);
    session.save(eventAfter);
    session.save(eventIn);
    session.flush();

    // Actual testing code excluded for brevity
} finally {
    session.delete(eventBefore);
    session.delete(eventIn);
    session.delete(eventAfter);
    session.flush();
    HibernateFactory.close(session);
}
```

This works, but you have to be vigilant and make sure you don't forget to clean up after yourself. An easier alternative is available if you're using a local testing database. You can use the `setUp()` method to reset the database to empty before each test:

```
protected void setUp () throws Exception {
    super.setUp();
    Session session = HibernateFactory.openSession();
    session.createQuery("delete Event").executeUpdate();
    HibernateFactory.close(session);
}
```

As you may know, the setUp() method is run before every test. Here you've overridden it so that it deletes all rows from your events table before every test. This ensures that no extra rows sneak into your queries. We use Hibernate's batch delete feature to remove the rows without having to load all the persistent objects into memory.

In the next section, we introduce an extension to JUnit specifically for testing database-related code.

10.4 Testing with DBUnit

Unit-testing database code presents some different challenges. To have effective tests, you must ensure that the database is in a consistent state before and after each test run. Throughout this chapter, you've been using Hibernate to set up and tear down your tests. Although this approach works, it could be argued that because you're actually testing Hibernate, you should use something other than Hibernate to set up the tests and confirm that operations performed by Hibernate have succeeded. This is where DBUnit comes in.

DBUnit, written by Manuel Laflamme, is designed to make reproducible database testing easier. It provides mechanisms to load test data, validate the state of database tables, and clean up once tests have run.

10.4.1 Loading test data

In the past, developers have had to load test data into databases using SQL scripts. The disadvantage of using SQL scripts for test data is that they can be difficult to maintain if the database structure changes. DBUnit allows you to create a DTD of your database schema and use an XML file to store test data. While typically more verbose than a SQL script, XML has the advantage of validating against the DTD, which informs you when your test data is out of date.

Creating the DTD

All of the tasks performed by DBUnit are performed through Ant tasks, including creating the DTD of the database schema. The dbunit task to create the DTD is shown here:

```
<target name="create-db-schema">
    <property file="hibernate.properties"/>
    <taskdef name="dbunit" classname="org.dbunit.ant.DbUnitTask"
        classpathref="runtime.classpath"/>
    <dbunit driver="${hibernate.connection.driver}"
        url="${hibernate. connection.url}"
        userid="${hibernate. connection.username}"
        password="${hibernate. connection.password}">
        <export dest="database-schema.dtd" format="dtd"/>
    </dbunit>
</target>
```

Here, you're getting the property values from the hibernate.proper-ties file in the example source tree. Executing this task creates a file named database-schema.dtd in the current directory. You then refer-ence the DTD in the XML file containing your test data.

Creating test data

DBUnit supports a few different XML formats. The easiest one to use is the flat XML format, in which each element represents a row of test data and the individual columns are represented by the attributes. For example, consider the following:

```
<dataset>
<!DOCTYPE dataset SYSTEM "database-schema.dtd">
    <events id="1937" name="Test Event 1"
        start_date="2005-01-27" duration="180"/>
</dataset>
```

This <dataset> element represents a single row of test data for the events table. The <dataset> element is the root element for the XML; all test data elements must be contained within <dataset> elements. Once you've created the test data, you can import it into the database.

Importing test data

Depending on how you choose to execute your tests, you could import the test data using Ant or programmatically. Let's look at how to use Ant first. The Ant task is shown here:

```
<target name="import-test-data">
    <taskdef name="dbunit" classname="org.dbunit.ant.DbUnitTask"
        classpathref="runtime.classpath"/>
    <dbunit driver="${hibernate.connection.driver}"
        url="${hibernate. connection.url}"
        userid="${hibernate. connection.username}"
        password="${hibernate. connection.password}">
        <operation type="INSERT" src="testdata.xml"/>
    </dbunit>
</target>
```

The `<operation>` element has the `type` attribute set to INSERT, which means the test data will be inserted into the tables. All options to the type attribute are shown in table 10.1.

Table 10.1 DBUnit Ant operations

Type Operation	Definition
INSERT	Inserts the contents of the dataset into the database.
UPDATE	Updates the data that exists in the database with the contents of the dataset.
DELETE	Deletes the contents of the dataset from the database.
DELETE_ALL	Deletes all rows of data from the database that are contained in the dataset.
REFRESH	Refreshes the contents of the database to match the dataset.
CLEAN_INSERT	Removes the contents of the database and inserts the contents of the dataset.
MSSQL_ INSERT	Performs special insert operation for Microsoft's SQL server.
MSSQL_REFRESH	Performs special refresh operation for Microsoft's SQL server.
MSSQL_CLEAN_INSERT	Performs special clean insert operation for Microsoft's SQL server.

Test data can also be loaded programmatically, which is valuable if you've created a base test case and store the data for each test case in separate files. We'll expand on the custom subclass of DatabaseTest-Case in the next section, but first, let's look at the method used to load the test data, shown in listing 10.6.

Listing 10.6 Importing test data programmatically

```
package com.manning.hq.ch10;

import org.dbunit.DatabaseTestCase;

import org.dbunit.dataset.IDataSet;
import org.dbunit.dataset.xml.FlatXmlDataSet;
import java.io.InputStream;

public abstract class ProjectDatabaseTestCase
    extends DatabaseTestCase {

    public ProjectDatabaseTestCase(String name) {
        super(name);
    }

    protected abstract String getDataSetFilename();

    protected IDataSet getDataSet() throws Exception {
        String file = getDataSetFilename();
        if (file == null) {
            return null;
        }
        else {
            InputStream fileStream =
                loadFromClasspath(file);
            InputStream dtdStream =
                loadFromClasspath("database-schema.xml");
            return new FlatXmlDataSet(fileStream, dtdStream);
        }
    }

    private InputStream loadFromClasspath(String s)
        throws Exception {

        ClassLoader cl =
            Thread.currentThread().getContextClassLoader();
```

Annotations:
- *Returns the name of the dataset file for a test case* → points to `protected abstract String getDataSetFilename();`
- *Gets the name of the file to load* → points to `String file = getDataSetFilename();`
- *Returns null if the filename is null* → points to `return null;`
- *Loads the dataset file from the classpath* → points to `loadFromClasspath(file);`
- *Loads the DTD for the database schema from the classpath* → points to `loadFromClasspath("database-schema.xml");`
- *Returns a FlatXmlDataSet object for the dataset and DTD* → points to `return new FlatXmlDataSet(fileStream, dtdStream);`

```
        return cl.getResourceAsStream(s);
    }
}
```

The getDataSet() method is inherited from DatabaseTestCase. You implement it to return a new FlatXmlDataSet object for a specific dataset file. Additionally, you add an abstract method, getDataSetFilename(), to be implemented by subclasses. The String returned by getDataSetFilename() tells the ProjectDatabaseTestCase which file to load for the specific test case. The loadFromClasspath(String) method is a utility method that loads a file from the classpath as an InputStream.

With the variety of operations available, it's easy to restore the database instance to a known state between test runs. Next, you'll expand on the ProjectDatabaseTestCase class and write a unit test that subclasses it.

10.4.2 ProjectDatabaseTestCase

You saw our ProjectDatabaseTestCase in the previous section. In this section you'll flesh it out and create a subclass suitable for testing your EventDao class. To begin, it's important to understand why you needed to subclass DBUnit's DatabaseTestCase in the first place.

In your unit tests thus far you have one XML file per test case, which allows you to isolate the test data for each test case. In our experience, having a massive XML file containing test data for all unit tests quickly becomes cumbersome. Having a base class for your tests cases to extend allows you to centralize the logic used to load the dataset. With the administration functions located in a superclass, your test cases can focus on testing functionality.

Listing 10.7 shows the complete ProjectDatabaseTestCase.

Listing 10.7 ProjectDatabaseTestCase

```
package com.manning.hq.ch10;

import org.dbunit.DatabaseTestCase;
```

```java
import org.dbunit.database.IDatabaseConnection;
import org.dbunit.database.DatabaseConnection;
import org.dbunit.operation.DatabaseOperation;

import java.io.InputStream;
import java.sql.Connection;
import java.sql.DriverManager;
import java.util.Properties;

public abstract class ProjectDatabaseTestCase
extends DatabaseTestCase {

    private static String driver =
        "hibernate.connection.driver_class";
    private static String url = "hibernate.connection.url";
    private static String username =
    "hibernate.connection.username";
    private static String password =
    "hibernate.connection.password";

    public ProjectDatabaseTestCase(String name) {
        super(name);
    }

    protected abstract String getDataSetFilename();

    protected IDataSet getDataSet() throws Exception {
        String file = getDataSetFilename();
        if (file == null) {
            return null;
        }
        else {
            InputStream fileStream =
                loadFromClasspath(file);
            InputStream dtdStream =
                loadFromClasspath("database-schema.xml");

            return new FlatXmlDataSet(fileStream, dtdStream);
        }
    }

    protected DatabaseOperation getSetUpOperation() {
        return DatabaseOperation.REFRESH;
    }

    protected DatabaseOperation getTearDownOperation() {
```

```
            return DatabaseOperation.DELETE_ALL;
        }

    protected IDatabaseConnection getConnection() throws Exception
    {
        Properties p = new Properties();
        p.load(loadFromClasspath("hibernate.properties"));

        Class.forName(p.getProperty(driver));
        Connection c =
            DriverManager.getConnection(p.getProperty(url),
                p.getProperty(username),
                p.getProperty(password));
        return new DatabaseConnection(c);
    }

    private InputStream loadFromClasspath(String s)
        throws Exception {

        ClassLoader cl =
            Thread.currentThread().getContextClassLoader();
        return cl.getResourceAsStream(s);
    }
}
```

The getConnection() method, returning an instance of DBUnit's IDatabaseConnection class, is also an abstract method inherited from DatabaseTestCase. You create a JDBC connection and wrap it with an instance of DatabaseConnection, another DBUnit class. While your Hibernate classes won't use the connection, your test code will use it to verify that your Hibernate operations actually impacted the database.

The base class also overrides two methods from DatabaseTestCase: getSetUpOperation() and getTearDownOperation(). These two methods define the operations that DBUnit will use to set up and tear down the database state before and after each test, respectively. This is significant because, as we've explained several times, you need to ensure the state of the database before and after each test. The default implementation is to refresh data before each test and delete everything after each test completes.

Now let's implement the new TestEventDao class.

TestEventDao

The updated version of the TestEventDao class, which subclasses ProjectDatabaseTestCase, is shown in listing 10.8.

Listing 10.8 Updated **TestEventDao** class

```
public class TestEventDao extends ProjectDatabaseTestCase {

    private EventDao eventDao;

    public TestEventDao(String name) {
        super(name);
    }

    public String getDataSetFilename() {        Defines the name of
        return "TestEventDao.xml";   <──────    the test data file
    }

    public void setUp() throws Exception {              Verifies the
        super.setUp();                                  number of
        eventDao = new EventDao();                       results
    }
                                            Retrieves the Events
                                              for a certain date
    public void testFindEventsFor () throws Exception {
        List eventsFor = eventDao.findEventsFor(7, 2005);   <─┐
        assertEquals("Should return 1", 1, eventsFor.size());  <─┘
        Event event = (Event) eventsFor.get(0);
        assertEquals("ID should be 1000", new Long(1000),    <─┐
        event.getId());                                         │
    }                                       Verifies that the Event id
}                                           matches your assertion
```

If you compare the testFindEventsFor() method with the one found in section 10.3.3, you can see that it skips loading the test data and restoring the state of the database. You're almost ready to run this test case.

Before you can test, you must define your test data. The XML file shown here contains three entries for the events table that are similar to the Event instances created when you used vanilla JUnit in section 10.3.3:

```
<dataset>
    <events id="1000" name="Test Event 1" start_date="2005-06-01"/>
    <events id="2000" name="Test Event 2" start_date="2005-07-01"/>
    <events id="3000" name="Test Event 3" start_date="2005-08-01"/>
<dataset>
```

The test data is stored in the TestEventDao.xml file and is loaded before your test runs. (You'll recall that the logic to load the file is in the ProjectTestCase class.) Once the test data is loaded, the test executes. If you have multiple tests in the test cases, the data is refreshed before each test.

However, we've only looked at a subset of DBUnit's functionality. You can also use DBUnit to verify the state of the database. Let's look at another test method:

```
public void testPersists() throws Exception {
    HibernateFactory.buildSessionFactory();
    Session session = HibernateFactory.openSession();
    Transaction trans = session.beginTransaction();
    Event event = new Event();
    event.setName("Another test event.");                    Creates a table
    session.saveOrUpdate(event);                           object that contains
    trans.commit();                                         data from the SQL
                                                                statement

    ITable table = getConnection().createQueryTable("events",  ⟵
        "select * from events where name='Another test event.'");
    assertEquals("Specified event not found.", 1,              ⟵
        table.getRowCount());               Verifies that only one
}                                           result was returned
```

The ITable class encapsulates the data retrieved by the SQL statement. You then use the ITable to ensure that only one row was retrieved from the events table. Why should you use DBUnit to verify the state of the database when you can do the same thing with Hibernate?

Our argument for using DBUnit to verify the state of the database is pretty simple. If you're testing your application code, which uses

Hibernate, you shouldn't also use that code to verify the state of the database. Think of DBUnit as an impartial witness to the state of the database.

10.5 Summary

If you want to make sure your code works correctly, test it. The best way to make sure your code works, and stays working, is to write automated unit tests that run every time you build your project. JUnit is even useful for testing databases and Hibernate.

In this chapter, we covered how you can get and install JUnit. We also looked at how to write simple unit tests, which can be used to test your class's domain logic. Because testing databases isn't as easy as testing simple classes, Hibernate has some specific items you want to test. These include verifying that classes are persistent, that mapping files are correctly written, that entities cascade correctly, and that queries are returning the objects you expect. Finally, we discussed a few general tips for testing databases, including using multiple databases, avoiding brittle tests, and resetting the database to known states between tests.

Much of the code we used was basic JUnit. The setup used in this chapter is effective but pretty simple, and you might want to be more elaborate. As a next step, for example, you can improve your unit tests by incorporating a more advanced developed database-testing framework, like DBUnit.

DBUnit provides methods to prepopulate the database with test data, as well as clean up after tests have been completed. When you move these responsibilities to an external framework, your test code can focus more on testing functionality and less on plumbing. Additionally, DBUnit provides classes and methods to access the state of the database, providing independent verification of the state of the database.

11

What's new in Hibernate 3

This chapter covers

- *Filtering persistent objects*
- *Creating mapping files with annotations*
- *Persistent events*

In Hibernate's short history, it has become one of the most popular persistence services for Java applications. When Hibernate 2 was released in June of 2003, it addressed most of the persistence problems developers commonly encounter. With the release of Hibernate 3 in March 2005, developers have a number of new features to take advantage of, such as filtering query results and utilizing stored procedures.

One of the focuses of Hibernate 3 is improved support for legacy database schemas, as well as support for stored procedures and using custom SQL statements. Another feature introduced in the latest release is the ability to persist Maps just as you would a JavaBean.

While the code examples in this book have included Hibernate 3 syntax when appropriate, this chapter gives you a more focused overview of many of the important new features found in Hibernate 3.

11.1 Filters

Suppose your application tracks sales for a company, and you only want to see sales for each person for the current quarter. You could probably handle this by writing an HQL statement to return the current results for the quarter, but calling an external query isn't ideal if the same business rule should be applied every time the results are viewed. Instead, it makes sense to apply a filter on the returned data at runtime. This is where filters come in.

Filters, or virtualization, allow you to apply filtering criteria to returned objects at the Session level. You can pass parameters to filters, and they work with classes or collections. To use filters, you first define them in the mapping files, and then enable a given filter by name when using the Session object. The filters are defined in the mapping definition, within the hibernate-mapping element:

```
<hibernate-mapping>
    ...
    <filter-def name="nameFilter">
        <filter-param name="nameFilterParam" type="string"/>
    </filter-def>
    ...
</hibernate-mapping>
```

With the filter defined, we can apply it to persistent classes and collections:

```
<class name="Event">
    ...
    <filter name="nameFilter"
        condition=":nameFilterParam = name"/>
            <set name="attendees">
            ...
            <filter name="nameFilter"
                condition=v:nameFilterParam = last_name"/>
    </set>
</class>
```

This code applies the filter to the name column in the events table, and to the last_name column in the attendees table.

To apply the filters, you must explicitly enable them at the Session level:

```
Filter f = session.enableFilter("nameFilter");
f.setParameter("nameFilterParam", "Plenary");
List results = session.createQuery("from Event").list();
```

This code enables the named filter and then sets the filter parameter. The results will only contain instances of Event with the name Plenary. You can also enable multiple filters per session.

Filters are one of a handful of improvements made to object mapping. The next section discusses a few of the more significant mappings.

11.2 Mapping improvements

Although the earlier versions of Hibernate handled the vast majority of mapping requirements, in a few corner cases it was lacking, particularly when Hibernate was introduced into a legacy database schema. We'll examine a few of the improvements in this section.

11.2.1 Multiple table mapping

One of the most significant improvements involves mapping a single persistent class to multiple tables. Ideally, you won't need to do this with new applications, but it's often required when you're working with legacy applications.

To support mapping a class to multiple tables, Hibernate adds the <join> element. Using the <join> element is straightforward:

```
<join table="event_detail">
    <key column="event_id"/>
    <property name="startDate" type="date"/>
```

```
<many-to-one class="Location" column="location_id"/>
    …
</join>
```

The following shows the `<join>` element in the context of the `Event` class:

```
<class name="Event" table="events">
    …
    <join table="event_detail">
        <key column="event_id"/>
        <property name="startDate" type="date"/>
        <many-to-one class="Location" column="location_id"/>
    </join>
</class>
```

Notice the `<key>` element. You've seen this element every time the parent object interacts with another table, typically with collections. In this case, the join table has a foreign key to the parent `Event` class.

The `<join>` element can be used inside the `class` or `subclass` element, and can contain the same elements as a class or subclass. You probably won't need to use the `<join>` element very often, but it can be useful in isolated cases with legacy databases.

11.2.2 Discriminator formulas

Discriminators, which we discussed in chapter 3, are used to determine the class type in an inheritance hierarchy. The discriminator value is typically stored in its own column in the table, but this is possible only if you're starting a project with Hibernate, or you're allowed to modify an existing schema.

If you are unable to provide a specific column for the discriminator value, you can use a snippet of SQL to determine the exact class type. Most of the time, the SQL will be a CASE statement returning a value to indicate the class type. The formula can be specified as an attribute to the discriminator element, or as a child element:

```
<discriminator type="string">
    <formula>
    case
        when class_type = 'network'
        then 'NetworkEvent'
        else 'Event'
        end
    </formula>
</discriminator>

<discriminator type="string" formula="…"/>
```

This example returns a string indicating the class type using a CASE statement. The returned string is actually the name of the class. Listing 11.1 shows a more complete mapping definition using derived discriminator values.

Listing 11.1 Derived discriminators

```
<hibernate-mapping>
    <class name="Event" discriminator-value="event">
        <discriminator type="string">
            <formula>
            case class_type
              when 'event' then 'Event'
              when 'network' then 'NetworkEvent'
              when 'food' then 'FoodEvent'
            end
            </formula>
        </discriminator>

        ...
        <subclass name="NetworkEvent"
            discriminator-value="network">

            ...
        </subclass>
        <subclass name="FoodEvent"
            discriminator-value="food">

            ...
        </subclass>
    </class>
</hibernate-mapping>
```

We still have a discriminator value, but it is derived from other values rather than being concrete. Derived discriminator values come into play with our next topic, union subclasses.

11.2.3 Union subclasses

When we discussed the various inheritance mapping strategies in chapter 3, one strategy we didn't discuss was the table-per-concrete-class concept. We avoided it because it is complicated to implement in Hibernate 2, and it does not support a number of polymorphic features, such as polymorphic one-to-many and joins, as well as outer-join fetching.

To address this shortcoming, Hibernate 3 introduces the new <union-subclass> element. Classes mapped with this element use the table-per-concrete-class strategy, but don't have the same limitations on polymorphic operations and joins.

The mapping for a union-subclass is shown here:

```
<hibernate-mapping>
    <class name="Event">
        <union-subclass name="NetworkEvent">
        ...
        </union-subclass>
        <union-subclass name="FoodEvent">
            ...
        </union-subclass>
    </class>
</hibernate-mapping>
```

Like the former table-per-concrete-class strategy, each subclass table contains all of the property columns, including the inherited fields. The primary difference is that the former method mapped all classes with the class element, which didn't preserve the inheritance hierarchy. The <union-subclass> element makes the table-per-concrete-class strategy much more usable and powerful.

11.2.4 Property references

When you're creating an association between two objects, Hibernate assumes that the association will be from the primary key of one object to the foreign key of the associated object. However, this isn't always the case, particularly in legacy database schema.

To address non-primary key associations, Hibernate 3 adds the property-ref attribute to the association elements, including <many-to-one> and <one-to-one>. This feature is best explained with an example.

Suppose you want to associate your Event class to the Location using the name of the Location, rather than the id. In that case, the <many-to-one> element in the Event definition would be

```
<many-to-one class="Location" property-ref="name"/>
```

The requirement on the referenced property is that it must be unique. Otherwise, the Event class could be associated to multiple Locations. Because of this limitation, the mapping definition for the Location class has to be modified:

```
<property name="name" unique="true"/>
```

If your legacy database doesn't require this feature, it's better to avoid it. Associations should be to primary keys whenever possible.

Most of the new features added to mapping definitions are designed to ease integration for legacy databases. The next feature we cover, dynamic classes, is designed to make development easier.

11.3 Dynamic classes

Throughout this book, we've discussed using Hibernate with domain models composed of plain old Java objects (POJOs). We can refer to domain models using POJOs as static domain models. The alternative is to use a dynamic domain model. Instead of POJOs, dynamic domain models use Maps to store properties and associations between persistent Maps. Dynamic domain models are useful when the domain model changes rapidly, or when the application is small.

The disadvantage of using dynamic domain models is that you lose the explicit strong typing found in static domain models. For instance, when you define a persistent object, you create getters and setters for the various properties:

```
public class Event {
    private Long id;
    private String name;
    ...
    public void setId(Long id) { this.id = id; }
    public Long getId() { return this.id; }
    public void setName(String name) { this.name = name; }
    public String getName() { return this.name; }
    ...
}
```

If you try to set a `java.lang.String` as the `id` property, you'll get a compile-time error. On the other hand, the `Map` interface currently only works with `Objects`, so you can set a `java.lang.String` as the value of an `id` property and the error will not be found until you attempt to persist the `Map`.

Despite the lack of strong typing, dynamic domain models can save you a good deal of time and allow you to test new ideas quickly. To declare a persistent `Map`, the new `dynamic-class` attribute has been created. Here is an example of mapping a persistent `Map`:

```
<dynamic-class entity-name="Event" table="events">
    <id name="id" column="id" type="long">
        <generator class="native"/>
    </id>
    <property name="name" type="string" length="50"/>
    <property name="startDate" type="date"/>
    <many-to-one name="location" class="Location"
        column="location_id"/>
</dynamic-class>
```

Once you've created the mapping document, using dynamic classes is straightforward:

```
Map m = new HashMap();
m.put("name", "Dynamic Event");
m.put("startDate", new java.util.Date());
m.put("location", myLocation);
m.put("type", "Event");
Session s = factory.openSession();
s.save(m);
s.connection().commit();
s.flush();
```

Setting the type property in the Map tells Hibernate the entity name. This is important because without the entity name, Hibernate won't know in which table to store the data. Once the Map is created and populated, it is persisted like static JavaBeans. Retrieving a dynamic class is simple:

```
Session s = factory.openSession();
Map m = s.get("Event", myEventId);
```

It is also possible to use dynamic classes as components. Dynamic components are effectively the same as static components. Dynamic classes can also be modified at runtime, providing a very powerful persistence solution.

11.4 Annotations

Java 5 (JDK version 1.5) introduced a new feature called annotations. Annotations were introduced in Java Specification Request (JSR) 175. Essentially, annotations allow you to insert metadata into your source files that can be interpreted by development tools and preprocessors to lighten the deployment burden for developers. Annotations are similar to XDoclet tags. The primary difference between XDoclet and annotations is that annotations aren't embedded in JavaDoc comments. Instead, annotations are actually part of the source code.

The set of annotations supported by Hibernate are taken from the EJB3 specification, which are in draft as of this writing. Let's look at an example of the Event class from chapter 1, this time using EJB annotations instead of a Hibernate mapping file (see listing 11.2).

Listing 11.2 Annotated Event class

```
@Entity      ❶
@Table(name="events")      ❷
public class Event {
    @Id(generate=GeneratorType.AUTO)      ❸
    @Column(name="uid")      ❹
    private Long id;

    @Basic      ❺
    @Column(length="100", unique="true")      ❻
    private String name;

    @Column(name="start_date")      ❼
    private Date startDate;

    private int duration;

    public void setId(Long id) { this.id = id; }
    @Column(name="uid",
    public Long getId() { return this.id; }
    public void setName(String name) { this.name = name; }
    public String getName() { return this.name; }
    public void setStartDate(Date startDate) {
        this.startDate = startDate;
    }
    public Date getStartDate() { return this.startDate; }
    public void setDuration(int duration) {
        this.duration = duration;
    }
    public int getDuration() { return this.duration; }
}
```

Let's take a closer look at this listing:

❶ Declares this object as a persistent entity

❷ Declares that instances of this persistent class should be persisted to the events table

❸ Declares the generator type should be AUTO

❹ Declares that the column for the primary key is called uid

❺ Declares that the name property should be persistent

❻ Declares that the length of the name column should be 100 chars, and that it should have a unique constraint

❼ Declares that the column for the startDate property should be named start_date

It's pretty easy to understand this listing if you've used XDoclet. However, some defaults are implied that require an explanation. You'll notice that the name property has a @Basic annotation. This means that the object should be persisted as a basic property. The @Basic annotation is optional and is implied if it's not present. Instead, you must intentionally declare fields as transient, using the @Transient annotation.

Assuming you didn't want the name property to be persisted to the database, you'd simply have

```
@Transient
private String name;
```

in your source file.

The @Column annotations allow you to configure column-specific attributes. The previous snippet demonstrates name, unique, and length, but there are many more to provide fine-grained configuration.

Once you have annotated classes, you can use a special version of Hibernate's `Configuration` class, `AnnotationConfiguration`. Let's look at the differences in creating a `SessionFactory` for annotated classes:

```
SessionFactory factory = new AnnotationConfiguration().
    .addPackage("com.manning.hq.ch11").
    .addAnnotatedClass(Event.class).
    .buildSessionFactory();
```

It's possible to use both annotated classes and standard mapping files with `AnnotationConfiguration`.

The introduction of annotations begs the question: should you use annotations or XDoclet? The answer depends on your environment and what you're doing. If you're not using Java 5, you'll need to use XDoclet for source code metadata. XDoclet works fine with Java 2. If you're using XDoclet for more than just Hibernate, you may want to stick with XDoclet until annotations exist for the other components, like Struts, Spring, and WebWork. Of course, you can mix the two approaches if that suits your application.

Hibernate's support for annotations is still being developed. The current development status can be found at www.hibernate.org/247.html. Now let's look at a frequently requested feature that shipped with Hibernate 3: stored procedures.

11.5 Stored procedures and SQL

One limitation of previous versions of Hibernate is the lack of support for stored procedures. Another desirable feature is custom SQL statements when objects are manipulated. Obviously, these two features are closely related, since any stored procedure or custom SQL would need to be declared in the mapping definitions.

Hibernate 3 provides the ability to specify custom SQL, including stored procedures, for various object operations, including inserting and updating objects and retrieving collections. We'll spend some time looking where this fits into the mapping definitions and how it can impact your development.

To use custom SQL or stored procedures when inserting, updating, and retrieving deleting objects, Hibernate 3 introduces the <sql-insert>, <sql-update>, and <sql-delete> elements, respectively. Where these elements fit into the mapping definition is shown in listing 11.3.

Listing 11.3 Custom SQL in a mapping definition

```
<class name="Event" table="events">
    <id name="id" column="id" type="long">
        <generator class="native"/>
    </id>
    <property name="name" type="string"/>
    ...
    <sql-insert>
    insert into events(name, id) values (?, ?)
    </sql-insert>
    <sql-update>
    update events set name=? where id=?
    </sql-update>
    <sql-delete>
    delete from events where id=?
    </sql-delete>
</class>
```

You'll notice that the SQL statements have ? placeholders. The placeholders are populated in the same order the property elements appear in the mapping definition, with the id column always appearing last. We hope that a future release will support named parameters in custom SQL, since ensuring fields are in the correct order can be tedious. Another thing to notice is the callable attribute. When callable is set to true, the SQL must be a stored procedure installed on the database.

Another feature that can be quite powerful is the ability to define a SQL statement that will be used whenever an instance of a persistent class is retrieved from the database by its primary key, like with Session.get(…) or Session.load(…). The mapping definition for the <loader> element is shown here:

```
<class name="Event" table="events">
    …
    <loader query-ref="events"/>
    …
</class>
```

The SQL query is defined at the Hibernate-mapping level:

```
<sql-query name="events">
    <return alias="e" class="Event"/>
    select name as {e.name}, id as {e.id} from events where id=?
</sql-query>
```

The <return> element defines the type of class returned and the alias of the class attribute values in the query. For instance, the class attribute declares that classes returned by the SQL query will be of type Event.

Despite the relative power of using custom SQL, you should only need to use it when you're dealing with legacy databases. The SQL generation performed by Hibernate should be sufficient for the majority of your persistence needs.

11.6 Persistence events

It's often desirable to know when certain things happen in an application, such as when objects are deleted or changed. In the past, this has been accomplished with the Interceptor interface. The Interceptor provides methods that are called when the Session instance performs certain actions, such as flushing a dirty object. While Hibernate 3 doesn't remove the Interceptor interface, it introduces an event architecture that can be much more granular than Interceptors.

The event architecture follows the familiar EventLister/EventObject pattern found throughout the Java SDK. Each of the operations performed by the `Session` interface fire corresponding events, which can be handled by the application. Some of the available event listeners are shown in table 11.1.

Table 11.1 Persistence events

Session Action	Associated Event
Automatic Session flush	AutoFlushEvent
	CopyEvent
Session.delete(…)	DeleteEvent
When an object associated with a Session has changed	DirtyCheckEvent
Session.evict(…)	EvictEvent
Session.flush(…)	FlushEvent
When collections are initially populated	InitializeCollectionEvent
Session.load(…) or as the result of a find(…) method	LoadEvent
Session.lock(…)	LockEvent
Session.refresh(…)	RefreshEvent
Session.replicate(…)	ReplicateEvent
Session.save(…) and Session.saveOrUpdate(…)	SaveEvent
Session.update(…) and Session.saveOrUpdate(…)	UpdateEvent

Suppose you want to log whenever an instance of the Event class has been loaded from the database. First, you must implement the Load-EventListener:

```
public class MyLoadEventListener implements LoadEventListener {
    public Object onLoad(LoadEvent e,
        LoadEventListener.LoadType type)
        throws HibernateException {
        log.info("Object loaded: " + e.getEntityName() +
```

```
                        "; id = " + e.getEntityId());
        }
    }
```

Your next step is to tell Hibernate to use your listener class:

```
<hibernate-configuration>
    <session-factory>
        <listener type="load"
            class="com.manning.hq.ch11.MyLoadEventListener"/>
        …
    </session-factory>
</hibernate-configuration>
```

Note that you're registering the listeners in the hibernate.cfg.xml file, not a mapping definition. Now, when an Event instance is loaded, the following is output to the log file:

```
INFO - Object loaded: Event; id = 4
```

Instead of just dumping something to the log file, you could have implemented a security manager to make sure only certain users can load Event instances. Another way to use events is for debugging. Suppose you have a collection that isn't getting populated as you expect. You can create an implementation of InitializeCollectionEventListener to log when a given collection is initialized.

Events are an interesting way to debug and manage your Hibernate applications. For example, your event-handling code could also integrate with Java Management Extensions (JMX) to create an administrative console. In the next section, we'll discuss another new feature in Hibernate 3: lazy properties.

11.7 Lazy properties

A common request from developers using Hibernate is the ability to lazily populate properties of persistent classes, similar to lazy collections. For instance, say you have an Event class that you want to display to a user. Your display doesn't include the start and end times of the Event, so there's no reason to populate it. This can be a powerful feature, but you need to see how it has been implemented in comparison to lazy collections.

Lazy population is fairly easy with collections, since Hibernate can transparently provide its own implementations of the collection interfaces. With properties, Hibernate can't step in at runtime to intercept each property because most of the properties are concrete classes, not interfaces. Instead, Hibernate must perform some compile-time processing, called instrumentation.

Instrumentation is the process of modifying bytecode to add additional operations, typically for debugging or testing purposes. Hibernate inserts instrumentation to intercept calls to lazy properties. When the interception is made, the property is populated transparently.

To create a lazy property, simply add the lazy attribute to the <property> element:

```
<property name="startDate" type="date" lazy="true"/>
```

Next, process your bytecode with an Ant task provided by Hibernate:

```
<taskdef name="instrument"
    classname="org.hibernate.tools.instrument.InstrumentTask"
    classpathref="project.class.path"/>
<instrument>
    <fileset dir="${build.dest}">
        <include name="**/*.class"/>
    </fileset>
</instrument>
```

The bytecode is modified to its current directory. If you've configured your classes to have lazy properties but the classes haven't had instrumentation added, Hibernate transparently disables the feature for that class.

While lazy properties require the extra step of adding instrumentation to bytecode, they allow you to be very specific when retrieving objects. The only thing to remember is that lazy properties, like lazy collections, require the `Session` to be open when the properties are populated.

11.8 Summary

With Hibernate's increasing adoption in enterprise applications, each new release must add features and address problems found in previous releases. Hibernate 3 is meant to address some of the shortcomings in previous releases, particularly in working with legacy databases. Other features, such as filters and dynamic classes, are designed to make developing with Hibernate easier.

Dynamic classes allow you to persist simple `Maps` of values. One of the main advantages of working with `Maps` is their flexibility: you can put any object into a `Map` and persist it. You aren't required to create explicit property accessors, as with POJOs.

Another feature we examined, lazy properties, allows the developer to specify properties that are not populated when the object is retrieved from the database. We also looked at filters, which return objects that pass certain criteria. Filters can be enabled or disabled at runtime, and can be passed parameters.

The features in Hibernate 3 should make it easier to quickly manage object persistence for any Java application, including legacy applications.

Appendix

The complete Hibernate mapping catalog

Using Hibernate in a project involves several disciplines. First, you have to understand how to build your object model and map it correctly to a database. Second, you need to understand how use the Hibernate library, along with database transactions, to safely store and update your objects. Finally, you must know the Hibernate Query Language (HQL) in order to efficiently retrieve your objects. Recognizing how each of these disciplines works together is the key to mastering Hibernate.

The intent of this appendix is to focus solely on the first discipline, mapping an object model. Hibernate has an extremely rich variety of mappings that it supports, and knowing which relationship to choose and how to express it can be a bit overwhelming. Both the XDoclet and Hibernate reference guides are fairly detailed, but we are aware of no complete guide that combines examples using XDoclet tags side by side with the mapping files. This appendix aims to fill that need. It doesn't cover the individual mapping attributes, which are already covered in detail in the Hibernate reference manual.

This appendix is written in the form of a catalog of mappings. Our hope is that developers will know the association they want, and will be able to quickly look up that association and quickly copy the syntax into their project. Like its inspirational parent, the catalog of patterns, this catalog too has its own format, which we will lay out next.

A.1 A sample association

Each mapping will usually start with a brief explanation of the relationship, followed by a UML class model diagram, to illustrate the relationship between the two classes, as shown in figure A.1.

Figure A.1
A sample class model

For relationships that can be both unidirectional and bidirectional, the first example will be unidirectional.

A.1.1 Unidirectional

The following sample Java code shows the persistent class(es):

```
package com.manning.hq.apdxA;
/**
 * @hibernate.class table="sample_class"
 */
public class ASampleClass {
    private Long id;

    /** @hibernate.id generator-class="native" */
    public Long getId() { return id; }
    public void setId(Long id) { this.id = id; }
}
```

Here we show the package name, but most examples will not (to save space). The following is the mapping file fragment itself, which is either handwritten or generated:

```
<class name="com.manning.hq.apdxA.ASampleClass"
    table="sample_class">
    <id name="id" column="id" type="java.lang.Long">
        <generator class="native"/>
    </id>
</class>
```

XDoclet is pretty verbose when generating files, which is irrelevant for regular usage. For writing a book, it's also a big waste of space. So in most cases, the mapping file will have whitespace condensed and, for clarity, some default XDoclet-generated properties may be stripped out as well. If not necessary for the point of illustration, the identifier field may be removed as well.

Table schema

To illustrate how the persistent objects will translate into database tables, we'll show a table schema to demonstrate how foreign keys link together:

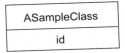

If an association has a bidirectional relationship, the following section will detail that relationship.

A.1.2 Bidirectional

This section examines the modifications necessary to make the association bidirectional and concludes the sample catalog entry. We begin with the many-to-one association.

A.2 Many-to-one

The most common object-to-object relationship is many-to-one (see figure A.2). It can be either unidirectional or bidirectional.

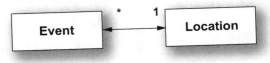

Figure A.2 Many-to-one relationship: Event to Location

A.2.1 Unidirectional

The following shows a many-to-one relationship: Event to Location:

```
public class Event implements Serializable {
    private Location location;
    /**
     * @hibernate.many-to-one column="location_id"
     */
    public Location getLocation() {
        return location;
    }
    public void setLocation(Location location) {
        this.location = location;
    }
}

public class Location implements Serializable{ }
```

The following illustrates a many-to-one mapping file:

```
<class name="com.manning.hq.apdxA.Event"  table="events">
    <many-to-one name="location" column="location_id"
        class="com.manning.hq.apdxA.Location" />
</class>
```

Table schemas

A single foreign key column in the events table links the two objects:

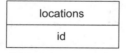

events	
id	location_id

locations
id

A.2.2 Bidirectional

Making a bidirectional link from Location to Event involves creating a one-to-many relationship, using either a Set or a Bag. Let's assume a simple Set in this case:

```
public class Location implements Serializable{
    private Set events = new LinkedHashSet();
    /**
     * @hibernate.set
     * @hibernate.collection-key column="location_id"
     * @hibernate.collection-one-to-many
    class="com.manning.hq.apdxA.Event"
     * @return
     */
    public Set getEvents() { return events; }
    public void setEvents(Set events) { this.events = events; }
}
```

The desired mapping files (which the above XDoclet would generate) should be similar to this:

```
<class name="com.manning.hq.apdxA.Location" table="locations">
    <set name="events">
        <key column="location_id"/>
        <one-to-many class="com.manning.hq.apdxA.Event"/>
    </set>
</class>
```

A.3 One-to-one

The one-to-one association (see figure A.3) is not as common as its similar many-to-one cousin, mainly because database semantics don't truly allow for it. There are two strategies: identical primary keys or unique foreign keys. (A foreign key always implies a many-to-one from at least one end.) These relationships need to be bidirectional to maintain the identical keys.

A.3.1 Identical primary keys

Here the relationship uses a special "foreign" key generation algorithm:

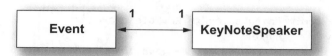

Figure A.3 One-to-one relationship: Event to KeyNoteSpeaker

```
/**   @hibernate.class table="keynote_speakers" */
public class KeyNoteSpeaker implements Serializable {
    private Long id;
    private Event event;

    /**
     * @hibernate.id generator-class="foreign"
     * @hibernate.generator-param  name="property" value="event"
     */
    public Long getId() { return id; }
    public void setId(Long id) { this.id = id; }

    /**
     * @hibernate.one-to-one constrained="true"
     */
    public Event getEvent() { return event; }
    public void setEvent(Event event) { this.event = event; }
}
/** @hibernate.class table="events" */
public class Event implements Serializable {
    private KeyNoteSpeaker speaker;

    /** @hibernate.one-to-one */
    public KeyNoteSpeaker getSpeaker() { return speaker; }
    public void setSpeaker(KeyNoteSpeaker speaker) {
        this.speaker = speaker;
    }
}
```

In the following code, KeyNoteSpeaker is the child class whose id is dependent on (and identical to) the parent Event:

```
<class name="com.manning.hq.apdxA.KeyNoteSpeaker"
   table="keynote_speakers">
  <id name="id" column="id" type="java.lang.Long">
     <generator class="foreign">
        <param name="property">event</param>
     </generator>
  </id>
  <one-to-one name="event"
     class="com.manning.hq.apdxA.Event"
     constrained="true" />
</class>

<class name="com.manning.hq.apdxA.Event" table="events">
  <one-to-one name="speaker"
     class="com.manning.hq.apdxA.KeyNoteSpeaker"
     constrained="false" />
</class>
```

Table schema

Since `events.id` and `keynote_speakers.id` must match, there is no need for a foreign key. This works well in many cases, except when you're using native key generation, which means the database is managing the key generation and foreign key violations become possible. In that case, you can try to use the next one-to-one strategy.

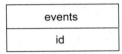
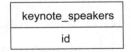

A.3.2 Foreign key one-to-one

The foreign key one-to-one is really a constrained many-to-one relationship, where one object is a many-to-one relationship to the other, using a unique foreign key to the other object. Unlike the primary key one-to-one, it can but does not need to be bidirectional.

Unidirectional

The following shows an Event with a foreign one-to-one relationship:

```
public class Event implements Serializable {
    private KeyNoteSpeaker speaker;

    /**
     * @hibernate.many-to-one column="keynote_speaker_id"
     *      unique="true"
     */
    public KeyNoteSpeaker getSpeaker() { return speaker; }
    public void setSpeaker(KeyNoteSpeaker speaker) {
        this.speaker = speaker;
    }
}
```

Because the `keynote_speaker_id` is unique, no other event can be associated with a single `KeyNoteSpeaker`. Here's the mapping file for this relationship:

```
<class name="com.manning.hq.apdxA.Event" table="events">
    <many-to-one name="keyNoteSpeaker"
        class="com.manning.hq.apdxA.KeyNoteSpeaker"
        column="keynote_speaker_id" unique="true" />
</class>
```

Note that as of XDoclet 1.2.3, a bug results in the generation of multiple `unique="true"` attributes. Until it's fixed, you can just ignore that attribute or handwrite the mapping file.

Table schema

Since there is now a foreign key link, a new column must be added to the events table.

events	
id	keynote_speaker_id

keynote_speakers
id

Bidirectional

The Event-to-KeyNoteSpeaker association can be made bidirectional by adding an event field to KeyNoteSpeaker and mapping it to point back to Event's keyNoteSpeaker field:

```
public class KeyNoteSpeaker implements Serializable {
    private Long id;
    private Event event;

    /**
     * @hibernate.id generator-class="native"
     */
    public Long getId() { return id; }
    public void setId(Long id) { this.id = id; }

    /**
     * @hibernate.one-to-one property-ref="keyNoteSpeaker"
     */
    public Event getEvent() { return event; }
    public void setEvent(Event event) { this.event = event; }
}
```

Note that KeyNoteSpeaker can also use a normal id generator now instead of the foreign one that we saw before. The newly generated KeyNoteSpeaker.hbm.xml file will contain the following:

```
<class name="com.manning.hq.apdxA.KeyNoteSpeaker"
    table="keynote_speakers">
    <id name="id" column="id" type="java.lang.Long">
        <generator class="native"/>
    </id>
    <one-to-one name="event" class="com.manning.hq.apdxA.Event"
        constrained="false" property-ref="keyNoteSpeaker" />
</class>
```

A.4 Components

The basic component is a one-to-one relationship between an entity and a child value object. The value object's data is contained with the parent table, and has no identity of its own. A component is typically unidirectional, but if necessary the component can have a reference to its parent class, as shown in figure A.4.

Figure A.4 Component: Location to Address

A.4.1 Unidirectional

A component has the property information in the component (`Address`) and the component relationship detailed in the parent entity object:

```java
/**
 * @hibernate.class table="locations"
 */
public class Location implements Serializable{
    private Long id;
    private Address address = new Address();

    /**
     * @hibernate.id generator-class="native" column="id"
     * @return
     */
    public Long getId() { return id; }
    public void setId(Long id) { this.id = id; }

    /**
     * @hibernate.component
     */
    public Address getAddress() { return address; }
    public void setAddress(Address address) {
        this.address = address;
```

```
        }
    }
    /** No hibernate.class tag or identity field needed. */
    public class Address implements Serializable {
        /**
         * A sample property, the name of a city.
         * @hibernate.property column="city"
         */
        public String getCity() { return city; }
        public void setCity(String city) { this.city = city; }
    }
```

The final result, either generated via XDoclet or written by hand, is a single mapping single file, the entity's hbm.xml file. For this example, it looks like this:

```
<class name="com.manning.hq.apdxA.Location" table="locations">
    <id name="id" column="id" type="java.lang.Long">
        <generator class="native"/>
    </id>
    <component name="address" class="com.manning.hq.apdxA.Address">
        <property name="city" type="java.lang.String"
            column="city" />
    </component>
</class>
```

Table schema

There's only a single table, since the component, Address, is bound by its parent, Location.

locations	
id	city

A.4.2 Bidirectional

To make a component bidirectional, you must add a field that refers to the parent object. The component mapping then gets a <parent>

element, which refers back to the original object. As of XDoclet 1.2.2, there is a @hibernate.parent tag, which generates the <parent> element. Specifying it on the location property binds the Location to the Address component, making the relationship bidirectional, as shown here:

```
public class Address implements Serializable {
    /**
     * @hibernate.parent
     */
    public Location getLocation() { return location; }
    public void setLocation(Location location) {
        this.location = location;
    }
}
```

The following is the mapping file for the Location and its contained Address component, which has a link back to the parent Location:

```
<class name="com.manning.hq.apdxA.Location" table="locations">
    <component name="address" class="com.manning.hq.apdxA.Address">
        <parent name="location"/>
        <!-- Other properties omitted -->
    </component>
</class>
```

Note that for XDoclet to generate the Location.hbm.xml correctly, you must specify the location field first before all the other properties on the Address object. Otherwise, the XDoclet will generate an invalid hbm.xml file (according to the DTD). The <parent> element has to come first, before the <property> elements.

A.5 Set: one-to-many

There are many flavors of collections, the most basic and common of which is the one-to-many set (see figure A.5). The basic contract of `java.util.Set` is that every element must be unique but there are no guarantees on the order. In Hibernate, each element of the one-to-many set is linked back to the parent object via a foreign key. Hibernate allows you to sort sets in memory, using a naturally sorted collection or at query time using an `order-by` clause.

Figure A.5 One-to-many set: Event to Speaker

A.5.1 Unidirectional

In a unidirectional set, the parent object has a collection, but the objects in the collection have no parent object field:

```
public class Event implements Serializable {
    private Set speakers = new LinkedHashSet();
    /**
     * @hibernate.set
     * @hibernate.collection-key column="event_id"
     * @hibernate.collection-one-to-many
     *      class="com.manning.hq.apdxA.Speaker"
     */
    public Set getSpeakers() { return speakers; }
    public void setSpeakers(Set speakers) {
        this.speakers = speakers;
    }
}
```

The `speaker` table will have an `event_id` column, which will link each Speaker instance to a single Event. The resulting mapping fragment should look like this:

```
<class name="com.manning.hq.apdxA.Event" table="events">
    <set name="speakers">
```

```
        <key column="event_id" />
        <one-to-many class="com.manning.hq.apdxA.Speaker" />
    </set>
</class>
```

Table schema

Each speaker needs its foreign key back to the events table:

speakers	
id	event_id

events
id

A.5.2 Bidirectional

The opposite end of a bidirectional one-to-many association is a many-to-one on the object in the collection. In this case, the Speaker object would have an Event field, which points back to the Event object. Here's the modified Speaker class with that field:

```
public class SpeakerBidirectional implements Serializable {
    private Event event;
    /**
     * @hibernate.many-to-one column="event_id"
     */
    public Event getEvent() { return event; }
    public void setEvent(Event event) { this.event = event; }
}
```

Note that the many-to-one column (event_id) must match the one declared column on the Event.speakers field. Here's what the mapping fragment will look like:

```
<class name="com.manning.hq.apdxA.Speaker" table="speakers">
    <many-to-one name="event"
        class="com.manning.hq.apdxA.Event"
        column="event_id" />
</class>
```

A.6 Set: many-to-many

Like all collections, Sets can handle both one-to-many and many-to-many associations. From the mapping file perspective there is not much difference, with only one element (or XDoclet tag) being swapped out. From the database perspective, it's considerably different, since it requires the use of an association table to hold the foreign keys. When persisting and querying, clients of the model class don't need to worry about this extra table, though, because Hibernate manages it under the covers. But you do need to consider this table when writing the mappings. Many-to-many Sets can be bidirectional; see figure A.6.

Figure A.6 Many-to-many set: Event to Attendee

A.6.1 Unidirectional

The unidirectional set consists of a Set field on one of the objects. In this case, our Event has a many-to-many relationship with Attendees. Attendees can go to many Events, and each Event has many Attendees:

```
public class Event implements Serializable {
    private Set speakers = new LinkedHashSet();
    /**
     * @hibernate.set table="as_event_to_attendee"
     * @hibernate.collection-key column="event_id"
     * @hibernate.collection-many-to-many
     *     class="com.manning.hq.apdxA.Attendee"
     *     column="attendee_id"
     */
    public Set getAttendees() { return attendees; }
    public void setAttendees(Set attendees) {
        this.attendees = attendees;
    }
}
```

As you can see, the <one-to-many> tag has been replaced with a <many-to-many> tag. In addition, the event_id is not stored in the attendee table, but in an association table, here called as_event_to_attendee.[1] The mapping file looks like the following:

```
<class name="com.manning.hq.apdxA.Event" table="events">
    <set name="attendees" table="as_event_to_speaker">
        <key column="event_id" />
        <many-to-many class="com.manning.hq.apdxA.Attendee"
            column="attendee_id" />
    </set>
</class>
```

Table schema

For a many-to-many relationship, three tables are needed: one table for each of the entities, Event and Attendee, and one association table for the many-to-many relationship.

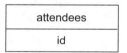

events
id

attendees
id

as_event_to_speaker	
event_id	attendee_id

A.6.2 Bidirectional

The bidirectional many-to-many Set puts another set on the object on the opposite end. In our current example, the Attendee would have a Set of Events. A bidirectional many-to-many set is going to result in quite a few queries when loading, especially if the number of Events and Attendees is large. So do some performance testing with the show_sql parameter on to check it. The following code is the modified Attendee with its Set of Events:

---

[1] The naming convention here of the association table, using as_ for a prefix, then the name of the tables being joined here, is strictly ours. We find it helps to distinguish between entity tables as the strictly associative ones.

```
/**
 *  @hibernate.class table="attendees"
 */
public class Attendee implements Serializable {
    private Set events = new LinkedHashSet();
    /**
     * @hibernate.set inverse="true" table="as_event_to_attendee"
     * @hibernate.collection-key column="attendee_id"
     * @hibernate.collection-many-to-many
   class="com.manning.hq.apdxA.Event" column="event_id"
     */
    public Set getEvents() { return events; }
    public void setEvents(Set events) { this.events = events; }
}
```

When dealing with a bidirectional many-to-many relationship, you have to mark one end of it as inverse. Which end you mark is your choice. By marking the set of Events on Attendee as inverse, you're telling Hibernate that the Event object is responsible for maintaining the relationship. Any changes made to the inverse end that aren't also made to the non-inverse end won't be saved.

The above code is virtually identical to that for the Event.attendees field, except that the columns are reversed. The attendee_id is now the key column and the outward foreign key is now event_id. Here's what the Attendee.hbm.xml file will contain:

```
<class name="com.manning.hq.apdxA.Attendee" table="attendees">
    <set name="events" table="as_event_to_attendee" inverse="true">
        <key column="attendee_id"/>
        <many-to-many
            class="com.manning.hq.apdxA.Event"
            column="event_id" />
    </set>
```

Most of the remaining collection types will follow this pattern, allowing both one-to-many and many-to-many associations.

A.7 Lists

Hibernate allows you to store Lists of entities, using a <list> element in the mapping file. The contract of java.util.List is that it maintains the order of insertion but has no guarantees that it won't contain duplicate elements. For Hibernate, this means it needs to store the index of each element in the database in its own column, which must be an integer type.

Figure A.7 One-to-many List: Speaker to EventSession

Hibernate doesn't support Lists as the "many" side of a bidirectional relationship. You have to use a set or bag if you want to take advantage of Hibernate's bidirectional features. Figure A.7 shows a diagram of the relationship between Speaker and EventSession.

A.7.1 Unidirectional one-to-many list

In our example, a single speaker will have multiple sessions that he is speaking at, within a single event. It's important to keep the sessions in order (since the Speaker has to perform at them in order). So our speaker will have a List of sessions. The Speaker looks like this:

```
public class Speaker implements Serializable {
    private List sessions = new ArrayList();

    /**
     * @hibernate.list
     * @hibernate.collection-key column="speaker_id"
     * @hibernate.collection-index column="session_index"
     * @hibernate.collection-one-to-many
    class="com.manning.hq.apdxA.EventSession"
     */
```

```
    public List getSessions() { return sessions; }
    public void setSessions(List sessions)
{this.sessions = sessions;}
    }
```

As you can see, this looks very much like a set mapping. The main difference is the addition of the @hibernate.collection-index tag, which specifies that the index column maintains the order of the sessions. In this case, the session_index column will exist in the event_session table. The mapping document looks like this:

```
<class name="com.manning.hq.apdxA.Speaker" table="speakers">
    <list name="sessions">
        <key column="speaker_id"/>
        <index  column="session_index" />
        <one-to-many class="com.manning.hq.apdxA.EventSession" />
    </list>
</class>
```

Table schema

The event_sessions table holds a foreign key back to the speakers table. It also has a column, session_index, that holds the order of the EventSessions within the list.

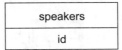

event_sessions				speakers
id	speaker_id	session_index		id

A.7.2 List of simple values

A List doesn't need to store entities; it can actually store simple values like Strings or Integers. To expand the object model, let's say that each Speaker has a list of telephone numbers, which you want to store as Strings. Simple values can't be bidirectional:

```
public class Speaker implements Serializable {
    /**
     * @hibernate.list table="phone_numbers"
     * @hibernate.collection-key column="event_id"
     * @hibernate.collection-index column="phone_index"
     * @hibernate.collection-element type="string"
     *     column="phone_number"
     */
    public List getPhoneNumbers() { return phoneNumbers; }
    public void setPhoneNumbers(List phoneNumbers) {
        this.phoneNumbers = phoneNumbers;
    }
}
```

Here you see a new XDoclet tag, @hibernate.collection-element, which declares that each value of the List is a String type. The resulting Speaker.hbm.xml looks like this:

```
<class name="com.manning.hq.apdxA.Speaker" table="speakers"
    <list name="phoneNumbers" table="phone_numbers">
        <key column="speaker_id"/>
        <index column="phone_index" />
        <element column="phone_number" type="string" />
    </list>
</class>
```

The <element> corresponds to the @hibernate.collection-element you saw in the previous listing. Now you can add phone numbers to the Speaker like so:

```
Speaker speaker = new Speaker();
speaker.getPhoneNumbers().add("867-5309");
```

Table schema

The phone_numbers table holds a foreign key back to the speakers table. It also has a column, phone_index, that holds the order of the

Strings within the list. The phone_numbers table doesn't represent an actual PhoneNumber entity but is just a collection of ordered strings.

phone_numbers		
speaker_id	phone_index	phone_number

speakers
id

A.7.3 Other lists

In addition to the List associations we've covered, these associations are possible:

- Unidirectional many-to-many lists
- Lists of components

A.8 Maps

Hibernate supports the use of Maps. The contract associated with a java.util.Map is that elements are stored and accessed (indexed) by a unique key, as opposed to order index (like a List). The values stored in the Map can be simple objects (like a String), an entity (like a Location), or a component (like Address). The index can be a simple value, entity, or component as well. Let's consider the entity first. Like Lists, Maps cannot be bidirectional. Figure A.8 shows a diagram of the relationship between Event and Room.

Figure A.8 One-to-many Map: Event to Room

A.8.1 One-to-many entity maps

In our next example, the Event has a number of rooms. Each room is its own unique entity, with a name and identity. For each event, the rooms are stored with a color code, such as "red", "blue", or "green". So Event will have a Map of Rooms, where the key is the color and the value is the Room:

```
public class Event implements Serializable {
    private Map rooms = new LinkedHashMap();
    /**
     * @hibernate.map
     * @hibernate.collection-key column="event_id"
     * @hibernate.collection-index
     *     column="room_color_code" type="string"
     * @hibernate.collection-one-to-many
    class="com.manning.hq.apdxA.Room"
     */
    public Map getRooms() { return rooms; }
    public void setRooms(Map rooms) { this.rooms = rooms; }
}
```

The key difference between a Map and a List is the need to specify the index type. In this case, the room color code is a simple string type. Since it's a one-to-many map, the event_id and room_color_code will go in the rooms table itself. Here's what the resulting mapping document will look like:

```
<class name="com.manning.hq.apdxA.Event">
    <map name="rooms">
        <key column="event_id"/>
        <index column="room_color_code" type="string" />
        <one-to-many class="com.manning.hq.apdxA.Room" />
    </map>
</class>
```

When you add new Rooms to an Event, you'll need to specify a unique color (for each event). Two different events could both have a "green" room, for example. The SchemaExport task will be an extreme help in this example, since it will make sure that the correct database constraints are generated.

Table schema

The rooms table holds a foreign key back to the events table. It also has a column, room_color_code, which uniquely identifies the room within the map. Because rooms are entities, they also have their own id column.

rooms		
id	event_id	room_color_code

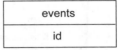

events
id

A.8.2 Many-to-many entity maps

Maps may also have a many-to-many association with an entity (see figure A.9). In this case, we could easily alter the Room relationship to fit it. This would involve specifying an association table, as well as replacing the one-to-many with a many-to-many. Here's what that class looks like:

Figure A.9 Many-to-many entity map: Event to Room

```
public class Event implements Serializable {
    private Map sharedRooms = new LinkedHashMap();
    /**
     * @hibernate.map table="as_event_to_rooms"
     * @hibernate.collection-key column="event_id"
     * @hibernate.collection-index
     *     column="room_color_code" type="string"
     * @hibernate.collection-many-to-many
     *     class="com.manning.hq.apdxA.Room" column="room_id"
     */
    public Map getSharedRooms() { return sharedRooms; }
    public void setSharedRooms(Map sharedRooms) {
        this.sharedRooms = sharedRooms; }
}
```

Here you're adding another field to Event, called sharedRooms, which is a many-to-many relationship with Rooms. The mapping file looks like this:

```
<class name="com.manning.hq.apdxA.Event">
        <map name="rooms" table="as_event_to_rooms">
        <key column="event_id"/>
        <index column="room_color_code" type="string" />
        <many-to-many class="com.manning.hq.apdxA.Room"
        column="room_id" />
    </map>
</class>
```

Table schema

As with all many-to-many relationships, you have an association table with dual foreign keys, which here also holds the map key: room_color_code.

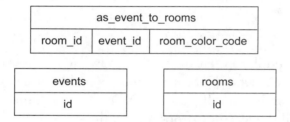

A.8.3 Map of components

Maps do not have to contain entities; like any other Hibernate collection, they can hold simple values (like Strings) or component objects. Let's consider an example where our Location has more than just two addresses but potentially a large number of them. You'll add a Map field to the Location object, which will hold Address components, with a key denoting the type of address (Billing, Mailing, Home Office, etc.).

Unlike components that are used via the @hibernate.component tag and <component> element, a collection of components needs its own table. This allows any number of components to be mapped back to the parent entity. You'll also see a new element, `<composite-element>`, which will be used instead of `<one-to-many>` or `<many-to-many>`. Collections of components are always one-to-many because they are coupled to their parent entity:

```
public class Location implements Serializable{
    private Map addresses = new LinkedHashMap();

    /**
     * @hibernate.map table="addresses"
     * @hibernate.collection-key column="location_id"
     * @hibernate.collection-index column="address_type"
     *     type="string"
     * @hibernate.collection-composite-element
     *     class="com.manning.hq.apdxA.Address"
     */
    public Map getAddresses() { return addresses; }
    public void setAddresses(Map addresses) {
        this.addresses = addresses;
    }
}
```

In this example, you can see the new tag, `@hibernate.collection-composite-element`. Here it defines the value of each map entry as an `Address` component. If you use XDoclet, the generated mapping file should pull the `Address` properties in the `<map>` element:

```
<class name="com.manning.hq.apdxA.Location" table="locations">
    <map name="addresses" table="addresses">
        <key column="location_id"/>
        <index column="address_type" type="string"/>
        <composite-element class="com.manning.hq.apdxA.Address">
            <property name="streetAddress"
              type="java.lang.String" column="street_address" />
        </composite-element>
    </map>
</class>
```

Table schema

The addresses table holds the foreign key back to the locations table, location_id. The address_type is the unique identifier within the map.

addresses		
location_id	address_type	streetAddress

locations
id

A.8.4 Maps with entity keys

A Map object allows the use of any object as a key. The only constraints are that it must override the equals() and hashCode() methods of the object. In the case of a Hibernate entity, the easiest way to define equals() and hashCode() is to use the primary key.[2] Instead of using an unsorted Set of Speakers, you want to store them according to a Room object. Since you want to use Room as a key, you must override both methods as well:

```
public class Event implements Serializable {
    private Map speakersByRoom = new LinkedHashMap();

    /**
     * @hibernate.map table="as_event_to_speakers_by_room"
     * @hibernate.collection-key column="event_id"
     * @hibernate.index-many-to-many column="room_id"
     *      class="com.manning.hq.apdxA.Room"
     * @hibernate.collection-many-to-many
     *      class="com.manning.hq.apdxA.Speaker"
     *      column="speaker_id"
     */
    public Map getSpeakersByRoom() { return speakersByRoom; }
    public void setSpeakersByRoom(Map speakersByRoom) {
        this.speakersByRoom = speakersByRoom;
```

---

[2] The strategy of using the primary key as the foundation for equality, while simple, does have its share of problems, since Hibernate typically generates the keys. For an in-depth discussion of this issues, see Christian Bauer and Gavin King's *Hibernate in Action* (Manning, 2004).

```
        }
    }
    public class Room implements Serializable {
        private Long id;
        public boolean equals(Object o) {
            if (this == o) return true;
            if (!(o instanceof Room)) return false;
            final Room room = (Room) o;
            if (id != null ? !id.equals(room.id) : room.id != null) {
                return false;
            }
            return true;
        }

        public int hashCode() {
            return (id != null ? id.hashCode() : 0);
        }
    }
}
```

Here you've implemented the two necessary methods on `Room` so that you can use it as a key in your map. In addition, to specify a `Room` object as a key, you've used a new tag, `@hibernate.index-many-to-many`. Notice that it breaks somewhat with the XDoclet naming convention; it should have probably been called `@hibernate-collection-index-many-to-many`, but that's a mouthful. The resulting Event.hbm.xml file looks like this:

```
<class name="com.manning.hq.apdxA.Event"  table="events">
    <map name="speakersByRoom"
    table="as_event_to_speakers_by_room">
        <key column="event_id"/>
        <index-many-to-many  class="com.manning.hq.apdxA.Room"
            column="room_id" />
        <many-to-many class="com.manning.hq.apdxA.Speaker"
            column="speaker_id"  />
    </map>
</class>
```

That's how you define this relationship, which is a pretty complicated one. You might never need a relationship this rich in your object model, but it's nice to know it can be done, should you require it. To illustrate how you might populate it, here's a short code sample to show it in action:

```
Event event = new Event();
Room room1 = new Room();
Room room2 = new Room();
Speaker speaker1 = new Speaker();
Speaker speaker2 = new Speaker();

session.save(event);
session.save(room1);
session.save(room2);
session.save(speaker1);
session.save(speaker2);

event.getSpeakersByRoom().put(room1, speaker1);
event.getSpeakersByRoom().put(room2, speaker2);
session1.flush();
```

You've created an event, a few rooms, and a few speakers. Then save all of them, which is important especially for the Room objects, so they won't have null ids. Next you put the speakers into the map using the Rooms as keys.

Table schema

This fairly complicated relationship has three entity tables, with an association table that links the three together. The room is actually the unique map key for the collections of speakers.

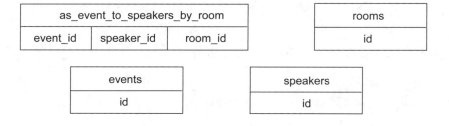

A.8.5 Other maps

Maps offer the most variety of association possibilities, not all of which we can cover here. As long as you know they are possible, it should be fairly easy to mix and match the collection tags/elements you've seen so far to build the association you want. Here's a list of other relationships that are possible but that we don't have space to cover:

- Maps with component keys and entity values (one-to-many or many-to-many)
- Maps with entity keys and component values
- Maps with entity keys and simple values
- Maps with simple keys and simple values

A.9 Arrays

Hibernate supports the use of arrays to store entities, components, and simple values. The two elements that it uses are `<array>` and `<primitive-array>`, the latter used only if non-object simple values are being stored (like `int`, `long`, or `boolean`).

A.9.1 Entity arrays

Suppose your `Event` had several speakers, featured as part of a round-table discussion panel. You might store them as an `Array` on the `Event` class, in a one-to-many relationship, as shown in figure A.10.

Figure A.10 One-to-many array: `Event` to `Speaker`

The `Event` class looks like this:

```
public class Event implements Serializable {
    private Speaker[] featuredSpeakers = new Speaker[0];
```

```
      /**
       * @hibernate.array
       * @hibernate.collection-key column="event_id_featured"
       * @hibernate.collection-index column="featured_speaker_order"
       * @hibernate.collection-one-to-many
       *    class="com.manning.hq.apdxA.Speaker"
       */
      public Speaker[] getFeaturedSpeakers() {
          return featuredSpeakers;
      }
      public void setFeaturedSpeakers(Speaker[] featuredSpeakers) {
          this.featuredSpeakers = featuredSpeakers;
      }
  }
```

Unfortunately you still need to specify the class on the @hiber-nate.collection-one-to-many tag, because XDoclet doesn't attempt to guess (even though it probably could from the return type):

```
<class name="com.manning.hq.apdxA.Event"  table="events">
    <array name="featuredSpeakers">
        <key column="event_id_featured"/>
        <index column="featured_speaker_order" />
        <one-to-many class="com.manning.hq.apdxA.Speaker" />
    </array>
</class>
```

Table schema

Arrays of entities and lists of entities are pretty much identical in usage and database schemas. There is a foreign key back to the parent table and a column that maintains the order.

Speakers				events
id	event_id_featured	featured_speaker_order		id

A.9.2 Primitive arrays

A regular <array> can be used to store simple value objects, but a special mapping is needed to store primitive values, like an int or long. Let's expand our object model by adding an array of room numbers, which are still available for guests to use. Rather than store entire room objects, you'll just store the room number itself. Here's what the Event class looks like:

```
public class Event implements Serializable {
    /**
     * @hibernate.primitive-array table="available_rooms"
     * @hibernate.collection-key column="event_id"
     * @hibernate.collection-index column="room_order"
     * @hibernate.collection-element column="room_number"
     *      type="integer"
     */
    public int[] getAvailableRooms() { return availableRooms; }
    public void setAvailableRooms(int[] availableRooms) {
        this.availableRooms = availableRooms;
    }
}
```

The @hibernate.primitive-array tag will be converted to a <primitive-array> element by XDoclet. A collection table is also needed here, available_rooms, to store these values. The Event.hbm.xml looks like this:

```
<class name="com.manning.hq.apdxA.Event"  table="events">
    <primitive-array name="availableRooms"
        table="available_rooms" >
        <key column="event_id" />
        <index column="room_order" />
        <element column="room_number" type="integer" />
    </primitive-array>
</class>
```

Here's a code sample to set the room numbers that are available:

```
Event event = new Event();
int[] rooms = new int[]{1, 200, 500};
event.setAvailableRooms(rooms);
session.save(event);
```

Table schema

The available_rooms table doesn't represent an entity, but is just an array of integers. There is no primary key, but there is a foreign key back to the events table. There is also a column for order, as well as the actual integer value.

available_rooms				events
event_id	room_order	room_number		id

A.9.3 Other arrays

Samples of other arrays include

- Arrays of components
- Array of simple value objects (String, Integer, etc.)
- Arrays of entities, many-to-many

A.10 Bags

The concept of a Bag may not be familiar to most Java developers, because there is no java.util.Bag interface in the Java core collections library. The contract of a Bag is a collection, which does not guarantee order and can contain the same object multiple times. In Hibernate, if you really want one, you can use either a List or a Collection to "fake" a Bag. Then you define a <bag> element, just like any other collection.

In Hibernate, Bags are very flexible, much like Sets, in that they allow bidirectional one-to-many and bidirectional many-to-many associations, which Lists and Sets do not. As with Sets, you can specify an order-by clause but no in-memory sort. This makes sense because there is no SortedBag interface, whereas a SortedSet interface exists.

A.10.1 Bags of entities: one-to-many, unidirectional

The simplest Bag we can show you is one that holds entity objects in a one-to-many association. To demonstrate it, let's rework our original Set of Speakers into a Bag of Speakers:

```
public class Event implements Serializable {
    private List bagOfSpeakers = new ArrayList();

    /**
     * @hibernate.bag
     * @hibernate.collection-key column="event_id_bag"
     * @hibernate.collection-one-to-many
     *      class="com.manning.hq.apdxA.Speaker"
     */
    public List getBagOfSpeakers() { return bagOfSpeakers; }
    public void setBagOfSpeakers(List bagOfSpeakers) {
        this.bagOfSpeakers = bagOfSpeakers;
    }
}
```

Note that while you're using a List as the actual field type for the Bag, you don't need to specify a @hibernate.collection-index tag. Bags have no index, so this column is unnecessary:

```
<class name="com.manning.hq.apdxA.Event"  table="events">
    <bag name="bagOfSpeakers">
        <key column="event_id_bag"/>
        <one-to-many class="com.manning.hq.apdxA.Speaker" />
    </bag>
</class>
```

With the bag mapped, you can go ahead and add elements to it, like so:

```
Event event = new Event();
Speaker speaker1 = new Speaker();
```

```
Speaker speaker2 = new Speaker();

event.getBagOfSpeakers().add(speaker1);
event.getBagOfSpeakers().add(speaker2);
```

Table schema

The table structure for Bags is just like a list, but without the order column:

A.10.2 Other bags

The Bag mapping has quite a few variations, most of which are mapped just like a Set. Here's a list, but we don't have enough space to describe them in detail:

- Bag of entities, many-to-many (unidirectional or bidirectional)
- Bag of entities, one-to-many, bidirectional
- Bag of simple values
- Bag of components

A.11 Subclasses

Hibernate supports several major types of subclass type: table-per-class (<subclass>), table-per-subclass (<joined-subclass>), and table-per-concrete-class (both <any> and <union-subclass>). In Hibernate 3, either <subclass> or <joined-subclass> can be used per hierarchy, but you can't mix in <union-subclass> too. So Event has two subclasses, ConferenceEvent and NetworkingEvent, and use <subclass> and/or <joined-subclass>. Figure A.11 shows a diagram of the class hierarchy containing Event and its subclasses ConferenceEvent and NetworkEvent.

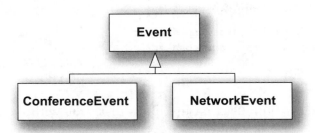

Figure A.11 Subclasses: Event with child ConferenceEvent and NetworkEvent

A.11.1 Table-per-class hierarchy strategy

To create a subclass (basic <subclass>), you need at least two classes: a superclass and a subclass. You have to mark them with the correct tags, and you need to specify a discriminator type so Hibernate knows what class each row is. Here are the classes:

```java
/**
 * @hibernate.class table="events" discriminator-value="Event"
 * @hibernate.discriminator column="class_name"
 */
public class Event implements Serializable {
    private Long id;
    /**
     * @hibernate.id generator-class="native" column="id"
     */
    public Long getId() { return id; }
    public void setId(Long id) { this.id = id; }
}

/**
 * @hibernate.subclass discriminator-value="ConferenceEvent"
 */
public class ConferenceEvent extends Event{ }

/**
 * @hibernate.subclass discriminator-value="NetworkingEvent"
 */
public class NetworkingEvent extends Event{ }
```

The parent class, Event, defines the column that will hold the discriminator value. Each subclass (as well as Event) has a different value that it will store in that column. When Hibernate loads a row, it looks at the value of the column and knows whether to instantiate an Event or a NetworkingEvent. Also, the id field demonstrates that the subclasses don't need to do anything other than extend Event. The superclass Event holds all the details.

```
<class name="com.manning.hq.apdxA.Event"  table="events">
    <id name="id" column="id" type="java.lang.Long">
        <generator class="native" />
    </id>
    <subclass name="com.manning.hq.apdxA.ConferenceEvent"
        discriminator-value=" ConferenceEvent " />
    <subclass name="com.manning.hq.apdxA.NetworkingEvent"
        discriminator-value="NetworkingEvent" />
</class>
```

As you can see, all the subclass mappings go into the Event.hbm.xml file; no ConferenceEvent.hbm.xml will exist. Subclasses can have their own properties, which will be defined inside the <subclass> element.

Table schema

One table holds all of the events, distinguished by the value in the class_name column.

events	
id	class_name

A.11.2 Table-per-subclass strategy

A joined subclass (<joined-subclass> element) works a bit differently from the <subclass> mapping. There will be a single top-level table, which holds all of the ids, and a table for every subclass. Since each subclass has its own table, Hibernate doesn't need a discriminator column to determine the class type. Expanding our object model, assume that there are several types of Rooms, including a SuiteRoom and a PenthouseRoom:

```
/**
 *  @hibernate.class table="rooms"
 */
public class Room implements Serializable {
    private Long id;

    /**
     * @hibernate.id generator-class="native" column="id"
     * @return
     */
    public Long getId() { return id; }
    public void setId(Long id) { this.id = id; }
}

/**
 *
 * @hibernate.joined-subclass table="suite_room"
 * @hibernate.joined-subclass-key column="room_id"
 */
public class SuiteRoom extends Room { }

/**
 *
 * @hibernate.joined-subclass table="penthouse_room"
 * @hibernate.joined-subclass-key column="room_id"
 */
public class PenthouseRoom extends Room { }
```

From the listing above, you can see that Room doesn't need the discriminator value. Instead, each joined subclass has to specify a key column, which joins back to the superclass table, in this case, room_id. And while it's currently not stated in the XDoclet documentation, a table attribute is available that lets you specify which table the subclasses map to.

```
<class name="com.manning.hq.apdxA.Room" table="rooms">
    <id name="id" column="id" type="java.lang.Long">
```

```
        <generator class="native" />
    </id>
    <joined-subclass name="com.manning.hq.apdxA.SuiteRoom"
        table="suite_room">
        <key column="room_id"  />
    </joined-subclass>
    <joined-subclass name="com.manning.hq.apdxA.PenthouseRoom"
        table="penthouse_room">
        <key column="room_id" />
    </joined-subclass>
</class>
```

If the subclasses had their own properties (which they likely would in a real example), they'd be defined normally with `<property>` elements, and they'd go right under the `<key>` element inside the subclass.

Table schema

For this relation three tables are needed: one for the parent, and one for each of the two subclasses.

rooms
id

suite_room	
id	room_id

penthouse_room	
id	room_id

A.11.3 Table-per-concrete-class strategy: any

The next inheritance strategy is one that is not commonly used. The table-per-concrete-class strategy makes use of the `<any>` mapping. Each concrete class has its own table, but unlike the `<joined-subclass>` there's no single table maintaining a common set of keys.

So if each table could theoretically have its own row "1," how does another table create a foreign key to it? Essentially, it needs what we refer to as a compound foreign key, with one column to store the name of table and one to store the foreign key. The fact that an object could join to any row in any table means conventional joins don't work. Therefore, several selects are needed to do what normal joins can do in one, so performance will be somewhat worse.

Although this mapping is a niche case, it has some neat uses, especially for databases that need to add new tables dynamically at runtime (as a content management system might do) or legacy databases. Hibernate 3 has a new way to handle the table-per-concrete-class strategy, <union-subclass>, but for 2.x, the <any> mapping is what's available. So let's explore what this looks like.

Our example for this section deals with event registration and payments. The Registration class will have any relationship to classes, which implement a PaymentDetails interface. Since the Event is going to be open, you need liberal payment options. So you'll accept both CreditCardPayments and BarterPayments. Both of these are structurally different; each gets its own table. Here's what the PaymentDetails interface looks like:

```
public interface PaymentDetails {    public Long getId(); }
```

The first subclass looks like this:

```
/**
 *  @hibernate.class table="credit_card_payments"
 */
public class CreditCardPayment
    implements Serializable, PaymentDetails {
    private Long id;
    private BigDecimal amount;
    private String currencyCode;
    /**
     * @hibernate.id generator-class="native" column="id"
     */
    public Long getId() { return id; }
    public void setId(Long id) { this.id = id; }
    /**
     * @hibernate.property
     */
    public BigDecimal getAmount() { return amount; }
    public void setAmount(BigDecimal amount) {
        this.amount = amount;
    }
    /**
```

```
   * @hibernate.property column="currency_code"
   */
  public String getCurrencyCode() { return currencyCode; }
  public void setCurrencyCode(String currencyCode) {
      this.currencyCode = currencyCode; }
}
```

And here's the second subclass:

```
/**
 * @hibernate.class table="barter_payments"
 */
public class BarterPayment implements Serializable, PaymentDetails
   {
   private Long id;
   private int numberOfCows;
   private int numberOfSheep;
   /**
    * @hibernate.id generator-class="native" column="id"
    */
   public Long getId() { return id; }
   public void setId(Long id) { this.id = id; }
   /**
    * @hibernate.property column="number_of_cows"
    */
   public int getNumberOfCows() { return numberOfCows; }
   public void setNumberOfCows(int numberOfCows) {
       this.numberOfCows = numberOfCows;
   }

   /**
    * @hibernate.property column="number_of_sheep"
    */
   public int getNumberOfSheep() { return numberOfSheep; }
   public void setNumberOfSheep(int numberOfSheep) {
       this.numberOfSheep = numberOfSheep;
   }
}
```

As you can see, both subclasses implement a very simple interface, Pay-mentDetails, and each has its own id and table. Nothing in the tables they use indicates they are subclasses. Next, let's look at the Registra-tion class, which actually has the <any> mapping:

```
/**
 * @hibernate.class table="registrations"
 */
public class Registration implements Serializable {
    private Long id;
    private PaymentDetails paymentDetails;
    /**
     * @hibernate.id generator-class="native" column="id"
     */
    public Long getId() { return id; }
    public void setId(Long id) { this.id = id; }
    /**
     * @hibernate.any id-type="long" meta-type="java.lang.Class"
     * @hibernate.any-column name="table_name"
     * @hibernate.any-column name="payment_id"
     */
    public PaymentDetails getPaymentDetails() {
        return paymentDetails;
    }
    public void setPaymentDetails(PaymentDetails paymentDetails) {
        this.paymentDetails = paymentDetails;
    }
}
```

The @hibernate.any and @hibernate.any-column tags specify the col-umn with the foreign key, and the column that holds the table name. Here we use the fully qualified class name as the table name. The three mapping files follow.

First, here's Registration.hbm.xml:

```
<class name="com.manning.hq.apdxA.Registration"
    table="registrations">
    <id name="id" column="id" type="java.lang.Long">
```

```xml
        <generator class="native"/>
    </id>
    <any name="paymentDetails" id-type="long"
        meta-type="java.lang.Class">
        <column name="payment_id" />
        <column name="table_name" />
    </any>
</class>
```

Next is CreditCardPayment.hbm.xml:

```xml
<class name="com.manning.hq.apdxA.CreditCardPayment"
    table="credit_card_payments">
    <id name="id" column="id"  type="java.lang.Long" >
        <generator class="native" />
    </id>
    <property name="amount" type="java.math.BigDecimal"
        column="amount" />
    <property name="currencyCode" type="java.lang.String"
        column="currency_code" />
</class>
```

And finally, BarterPayment.hbm.xml:

```xml
<class name="com.manning.hq.apdxA.BarterPayment"
   table="barter_payments">
    <id name="id" column="id" type="java.lang.Long" >
        <generator class="native" />
    </id>
    <property  name="numberOfCows"  type="int"
        column="number_of_cows" />
    <property name="numberOfSheep"  type="int"
   column="number_of_sheep" />
</class>
```

A Registration object can be assigned either a CreditCardPayment or a BarterPayment, and each object is stored in its own table.

Table schema

Here's what the table structures would look like:

Registrations		
id	payment_id	table_name

credit_card_payment		
id	amount	currency_code

barter_payment		
id	number_of_cows	number_of_sheep

To further highlight the data that is actually added to the database, suppose you wrote the following code:

```
Registration r = new Registration();
CreditCardPayment cc = new CreditCardPayment();
r.setPaymentDetails(cc);
cc.setAmount(new BigDecimal(34.50));
cc.setCurrencyCode("US");
session.save(cc);
session.save(r);
session.flush();
```

You'd get something like the following rows in the database:

Registrations		
id	payment_id	table_name
100	102	com.manning.hq.apdxA.CreditCardPayment

credit_card_payment		
id	amount	currency_code
102	34.50	US

So you can see some sample data, as well as what the "compound foreign key" looks like.

Non-class-based discriminators

Finally, you don't have to use a fully-qualified class name for the table, but since XDoclet 1.2.3 doesn't have a tag for the <meta-value> element, you'll need to handwrite the mapping file. If you want to use string keys, like "cc" or "bp" instead, here's how the mapping file would look:

```
<class name="com.manning.hq.apdxA.Registration"
    table="registrations">
<id name="id" column="id" type="java.lang.Long">
    <generator class="native"/>
</id>
<any name="paymentDetails" id-type="long" meta-type="string">
    <meta-value value="cc"
        class="com.manning.hq.apdxA.CreditCardPayment"/>
    <meta-value value="bp"
        class="com.manning.hq.apdxA.BarterPayment"/>
    <column name="table_name"/>
    <column name="payment_id"/>
</any>
</class>
```

As you can see, <meta-value> allows non-class values to be used as the discriminators. In addition, you must change the meta-type attribute back to string rather than java.lang.Class.

Other possible relationships

In addition to the <any> relationship are several other variations of the table-per-concrete-class strategy, including

- <many-to-any>, which is supported by the @hibernate.many-to-any and @hibernate-many-to-any-column tags
- <index-many-to-any>, for which no tag is available as of XDoclet 1.2.3, so a merge point will be necessary

Both of these variations allow for very loose relationships between tables. You will probably need them even more rarely than <any> because they are very complex and uncommon cases, but handy when you need them.

A.11.4 Table-per-concrete-class strategy: union

A new relationship added in Hibernate 3 is the <union–subclass> relationship. Like the <any> relationship, it uses a single table for each concrete class, but doesn't use a compound foreign key. Since the primary key has to be shared across all the tables, you can't use the identity key generation scheme. Also, because it's a new relationship, XDoclet doesn't yet support it, so handwriting the mapping file will be necessary. We'll use the same classes as the <any> mapping and the interface PaymentDetails, with subclasses UnionCreditCardPayment and UnionBarterPayment. Here's what UnionBarterPayment looks like:

```
public class UnionBarterPayment implements PaymentDetails {
    private Long id;
    private int numberOfCows;

    public Long getId() { return id; }
    public void setId(Long id) { this.id = id; }

    public int getNumberOfCows() { return numberOfCows; }
    public void setNumberOfCows(int numberOfCows) {
        this.numberOfCows = numberOfCows;
    }
}
```

And UnionCreditCardPayment is next:

```
public class UnionCreditCardPayment implements PaymentDetails {
    private Long id;
    private BigDecimal amount;

    public Long getId() { return id; }
    public void setId(Long id) { this.id = id; }

    public BigDecimal getAmount() { return amount; }
    public void setAmount(BigDecimal amount) {
        this.amount = amount;
    }
}
```

Finally, a single mapping file is used, called PaymentDetails.hbm.xml, that has mappings for both classes. Here's what it looks like:

```xml
<hibernate-mapping>
    <class name="com.manning.hq.apdxA.PaymentDetails"
        table="payment_details">
        <id name="id" column="id" type="java.lang.Long">
            <generator class="increment"/>
        </id>
        <union-subclass
            name="com.manning.hq.apdxA.UnionBarterPayment"
            table="union_barter_payments">
            <property name="numberOfCows"
                column="number_of_cows"/>
        </union-subclass>
        <union-subclass
            name="com.manning.hq.apdxA.UnionCreditCardPayment"
            table="union_cc_payments">
            <property name="amount" column="amount"/>
        </union-subclass>
    </class>
</hibernate-mapping>
```

Note that we used the increment key generation strategy, but anything besides identity should work.

Table schema

Here's what the table structures would look like:

payment_details
id

union_cc_payments	
id	amount

union_barter_payments	
id	number_of_cows

Union subclasses allow the table-per-concrete strategy without having to be used as a relationship, like the <any> mapping.

A.12 Summary

The appendix has summarized and detailed most of the common associations that Hibernate permits. We've given examples of the mapping elements and how you can use XDoclet tags to generate them. This appendix is not meant as a replacement for the Hibernate manual, but as a supplemental catalog. You should be able to look up the association you want, find the mapping details, and then turn to the Hibernate manual or XDoclet to fill in the details.

Index

Symbols
< 182
<= 182
<> 182
= 182
> 182
>= 182

A
Active code generation 307
agile methodology 324
all-delete-orphan 147
and 182
AnnotationConfiguration 357
annotations 354
  and XDoclet 357
anonymous inner class
  using for callbacks 207
Ant 2, 26, 186
  build file 36
  configuring for XDoclet 280
  debugging output 41
  extracting 30
  inserting into XDoclet tags 309
  installing 30– 31
  obtaining 30
  running from command line 39– 41
  setting up 27

ANT_HOME environment variable 31
<antcall> element 309
any 182
<any> mapping 401
Apache commons connection pool 210
Apache Software Foundation 30
appenders for log4j 104
ApplicationContext 210, 216
  applicationContext.xml 208, 210
array 132
  entity 392
  of primitive values 394
  other possible types 395
  persistent. *See* collections
  relationships 392
Aspect Oriented Programming 203, 215
assertFalse 317
AssertionFailedError 317
assertions 316
assertTrue 317
association
  outer-join property 24
  relational vs. object 5
  table 378
  unidirectional 60
attributes
  used by XDoclet tags 278
@author tag 277
auto_increment fields 107

AutoFlushEvent 360
automated unit tests 313
    benifit of 345
automatic dirty object checking 197

B
Bag
    one to many, entity, unidirectional 396
    other possible types 397
    relationships 395
    See also collections, Bag
<bag> element 395
@Basic 355
BasicDataSource
    apache commons 208
<batchtest> element 320
<bean> element 211
best practices, organizing your projects
        with 189
between 182
bidirectional associations 142
    inverse end 143
    many-to-many 143
        inverse 145
boilerplate code problem 196, 201
brittle tests, avoiding 333, 345
build file 31
    default name for 40
    reusing 42, 46– 48
    specifying name of 42
build process 30
build.xml. *See* Ant, build file
business logic 198
buzzword compliance 203

C
C3P0 74
cache 24, 79
    query results 24
    second-level and HQL 164
    second-level caches. *See* second-level
        cache
    session based 328
    Session vs. second-level 79

transactional 81
    usage attribute 80
cache provider 79– 82
    cache.provider_class 79
    collections and classes 80
callbacks 206– 207
Cartesian product 14, 172
cascade 64– 66
    attribute for hibernate.many-to-one tag
        293
    attribute for hibernate.set tag 303
    avoid need to manually save objects 116
    configuring 65
    executed 65
    for many-to-one relationships 115
    save 17
    types 65
CASE 349
casting, performed by DAOs 201
CDATA 167
CGLIB 62
checked exceptions, converting to
        unchecked 108, 192, 205
class attribute
    for hibernate.component tag 295
    for hibernate.many-to-one tag 293
    for mapping files 94
class element 57
class files, output location 41
class level comments, as valid location for
        XDoclet tags 283
class tag. *See* hibernate.class tag
class type 349
classes, running in Ant 44
ClassNotFoundException
    thrown on misnamed class 305
classpath
    configuring to include XDoclet 281
    defining in build file 42
ClasspathXmlApplicationContext 211
clean target 45
CLEAN_INSERT operation 338
closing sessions
    with a helper class 111

code duplication, avoiding 215
code generate, hbm files 274
code generation tool
    Xdoclet as a 312
code samples for XDoclet 280
collections 63– 64
    accessing by index 180
    Bag 125, 136
        as List 136
    cascades 145
    Collections semantics 125
    element 131
    elements of 177
    filters 141
    generating with xdoclte 300
    Hibernate implementation of 126
    Hibernate support for 123
    idbag 137
    index 125
        map 133
    index-many-to-many 134
    interface 127
    key 129
    key element 64
    lazy 23, 138
        populating 138
        populating in web tier 139
        retrieving 173
    list 132
    many-to-many 130
        column attribute 130
    map 133
    of value types 131
    one-to-many 128
    persistent behavior 125
    persistent types 64
    set 127, 131
    sorting 139
    table attribute 130
@Column 355
column attribute
    for hibernate.collection-key 305
    for hibernate.id tag 284

    for hibernate.many-to-one tag 293
    for hibernate.property tag 287
<column> element 290, 292
column tag 282
comments, value of XDoclet tags 275
Commons Logging 102
    homepage for 104
Comparable 140
    vs. Comparator 141
Comparator 140– 141
compareTo(Object) 140
component 89, 116, 124
    bidirectional 374
    generating multiple with XDoclet 298
    having no identity 117
    mapping catalog for 373
    mapping in .hbm.xml file 119
    multiple identitical 300
    reasons to use one 121
    unidirectional 373
    using multiple 121
<component> element 119, 297, 299
component tag
    similiarity to many-to-one relationship
        297
CompositeUserTypes 147, 154
    assemble(...) and disassemble(...) 157
    second-level cache 158
    Serializable 154
    vs. components 158
    vs. UserType 154
Configuration
    addJar(...) 67
configuration
    application server 55
    basic 53– 56
    cache element 80
    cache providers 79– 82
    central file 208
    connection pools 74– 76
        configuring specific 75
    connection properties 54
    connection.datasource 55
    database connections 53

configuration *(continued)*
  dialect 54
  dialect property 54, 56
  Hibernate 45
  JDBC connections 53
  JNDI DataSource 55
  mapping 55
  mapping element 55
  transactions 76– 78
Configuration class 52
  addClass(...) 67
  addFile(...) 67
  adding classes dynamically 68
  configure() 67
connection
  closing manually 108
  configuring for database 95
  properties 54
connection pool 54, 74– 76
  adding new 75
  default 75
connection.datasource property 55
Connector/J 34
consistent state 336
convenience methods 206
CONVERT 170
cooperating tags 301
copy and paste reuse 196
CopyEvent 360
core patterns, as defined by Sun 190
create, read, update and delete. *See* CRUD
Criteria 183
  alternative to HQL 183
  limitations 184
CRUD 192, 201
CURRENT_TIMESTAMP 176
custom types 147
  purpose 147
  UserType 148

D
Data Access Object pattern (DAO) 190
  per class as a style of DAO 192
  simple implementation of 193

database
  changing structure 336
  configuring connection 95
  portability of 291
  setting up 31– 34
  sharing between tests 335
  testing 324
DatabaseConnection 342
DatabaseTestCase 339– 340
<dataset> element, for DBUnit 337
DataSource 74
dates
  querying based on 329
  working around JDK API 99
DBCP 74
DBUnit 336, 345
  creating test data 337
  disadvantages of SQL scripts 336
  generating DTD 336
  importing test data 337
  loading test data 336
  operations 338
  verifying state of the database 345
<dbunit> task 336
debugging, for Ant property substitution 310
default attribute in Ant 37
DELETE operation 338
DELETE_ALL operation 338
DeleteEvent 360
depends attribute 38
deploying applications
  against multiple databases 331
description message
  of asserts 318
destdir attribute 41
detached objects
  problem of 197, 202
  updating 206
dialect
  attribute for 311
  property for 54, 56
  specifying in config file 96

directory, for projects 35
DirtyCheckEvent 360
discriminator 350
  column 398
  derived 350
  formulas 349
  non-class based 407
  See also inheritance
distinct 177
documentation, via XDoclet tags 275
domain layer 198
domain logic
  testing 345
  using a component to encapsulate 121
domain model 10, 20
  using Hibernate for 35
domain objects
  testing of 315
drivers. *See* JDBC, drivers
drop tables, using SchemaExport task
  100
dtd
  for .hbm.xml files 93
  for hibernate.cfg.xml 95
duplication
  avoiding in build files 42
duplication problem
  potential for with simple DAOs 196
  potential of 201
dynamic classes 352
dynamic domain model 352
  advantage 353
  disadvantage 353
  retrieving 354

E
echo task 39
EHCache 79
  configuring 81
ehcache.xml 81
EJB3 355
Enterprise JavaBeans (EJB) 20
  XDoclet tags for 277

entities, verify they persist 325
@Entity 355
  entity object vs. persistent object 134
entity objects 89
entity-name 353
environment
  managed 52
  nonmanaged 52
equality
  strategy based on identity 389
equals() method 389
EventLister 360
EventObject 360
events 359
EvictEvent 360
evils of duplication, avoiding 312
exception handling, managing
  with DAOs 191
exceptions, thrown from failed
  assertions 316
excess objects, in the database during
  testing 330
excise 204
exists 182
explicitness 195, 213
expressions. *See* HQL, expressions
extension points
  for XDoclet 312
extract Hibernate utility class,
  refactoring of 108
Extract SchemaExport task
  refactoring of 111
Extreme Programming 324

F
failure messages 317
false negatives 330
false positives
  avoiding 329
fileset element 46
filter-def 347
filtering, with ant 332

filters 347
    applying 347
    See also collections, filters
finally block
    using to delete objects during tests 335
finely grained objects 121
FlatXmlDataSet 340
flush, session state to the database 99
FlushEvent 360
foreign key 3
    automatically mangaged by hibernate
        122
    compound 401, 406
    generation algorithm 368
    unsupported by all MySQL versions
        106
    using to specify relationships 94
formatters 319
FROM 171
functions. *See* HQL, functions

G

generator 58–59
    assigned 58
    native 59
generator-class attribute 284
getSetUpOperation() method 342
getTearDownOperation() method. 342
getter/setter 92
GROUP BY. *See* HQL, GROUP BY

H

handwritten, avoiding need for 312
hashCode() method 389
HAVING 182
HBM files. *See* mapping definition
hbm.xml
    necessary evil of 274
    specifying location for 93
    See also mapping definition
helper class, creating one for
        hibernate 108
hibernate.many-to-any tag 407
Hibern8IDE 186

Hibernate
    completeness 22
    connecting 42
    documentation 364
    flexibility 20
    home page 28
    instead of JDBC 7
    mapping document 21
    obtaining 28
    performance 23
    persistence with 20–24
    primary classes 52
    runtime configuration file 21
    simplicity 20
Hibernate in Action 1
Hibernate manual
    not a replacement for 410
Hibernate Query Language. *See* HQL
Hibernate Reference documentation 311
hibernate.any-column tag 404
hibernate.array tag 304
hibernate.bag tag 304
hibernate.cfg.xml 53–56, 95
    alternative to 208
    and hibernate.properties 53
    generating 310
hibernate.class tag 278, 283
    using to generate hibernate.cfg.xml 310
hibernate.collection-composite-element
        tag 388
hibernate.collection-element tag 383
hibernate.collection-index tag 382
hibernate.collection-key tag 301, 304
hibernate.collection-many-to-many
        tag 303
hibernate.collection-one-to-many
        tag 301, 305
hibernate.column tag 289, 301
    needing in conjuction with hiber-
        nate.component tags 300
    reasons to use 290
hibernate.component tag 295
hibernate.id tag 284, 301

hibernate.index-many-to-many tag 390
hibernate.list tag 304
hibernate.many-to-one tag 292, 301
hibernate.map tag 304
hibernate.parent tag 375
hibernate.primitive-array tag 304, 394
hibernate.properties 53
hibernate.property tag 287, 301
  used by hibernate.componet tag 295
hibernate.set tag 301, 303
Hibernate.STRING 152
hibernate23.jar
  adding to classpath 44
HibernateCallback 207
<hibernatecfg> subtask 311
HibernateDaoSupport 211, 213
hibernatedoclet task 281, 308, 310
hibernate-many-to-any-column tag 407
hibernate-mapping
  package 57
hibernate-mapping element 57
hibernate-mapping-2.0.dtd 278
HibernateTemplate 205, 211, 216
hilo key generation 309
HQL 23, 54, 70
  alias 171
    naming convention 172
  alternatives to 183
  avg 176
  consolditing in one place 191
  debugging 169
  displaying generated SQL. See show_sql
  executing 163, 168
  expressions 179
    maxElement(...) 180
    maxIndex(...) 180
    minElement(...) 180
    size(...) 179
  for efficient retrieval 364
  functions 176
    aggregate 176
    elements(...) 177
    for indexed collections 180
    scalar 176

GROUP BY 182
join 172
  alias for 177
  types of 172
joined objects 174
limiting results. See Query, maxResults
max 176
min 176
named queries 167
  advantage of 167
new. See HQL, returning new objects
ORDER BY 182– 183
outer-joins 168
paramaters, positional 165
parameters, named 166
properties 178
  class 178
  class, return type 179
  id 178
  size 179
query parameters 23
query substitutions 169
querying objects 171
querying on object properties 71
returning new objects 175
returning specific fields. See HQL,
    SELECT projection
SELECT 174
  projection 174
  returned values from 174
similar to SQL 162
similiar to SQL 22
sum 176
WHERE 179
why needed 161
HQL queries, verify they work 325
HTML
  converting test results to 321
  generated by Javadoc 276

I
iBATIS 8
@Id 355

id
  column attribute 58
  element for 58
  mapped attribute and property type 59
  tag for 282
  unsaved-value attribute 58–59
IDatabaseConnection 342
idbag 125
  performance 138
IDE. *See* Integrated Development Environment (IDE)
identical primary keys, one-to-one 368
identity
  as defining charactership of entities 90
  key generation for 309
  relational vs. object 4
impedance mismatch. *See* object/relational impedance mismatch
import task 42, 47
in 182
increment key generation 409
index attribute
  for hibernate.column tag 290
indexes 132
  automatically generated by schemaexport 105
  for lists and arrays 132
  for maps 133
  storing in database column 381
<index-many-to-any> element 407
inheritance 83–86, 351
  discriminator element 84
  relational vs. object 5
  table per class 83–85
  table per concrete class 83
  table per subclass 83, 85–86
InitializeCollectionEvent 360
InitializeCollectionEventListener 361
inner join fetch 173
INSERT operation 338
instrumentation 362
Integrated Development Environment (IDE) 35

Interceptor 359
inverse 142, 380
inverse attribute for hibernate.set tag 304
isolation
  making sure code works in 313
  providing with multiple databases 331
  testing in 324
ITable 344
iterative development
  using XDoclet 289

J
JAR files
  adding to classpath 42
  organizing for resuse 43
Java 1.4, lacking metadata capability 274
Java 5 354
Java Beans 208, 211
Java Blueprints 190
java source, parsing 276
java task 39, 48
Java Transaction API. *See* JTA
JAVA_HOME 27
JavaBean, specifications for 92
javac task 39, 48
JavaDoc 275
  basics of 276
javadoc comments 276–277
JBDC, transactions 77
JBoss 52
JDBC
  avoiding the need for 31
  connection 342
  database connections 53
  drivers 34
  persistence with 9–20
JDBC Datasources 202
JDK 27
JDO
  changing ORM implementations to 191
  XDoclet tags for 277
join 113, 168, 348
  See also HQL, join

join table 6
<joined-subclass> element 399
JSR-175 354
JTA 76
    transactions 77–78
<junit> task 319
JUnit 2
    as the defacto standard for testing 314
    homepage of 318
    installing 318
    providing support structure to run tests
        315
junit.jar 318
    bundled with Ant 321
<junitreport> task 319–320

K
karma, generated by testing 319
key 349
key column
    naming for correct object 305
<key> element 302
key generation
    configuring with Ant 309
known state, reseting database to 335,
        345

L
labor intensive style of manual testing 314
Layer Supertype pattern 190, 197–198,
        212
layering your application 198
lazy 362
lazy attribute for hibernate.set tag 304
lazy collections in a web application 139
LazyInitializationException 139
legacy database. *See* object/relational map-
        ping (ORM), when to use
length
    for hibernate.column tag 290
    for hibernate.id tag 284
    for hibernate.property tag 287
levels, for logging 103
light weight container 202, 208, 215

like 182
LinkedHashMap 140
LinkedHashSet 140
LinkedList 126
Linux
    getting Hibernate for 28
    installing Hibernate for 29
list 381
    one-to-many, unidirectional 381
    simple values 382
listener 361
load method 114
loader 359
LoadEvent 360
LoadEventListener 360
local database, for developer testing 331
LocalSessionFactoryBean 210
    Spring 209
LockEvent 360
log4j 44, 102
    configuring 45
    homepage for 104
    properties file 102
log4j.properties
    configuring 103
logging JDK 1.4 102
logging, with Log4j 45

M
managed environment 52
manual testing 313
Manuel Laflamme 336
<many-to-any> element 407
many-to-many 5
<many-to-many> element 303
many-to-many list 300
many-to-one association, lazy 61
<many-to-one> element 294
many-to-one element 60–61
    column attribute 61
    example 61
    object references between persistent
        objects 61

many-to-one relationship 89, 122, 366
  bidirectional 367
  unidirectional 367
Map 133
map 384
  entity keys 389
  many-to-many, entity 386
  of components 387
  of possible types 392
  one-to-many, entity 384
  See also collections, map
mapping definition 56–66
  multiple files 56
  naming convention 56
mapping element 55
mapping file 31, 55
  generating with XDoclet 282
  location 64
MappingException 57
max_fetch_depth 168
memory management 204
merge directory 307
merge points 306
metadata 354
<meta-value> element 407
mkdir task 39
Mock objects 324
modular build files 49
MS SQL Server 31
MSSQL_ INSERT operation 338
MSSQL_CLEAN_INSERT
    operation 338
MSSQL_REFRESH operation 338
multiple databases 345
  using for testing 331
multiple objects, for a single table 122
multiple tables
  mapping objects to 348
  spanning with associations 122
MVC web framework, Spring 203
MySQL 26–27, 31, 170
  adding to Windows path 33
  bin directory 32

drivers 34
  obtaining 32
  show databases 33
  starting from command line 33
  supporting of subselects 32
  testing 32
  website 34
mysql console, showing table data
    from 107

N
name attribute
  for hibernate.column tag 290
  in Ant 37
named parameters 358
naming convention
  for association tables 379
  for test methods 317
  for tests 316
native key generation
  problems with one-to-one 370
network latency 331
nonmanaged environment 52
nonstrict-read-write cache, usage 81
NonUniqueObjectException 73
not 182
not null
  for hibernate.column tag 290
  for hibernate.many-to-one tag 293
now() 176

O
object
  persisting 68–70
  retrieving 70–72
object graph 9
  deleting 18
  obtaining 88
  persisting to relational model 15
  querying 19
  retrieving using JDBC 11
object model, building and mapping with
    Hibernate 364
object/relational impedance mismatch 4

object/relational mapping (ORM) 7
  when to use 8
one-to-many 5
<one-to-many> element 302
one-to-many set 300
one-to-one 5
one-to-one relationship 368
  bidirectional 372
  foreign key 370
  unidirectional 370
Open Closed Principle 192
<operation> element, for DBUnit 338
or 182
Oracle 31, 170
ORDER BY. *See* HQL, ORDER BY
order-by 140
order-by attribute, for hibernate.set
    tag 304
outer-join property 24
overriding targets when importing build
    files 113

P
package
  scoped methods for testing 326
  structure matching merge directory
      to 307
  to locate tests in 326
paged results. *See* ScrollableResults
@param tag 277
parameters, using in Ant 43
<parent> element 375
passive code generation 307
path element 36, 38, 46
patterns
  catalog of 364
  for logging 104
  organizing your projects with 189
Patterns of Enterprise Application
    Architecture 198
persistence 9, 17– 19, 22
  definition 3
  events 359
  layer for 198

make objects persistent 68– 70
object
  update(...) 69
object vs. entity 134
testing of persistent objects 327
with Hibernate 20– 24
with JDBC 9
plain old Java object (POJO) 19
polymorphic association 86
polymorphism
  XDoclet tags for handling 283
prefix attribute for hibernate.component
    tag 295, 298
PreparedStatement 165, 168
  class 19
  interface 71
presentation layer 198
primary key 3
  assigned by Hibernate 328
  associations 352
  automatic setting of 114
  loading objects by 113
primitive types vs. object types 69
<primitive-array> element 392
programmatic configuration,
    avoiding 208
project element 37
project, setting up 34– 41
projection 174
properties 59– 60
  available data types 60
  lazy 361
  name attribute 59
  querying specific 171
  references 352
  resolving 41
  substitution using Ant/XDoclet 306,
      308, 312
  type attribute, determined at
      runtime 60
property element
  generated by XDoclet 289
  in Ant 36– 37
  property level tag for XDoclet 282, 285

PropertyAccessException 69
protected methods
    as used in supertypes 198
Proxool 74
proxy 24, 62– 63
    defining 62
    populated by ID 63

Q
Quality Assurance 313
queries testing 329
query 164
    building inside callback 207
    features 164
    iterate(...) 164
    maxResults 164
    query.substitutions property 169
    setEntity(...) 181
    substitutions property. *See* HQL, query
        substitutions
QueryException 171, 179

R
read-only cache, usage 81
read-write cache, usage 81
refactoring
    extract component 117
    extracting common resource handling
        code 196
    for simplifying resource code 108
references, debugging 48
REFRESH operation 338
RefreshEvent 360
Registry pattern 213
relational database 3
relational identifier 4
relational model 3
ReplicateEvent 360
<report> element 321
reports directory 322
reset the database 328
resource clean up, managed by DAOs
    191
ResultSet 19, 168

retrieving objects 70– 72
return 359
@return tag 277
reusing build files 42, 46– 48
reverse engineer, XDoclet tags from
        Hibernate elements 311
robust tests 334
ROI 298
rollback
    transaction with a helper class 111
rollbacks
    handling 99
root element 37
root logger 104
rule of XDoclet Collections 302
RuntimeException, automatic converting
    to 215

S
sample data, loading using Hibernate 96
SaveEvent 360
save-update 146
    cascading 116
scalar values. *See* HQL SELECT, projec-
    tion
SchemaExport 292
    importing in ant 112
    specifying needed resources 101
    task 89, 99, 289
    tool 122
SchemaUpdate task 106, 289
ScrollableResults 165
second-level cache 79
SELECT
    optional in HQL 162
    See also HQL, SELECT
servers, deploying for multiple 332
Session
    cache 72– 74
    cache, adding objects to 73
    clear() 74
    closing by HibernateTemplate 205
    contains() 73

Session *(continued)*
  createCriteria(...) 184
  creating multiple for testing 328
  evict(...) 73
  find(...) 71, 163
  find(...) vs. iterate(...) 163
  flush() 69
  instance of 52
  iterate(...) 163
  iterate(...) efficiency 163
  load(...) 70
  passing around 197
  per operation, as a responsibilty of
      DAOs 192
  save(...) 68
  saveOrUpdate(...) 69
  thread safety 66
  update() 69
session level object cache 197
SessionFactory 52
  building using hibernate.cfg.xml 99
  configuring 66– 68
    using hibernate.cfg.xml 95
  why to avoid frequent creation of 107
set
  many-to-many 378
  many-to-many, bidirectional 379
  many-to-many, unidirectional 378
  one-to-many 375
  one-to-many bidirectional 377
  one-to-many, unidirectional 376
  See also collections, set
<set> element 302
setting up projects 34– 41
setUp() method 328
  using to clean out database 335
show_sql 169
single transaction per operation as a
    responsiblity of DAOs 192
Singleton pattern 215– 216
size, declaring for columns 291
some 182
sort attribute for hibernate.set tag 304

sorting
  sets at query time 376
  sets in memory 376
sourceforge.net, hosting XDoclet 276
Spring 2, 190
Spring framework 202
SQL 3
  create database 33
  create table 99
  custom 357
  dialects 55
  generated by Hibernate. *See* show_sql
  generating tables 274
  Hibernate abstraction 22
  using DAO pattern for 191
SQL scripts, using to load data 336
sql-delete 358
SQLException
  parsing output from 215
sql-insert 358
sql-type attribute
  for hibernate.column tag 290
sql-update 358
stack trace, denoting assertion failure 318
Statement class 19
static domain model 352
static field, storing SessionFactory in 111
stored procedures 357
strong typing 353
strongly typed 213
  DAOs 193
Struts 2
  XDoclet tags for 277
stubbing out components 324
stylesheet, XSLT 320
<subclass> element 398
subclasses
  catalog of 397
subselects 162
  See also MySQL, supporting of subse-
    lects
suite, as collection of tests 317
Sun 27

surrogate key 8
Swing 52
SWT 52
syntax check, HQL 325
System.out.println, testing with 313

T
@Table 355
table attribute 278
    for hibernate.set tag 303
table per class hierarchy
    subclass mapping 398
tables
    creating with SchemaExport 99
    per concrete class 351, 401
    per subclass 399
    schemas 366
Tapestry 2
target element 36, 38
task element 36, 39
taskdef task 102
tearDown() method 328
templates 203–204
test data, loading 336
test everything that could possibly
        break 314
test infecting 318
test properties files 332
test results
    as xml file 320
    shouldn't affect other tests 335
TestCase class 316
testing directory 326
testing persistence layer, how to do it 324
testing task, adding to build file 323
tests, organizing 326
TEXT column type 291
Thread Local Session pattern 197
threading 78
@throws tag 277
tips for testing databases 331
transaction 76–78
    automatically flushing Session 77
    benefits of JTA 78

commiting by HibernateTemplate 205
configuring for JTA 77
handled by HibernateTemplate 205
JDBC 77
jta.UserTransaction 77
managing with DAOs 191
transaction.factory_class 77
transaction.manager_lookup_class 77
Transaction API 215
transactional cache usage 81
@Transient 356
transient 146
TransientObjectException
    thrown when cascades aren't specfied
        115
TreeCache 81
truncate data 291
type 354
    for hibernate.property tag 287
type attribute for hibernate.id tag 284

U
UML diagrams 365
union subclass 351, 402, 408
    differences 351
unique 352
    for hibernate.column tag 290
    for hibernate.many-to-one tag 293
    for hibernate.property tag 287
unique-key attribute
    for hibernate.column tag 290
Unix
    getting Hibernate for 28
    installing Hibernate for 29
unsaved-value 284, 286
    impacting save or update 69
UPDATE operation 338
UpdateEvent 360
updating database schema 120
UserType 147, 153
    bridges persistence 151
    multiple columns 154
    nullSafeGetSet(...) 151

UserType *(continued)*
  Serializable 151
  sqlTypes() 151

V
validating DTD for database 336
VARCHAR, converts to Strings 105
verifying
  classes persist 324, 345
  entities cascade 325
  fields map correctly 325
version control, not checking derived files
    into 322
version, changing in build file 43
virtualization. *See* filters

W
WebSphere 52
Webwork 2
  XDoclet tags for 277
WHERE. *See* HQL, WHERE

whitespace condensing 366
Wiki 28
Windows
  getting Hibernate for 28
  installing Hibernate for 28
wiring objects 208
workarounds for XDoclet 306

X
Xalan 320
XDoclet 2, 354
  documentation 364
  homepage of 279
  using to generate .hbm.xml files 275
  working at build time 280
XDoclet Hibernate Tag Reference 311
xdoclet.version path 280
XML file, splitting up into multiple data
    files 340
XML formats for DBUnit 337
XSLT 320

MORE TITLES FROM MANNING

Hibernate in Action
   by Christian Bauer and Gavin King
   ISBN: 1-932394-15-X
   400 pages, $44.95
   August 2004

WebWork in Action
   by Patrick Lightbody and Jason Carreira
   ISBN: 1-932394-53-2
   400 pages, $44.95
   September 2005

For ordering information on these and other Manning titles,
go to www.manning.com

MORE TITLES FROM MANNING

Spring in Action
   by Craig Walls and Ryan Breidenbach
   ISBN: 1-932394-35-4
   472 pages, $44.95
   February 2005

JavaServer Faces in Action
   by Kito D. Mann
   ISBN: 1-932394-12-5
   774 pages, $49.95
   October 2004

For ordering information on these and other Manning titles,
go to www.manning.com

MORE TITLES FROM MANNING

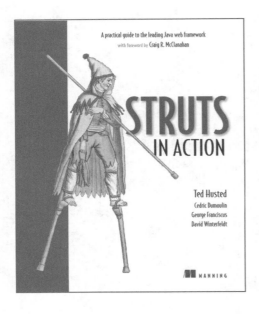

Struts in Action
Building web applications with
the leading Java framework
by Ted Husted, Cedric Dumoulin,
George Franciscus, and David Winterfeldt
ISBN: 1-930110-50-2
672 pages, $44.95
November 2002

Struts Recipes
by George Franciscus and
Danilo Gurovich
ISBN: 1-932394-24-9
520 pages, $44.95
December 2004

For ordering information on these and other Manning titles,
go to www.manning.com

MORE TITLES FROM MANNING

Java Development with Ant
    by Erik Hatcher and Steve Loughran
    ISBN: 1-930110-58-8
    672 pages, $44.95
    August 2002

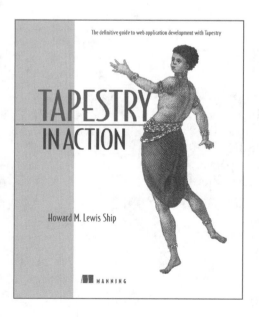

Tapestry in Action
    by Howard M. Lewisship
    ISBN: 1-932394-11-7
    580 pages, $44.95
    March 2004

For ordering information on these and other Manning titles,
go to www.manning.com

MORE TITLES FROM MANNING

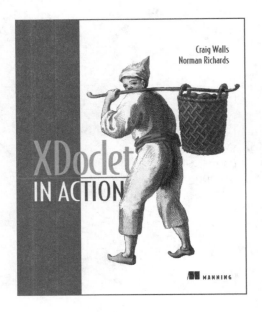

XDoclet in Action
 by Craig Walls and Norman Richards
 ISBN: 1-932394-05-2
 624 pages, $44.95
 December 2003

JUnit in Action
 by Vincent Massol
 with Ted Husted
 ISBN: 1-930110-99-5
 384 pages, $39.95
 November 2003

For ordering information on these and other Manning titles,
go to www.manning.com